Adam Smith and Modern Economics

To my wife Ann

Adam Smith and Modern Economics

From Market Behaviour to Public Choice

Edwin G. West

Professor of Economics
Carleton University
Ottawa, Canada

Edward Elgar

Published by
Edward Elgar Publishing Limited
Gower House
Croft Road
Aldershot
Hants GU11 3HR
England

Edward Elgar Publishing Company
Old Post Road
Brookfield
Vermont 05036
USA

British Library Cataloguing in Publication Data

West, Edwin G.
  Adam Smith and modern economics: from market behaviour to public choice.
  1. Economics. Theories of Smith, Adam, 1723–1790
  I. Title
  330.153

ISBN 1 85278 313 3

Printed in Great Britain by
Billing & Sons Ltd, Worcester

Contents

Figures and Tables

Figures

Tables

Acknowledgements

Among my colleagues at Carleton University, I want especially to thank T. K. Rymes, P. Nicholas Rowe, S. Ferris, D. Allen and J. Galbraith. I am grateful too for helpful discussion over the years with Mark Blaug, George Stigler, Robert Dimand, Gary Anderson and Ronald Bodkin.

In Chapters 2, 7, 8 and 9 I have drawn, more or less freely, upon previously published work and I should like to thank Kluwer Academic Publishers, *History of Political Economy* and the *Canadian Economic Journal* for permitting me to do so. With respect to Chapter 10 I wish to thank Laurence Iannaccone for useful discussion and permission to quote from his ongoing work on the economics of religion.

1. Introduction

Appearing, as intended, in 1990 this volume marks the bicentenary of the death of Adam Smith. Another evaluative work such as this, after the distinguished studies collected in Glasgow in 1976 to commemorate the bicentenary of Smith's *The Wealth of Nations*, might well be justified if for no other reason than the fact of its fresh relevance in this new age of deregulation, privatization and Perestroika. The current dramatic collapse of centrally directed East European economies has brought new popular demands there for what look remarkably like Smithian type free markets, free mobility and indeed 'natural liberty'. The main motivation for this book, however, stems from the fact that over the past 14 years the professional literature has produced a host of new references to Smith that bring interesting new light on his economic analysis and give further important evidence of the inspirational quality of his work. The main focus here accordingly will be on newly-found relationships between Smith's writing and a variety of emerging modern concepts or theories. These include the principal/agent problem, moral hazard, implicit contracts, the monetary approach to the balance of payments, credit rationing, the theory of screening and sorting, rent seeking, hierarchical modes of production, human capital, the theory of non-profit organization, the theories of public goods and externalities and the theory of balanced growth. Students in need of some grounding in these modern concepts may indeed find an introduction to them, through the eyes of Adam Smith, to be a good preparation for the current textbook treatment.

It must be emphasized before proceeding that Smith would probably be surprised by any interpretation of his career as having been first and foremost in economics. He lived at a time when an individual could hold sway over a wide domain of knowledge. Besides being an authority on poetry, aesthetics and literary appreciation, Smith viewed himself primarily as a philosopher. In his first major work, *The Theory of Moral Sentiments* (1759), he made a full investigation into ethics and social philosophy. Smith was also a classical scholar and there is an obvious connection between his philosophical writing and that of the early Stoics. At his death he left a library approaching 3000 volumes, only one-fifth of which related to political economy and history, the rest being on philosophy, law, literature, art and geography.

With this information before us it is understandable that Donald Winch pointedly asks 'How much can now be learned from Smith by treating him from a Whig-Historical perspective within which the main issue is one of deciding in what respects he anticipated or foreshadowed, or failed by a large or small margin to foreshadow, what later generations of economists regard as significant?'[1] One must, of course, be constantly aware that Smith worked with concepts, language, and outlook that were peculiar to the 18th century, and special care must obviously be taken to avoid anachronistic interpretations. Nevertheless, while no one can deny the legitimacy of examining Smith from the standpoint of history and other disciplines, it should be emphasized that the central concern of this volume is his connection with economics. And the fact that several recent articles presenting new economic analysis continue to find it necessary to quote from *The Wealth of Nations* to support their findings is surely an interesting phenomenon in its own right. Bringing Smith, as it were, into the fellowship of modern practitioners, often helps to trigger new insights relevant to current circumstances; but it also frequently produces a better understanding of *The Wealth of Nations*.

During the 1976 bicentenary, George Stigler reviewed what he called the 'Successes and Failures of Professor Smith' down to that year.[2] He used as his evaluation benchmark the acceptance or non-acceptance of Smith's theory by his successors. By this criterion it will be maintained that Smith's 'score' has improved significantly since Stigler wrote. This is not to say, of course, that all of Smith's failures have been eradicated! Indeed, in order to achieve proper balance, it is always important to list the shortcomings that persist. One must agree with Stigler, in particular, that Smith's most important analytical failure was his postulated hierarchy of employments of capital that appears in Book II, Chapter 5 of *The Wealth of Nations*, and this despite the valiant rescue attempt by Marion Bowley.[3] At the top of Smith's hierarchy, it will be remembered, was agriculture: 'no equal capital puts into motion a greater quantity of productive labour than that of the farmer', a statement that still suggests strongly the influence of Smith's 18th-century French economist friends. If this error had been incorporated into the theoretical system of *The Wealth of Nations*, the invisible hand and natural liberty argument would have collapsed. Fortunately for Smith he did not do so and his hierarchy argument remains an awkward excrescence.

Another important failure is Smith's labour command theory of demand, the theory whereby an individual values a commodity in his possession by the quantity of other people's labour or 'toil and trouble' that he can buy with it in the market. This theory assumes an equal disutility of labour at all times and at all places, an assumption that is surely indefensible.

Smith has, of course, also been heavily criticized for 'playing down' demand analysis in his theory of price. According to Hutchison and O'Brien, for example, Smith maintained that 'utility', which may be called 'value in use' was *not* a necessary prerequisite for value in exchange.[4] This is because goods 'which have the greatest value in exchange' may have *no* 'value in use'.[5] This treatment excluded a role for *subjective* utility and individual choice and this role is essential in societies enjoying the 'natural liberty' that Smith was always urging. This subject, however, appears to remain somewhat controversial. Certainly the last word on it has probably yet to be heard. In the meantime, a reading of the defense of Smith's treatment of demand by Hollander is strongly recommended.[6]

Another area of ongoing criticism concerns Smith's saving and investment analysis of Volume II, Chapter 3 of *The Wealth of Nations*. In it he condemns luxury expenditures, praises frugality, denies hoarding and in crucial ways departs radically from the ideas of Hume, Steuart, Quesnay, Mandeville and Boisguilbert. Smith's assertion that 'what is annually saved is as regularly consumed as what is annually spent, and nearly in the same time too', continues to appal today's typical macro-economist.

With respect to monetary economics Smith concluded: 'Upon every account, therefore, the attention of government never was so unnecessarily employed, as when directed to watch over the preservation or increase in the quantity of money in any country.'[7] This statement again well illustrates Smith's belief in the power of the self-adjusting model. Such reasoning was deficient, according to the late Sir John Hicks, primarily 'because the model paid no attention to plans and expectations'. Consequently, Hicks argues,

> ... it neglected uncertainty and liquidity; so that the bridge between real theory and monetary theory, of the possibility of which Hume had some inkling, remained unbuilt. The only monetary theory which could match the static real theory was one which concentrated upon the more mechanical aspects of the monetary system; this is just what the 'classical' Quantity Theory was. The responsibility for all this goes back to Adam Smith; it is the reverse of his great achievement.[8]

Any evaluator of an economist's successes and failures who, like Stigler, uses the criterion of the acceptance or unacceptance of his theory by his successors, would clearly declare Smith's macro-economics a failure, at least if Hicks and his followers are reasonably representative successors. This does not mean, however, that there is no room for further debate. Chapter 6 will accordingly raise some questions that are relevant especially to the traditional reception of the money and banking part of Smith's macro-economics. It will be shown in particular that the growing advocacy today of free (note-issuing) banking under a commodity reserve system throws new light on Smith's championship of the banking system that prevailed in his native Scotland.

As for the charge that Smith neglected uncertainty it seems fair to point out that he was not completely unaware of its importance. In his words: 'In all the different employments of stock, the ordinary rate of profit varies more or less with the certainty or uncertainty of the returns'.[9] But with respect to one particular kind of uncertainty, Smith was evidently much more alert than the average 20th-century economist who advocates government stabilization policies. Politicians and administrators who comprise government have their own particular self-interests to serve and Smith viewed the chances that these would coincide with the 'public interest' as constituting the greatest uncertainty of all. For some kind of parallel to this view, Chapter 6 refers to an article by Barro and Gordon (1983) and another by Shughart and Tollison (1983) both of which predict a tendency and inevitable incentive of modern governments to engineer positive inflation at all times. The reasoning of the latter authors is based on the recently-developed discipline called public choice. Smith's affinity with this new branch of economics is, appropriately enough, the subject of Chapter 7.

Chapter 6 also examines Smith's surprising acquiescence to usury laws. Bentham's *Discourse on Usury* attacked Smith in his own lifetime on the grounds that officially fixing the price of capital contradicted his general advocacy of 'natural liberty'. Also examined is the extension of the Benthamite critique by Garrison (1985), and the attempts by Buchanan (1976) and Jadlow (1977) to rationalize Smith's usury policy in terms of external economies from increased capital formation.

More interesting still is the opinion of Stiglitz (1987) that Smith's position is consistent with the treatment of the interest rate as a screening device. Banks may realize from experience that the higher the interest rate the higher the probability of lenders defaulting. Nevertheless, banks will trade-off the lower probability of success of one project with the higher rate of interest charged and it will often be rational for them to lend, indeed, for the higher-risk project. At the same time, according to Stiglitz and Weiss (1981), such expected private returns may be less than expected *social* returns and a usury law could increase net national output.

Whether such new light on Smith's position on usury will change 'failure' into 'success' remains to be seen. For our part we close Chapter 6 with what we believe to be serious remaining questions and problems especially with the Stiglitz interpretation. But even though we would, on balance, judge that this episode in *The Wealth of Nations* will ultimately be a failure (on Stigler's criterion) we must admit that the necessary intellectual travail has been rewarding and stimulating.

On the positive side, Stigler refers to 'one overwhelming important triumph' of Smith. He put into the centre of economics the systematic analysis of the behaviour of individuals pursuing their self-interest under conditions of competition. 'This theory was the crown jewel of *The Wealth of Nations*, and it became, and remains to this day, the foundation of the theory of the allocation of resources'.[10] It has recently been recognized that the 'systematic analysis' of the invisible hand mechanism that Smith placed at the centre of the stage is more than an exercise in normative economics. It can also be presented in terms of a set of refutable hypotheses concerning the influence on national output (and its growth) of a series of measurable independent variables such as the extent of political (civil) rights, the presence of private property rights and market versus government allocation of resources. Chapter 2 summarizes an empirical test on these lines across 115 countries relating to 1960 until 1980. The findings are unambiguously favourable to Smith's propositions. This is perhaps one of the most important examples suggesting a net improvement in Smith's standing since 1976.

With regard to international trade theory, neoclassical static analysis has been dominant until recently. Chapter 3 shows however that modern theorists appear now to be returning to issues raised by Smith. Capital accumulation, population growth and technological change are all being freshly incorporated into highly sophisticated formal models of trade and development. Modern specialists also emphasize reasons for international trade that are quite separate from the neoclassical theory of static comparative advantage. Economies of scale are now seen as an inducement to trade in its own right. But Adam Smith recognized this in 1776. He emphasized that trade led to new divisions of labour and therefore implicitly to what we now call economies of scale. And the invisible hand would see to it that most of such economies would be captured.

It is true that trade theorists are also currently occupied with problems of imperfect competition that are associated with scale economies. But arguments urging governments to respond by undertaking 'strategic trade policies', a kind of neo-mercantilism, are now being increasingly challenged via a resuscitated political economy approach. This approach typically points to the danger of arbitrary welfare benefits and losses from such government intervention that stem from differential powers of political lobbying across different groups in society. The abundant awareness of such 'rent-seeking' in *The Wealth of Nations*, it will be shown in Chapter 9, makes another interesting parallel to current economic thinking.

One of the most important mainsprings of economic progress in *The Wealth of Nations* was the division of labour. Stigler regretted in 1976 that Smith's impressive writing on the subject had not been taken up by successors. For this reason, Stigler concluded, Smith's analytical efforts on the division of labour must be considered a failure, albeit an 'improper failure'. Division of labour analysis, however, has received more serious attention by several economists since Stigler wrote. Chapter 4 reports the progress to date and shows that, in particular, the relationship between worker specialization and increasing returns to scale is now much more clearly understood than it was in 1976.

The provocative and influential suggestion by Berle and Means in the 1930s, that modern capitalism is hindered by the separation of management and control in large corporations, received a new evaluation by economists in the 1980s. As shown in Chapter 5, the authority of Adam Smith was frequently appealed to during this debate. But, as also observed, Smith has been wrongly interpreted on this subject by many scholars. A close examination of his reasoning shows in fact a sophisticated anticipation of what in modern economics has come to be called the principal/agent problem. This chapter also looks at the implicit theory of the firm in Smith's work. It is shown that, even if it is of an embryonic kind, there *is* a theory of organization in *The Wealth of Nations* and for this reason, also, Smith's treatment is more comprehensive than that of most neoclassical writing.

The most important linkage with modern economics has already been mentioned: the rich provision of implicitly and often explicitly testable hypotheses. Such contribution to positive economics has been neglected in the past partly no doubt because in Smith's day the necessary data with which to test his propositions were not present. Now that much pertinent evidence is becoming available, new credit is due to Smith when modern scholars successfully or fruitfully use it to test his arguments in a modern setting and in the modern scientific manner. Indeed such exercises in themselves are included here in the term 'modern economics'. The most ambitious of these exercises is the previously mentioned modern test of the central 'invisible hand' proposition reported in Chapter 2. An equally striking example, however, (in Chapter 10) is the use of modern data to test Smith's hitherto neglected economic theory of religion.

All the chapters of this book give evidence, therefore, that Smith is in many senses a 'modern economist'. But perhaps this is another way of saying that *The Wealth of Nations* is a classic. Smith, the man, died two centuries ago; but his work clearly enjoys continuous and robust survival.

Notes

1. Winch, in Thweatt (1988), p. 45.
2. Stigler (1976).
3. Bowley, in Skinner and Wilson (1975).
4. Hutchison (1988), O'Brien (1978). Schumpeter (1955) made the notorious claim

that *The Wealth of Nations* did not contain even a single analytic idea that was new in principle. He was, however, thin on supporting quotations. For more documented support of Schumpeter's view see Rashid (1989). The implication of the subsequent chapters of this book is that the Schumpeterian judgment needs to be complemented at least by an evaluation of the ways in which Smith's work has inspired modern developments in theory; developments that have indeed occurred since Schumpeter wrote.

5. Smith (1976), p. 44.
6. Hollander (1973), Chapter 4.
7. Smith (1976), p. 437.
8. Quoted in Hutchison (1988), p. 369.
9. Smith (1976), p. 127.
10. Stigler (1976), p. 1201.

2. Smith and Modern Positive Economics

As Mark Blaug has observed, economists in the 1950s and 1960s learned their methodology from Karl Popper and their main source was Friedman's 'Essay on the Methodology of Positive Economics'. Friedman's emphasis was on a theory, deduced from assumptions, realistic or otherwise, that culminates in predictions that are falsifiable. For it was Popper's main innovation to have shifted the emphasis in science from verification to falsification. The Popperian view of science indeed is that of an 'endless dialectical sequence of conjectures and refutations'.[1] Popper is a 'sophisticated' rather than a 'naïve' falsificationist, meaning that he does not discard a theory after a single failure to pass a statistical test. What he calls for is a whole series of attempted refutations. The question immediately arises whether Adam Smith's propositions are falsifiable in Popper's sense. Before addressing this question, however, it will be helpful to examine some views of other writers concerning Smith's general handling of evidence.

Samuel Hollander shows that several 19th-century observers were critical of Smith as an empiricist.[2] John Rae, for instance, objected in 1834 that Smith failed to justify his axioms empirically. Alfred Marshall believed that history provided Smith with 'illustrations' to make his exposition more palatable, but 'close induction' from the evidence was largely absent. J.E. Cairnes had a similar view of Smith.

Drawing upon Smith's posthumously published *Essay on the History of Astronomy*, Hollander's article concludes that while the deductive aspects of Newton's method are certainly reflected in Smith's model building, and especially in his mechanism of investment priorities, ultimately there is a divergence from Newton on the *uses* of theory. In the end, Smith 'had little confidence in testing procedures for the verification of the deductions drawn from econ-

9

omic models. In the last resort, the results derived would inevitably be "conjectural inference".'

Similarly, D.P. O'Brien is doubtful whether we can explain the longevity of Smith's economics by success in the falsification (Popperian) sense. For, in O'Brien's opinion, Smith's ideas were not subjective to a testing programme. Unlike Ricardo, 'Smith offered very few unambiguous predictions which would invite attempts at falsification'.[3]

O'Brien finds it interesting instead to read Adam Smith in terms of T.S. Kuhn's 1970 book *The Structure of Scientific Revolutions.* Kuhn's 'paradigm replacement process', according to O'Brien, is in many ways a more illuminating way of looking at Smith's economics. Considered as 'a pair of spectacles through which we see the world', the Kuhnian paradigm usefully limits our view as to the proper area of scientific concern. Thus the Marginal Revolution, and later the Keynesian Revolution, are sometimes described as the kind of changes of focus or paradigm shifts in economics that constitute what Kuhn calls scientific revolutions.

The Wealth of Nations provided a paradigm of 'the self-interest pursuit and decentralised decision-taking in a growth context viewed as producing a relatively best state of affairs and relatively efficient allocation of resources'. Yet, O'Brien points to an interesting deficiency in Kuhn's analysis when applied to Smith. Even if we accept that Ricardo's version of classical economics presented a 'paradigm switch', there seems to be no provision within Kuhn's apparatus for the old paradigm to come back and replace the new one. But that is what happened in the 19th century. For not only did Ricardian economics go into severe decline after the 1830s, but the attack on the Corn Laws in 1846 probably owed as much to the restored influence of Adam Smith (now represented by J.R. McCulloch).

O'Brien believes that Kuhn's approach is more successful in explaining post-1870 development. For then the Smithian spectacles were gradually replaced, as economists switched from preoccupation with growth to the problem of static optimization. At the same time there was a change in the range of economics. Population, for instance, a subject to which Smith had paid much attention, faded from attention.

This partial defence by O'Brien of Kuhn's paradigm model will be persuasive only to those who believe, as apparently O'Brien does, that Adam Smith's economics was dealt the final 'body-blow' with the arrival of the neoclassical system. But consider O'Brien's single example of population. It is strongly arguable that it was Malthus's version of population theory in classical economics, not Smith's, that suffered the downfall in the late 19th century. Smith proposed that population lagged changes in capital so that, as Stigler points out the wage rate of unskilled labour was given by:

wage rate = subsistence level + λ ($\triangle$[capital]/ $\triangle$[time])

where $\lambda > 0$. Stigler argues that this provided a greatly plausible wage theory. But it was vanquished by Malthus's simple theory which set $\lambda = 0$.[4]

Several other writers have recently been defending Smith against neoclassical 'victory claims', and these will be referred to later in this book. Most of them stress the return and resilience of the Smithian paradigm in the 20th century. Such champions of Smith will find more significant O'Brien's first, not second, thoughts, namely that Kuhn's system includes no provision for old paradigms to come back and replace new ones.

Blaug presents a case for viewing the so-called Marginal Revolution of the 1870s not as a scientific revolution, or paradigm switch, but as a 'progressive problem shift' and one that was more a reaction against Ricardo than against Adam Smith. 'The Ricardian system was itself a "progressive problem shift" in the Smithian research program motivated by the experiences of the Napoleonic wars and was designed to predict the "novel fact" of the rising price of corn, leading in turn to rising rents per acre and a declining rate of profit.'[5]

The Ricardian episode, according to Blaug, was in any case largely a British affair. There is no evidence, he claims, of any widespread sense of increasing dissatisfaction on the European continent around 1870 with classical economic doctrine conceived broadly on the lines of Adam Smith. The attempt by Menger and Walras to concentrate attention on the problem of price determination could be seen,

> and indeed was seen, as an improvement rather than an outright rejection of Adam Smith ... In other words, whatever we say about Jevons and the British scene, there was not a Marginal Revolution on the Continent: There was a 'problem shift', possibly even a 'progressive problem shift', if predictions about 'the price of an egg' may be regarded as more testable than predictions about the effects of giving free rein to the workings of the invisible hand.[6]

But, ultimately, Blaug has misgivings about the applicability of a philosophy of science grounded in the history of the physical sciences to a social science like economics. Among other things, there is nothing in the physical sciences that corresponds to theories which deduce a social optimum from value judgements. And these theories are common, for instance, in welfare economics. But where value judgements are blended in with an economist's analysis, he is likely to be very tenacious in his hold on his particular theory. If we pursue Blaug's line of thought we will not be surprised if economists take the opportunity to dub 'degenerating' those research programmes that they dislike but are unable to criticize effectively. Such is the crucial question raised by Ludwig Lachman: 'But when we face a state of degeneration, who can tell whether and when a resuscitator will arise?'[7]

The continued survival of the Smithian analysis raises the question whether his particular style of thought ever was 'degenerate', however described. According to Gordon, 'Smith's postulate of the maximizing individual in a relatively free market ... is our basic paradigm ... economics has never had a major revolution; its basic maximizing model has never been replaced ... it is, I think, remarkable when compared to the physical sciences that an economist's fundamental way of viewing the world had remained unchanged since the eighteenth century.'[8] A similar view is expressed by Coats.[9] Blaug goes further and expresses the view that every economist feels in his bones that the invisible hand theorem 'is almost as relevant to socialism as to capitalism, coming close indeed to a universal justification for the role of the market mechanism in any economy'.

But to return to the earlier discussion of positive economics, many will argue that it is one thing for Smith to present a comprehensive vision of a market system, but it is quite another for him to offer it in the modern terms of refutable hypotheses. It will be argued next, however, that, despite the scepticism of the writers previously mentioned, Smith comes closer than is usually recognized towards the scientific requirements of Popper and Friedman. We are not alone in this view. Hutchison, for example, argues that 'for Smith "self-adjustment" was not assumed as a hypothetical abstraction, but was asserted as an imprecise and qualified empirical theory, open in principle, to refutation, regarding how particular markets processes actually and usually worked out'.[10] And with respect to the theory of organization, Anderson and Tollison are more explicit: 'In effect,

Smith framed an explicitly testable hypothesis concerning the efficient organization of the firm, and in this respect he cannot be accused of woolly reasoning or bad economics.'[11]

It should be emphasized that Friedman demands a theory that culminates in predictions that are falsifiable (refutable) by *systematic* data. But Smith was writing at a time when this was largely unavailable. There was not even a census of population, let alone a set of national accounts. Yet even if Smith was deprived of the reliable data sources we have today it was still possible for him to produce predictions that a later age could attempt to test. It will be maintained in this and following chapters that this is indeed the case and that, in particular, his central 'invisible hand' discussion did culminate in a falsifiable set of predictions. Furthermore, these predictions withstood important empirical tests in the late 1980s.

To demonstrate, it will be necessary to return to the basic economic vision in *The Wealth of Nations*. Smith felt that the greatest aggregation of wisdom was contained in the decentralized decisions of individuals trying, under a system of what he called 'natural liberty', to obtain the most from their separate capitals. He believed, correspondingly, that this system of minimum government intervention, or *laissez-faire* as it came to be known in a looser and more popular language, would lead to the highest level of national income or what Smith called 'the annual revenue'. Regulations designed to stimulate foreign trade, he insisted, would reduce the national income. And the national income, after all, was simply the sum of all individual incomes from trade. Self-interest, therefore, led to social interest, in so far as social interest was equated with maximizing national wealth. It is this train of thought which led Adam Smith to produce the famous invisible hand proposition. But it is important always to remember that the proposition is accompanied by the conditions of natural liberty and minimum government, conditions that will be fully explored in Chapters 7 and 8.

But the annual revenue of every society is always precisely equal to the exchangeable value of the whole annual produce of its industry, or rather is precisely the same thing with that exchangeable value. As every individual, therefore, endeavours as much as he can both to employ his capital in the support of domestic industry, and so to direct that industry that its produce may be of the greatest value; every individual necessarily labours to render the annual revenue of the society as great as he can. He generally, indeed, neither intends to promote the public interest, nor knows how much he is promoting it. By preferring the support of domestic to that of foreign industry, he intends only his own security; and by directing that industry in such as a manner as its produce may be of the greatest value, he intends only his own gain, and he is in this, as in many other cases, led by an invisible hand to promote an end which was no part of his intention. Nor is it always the worse for the society that it was no part of it. By pursuing his own interest he frequently promotes that of the society more effectually than when he really intends to promote it. I have never known much good done by those who affected to trade for the public good. (p. 456)

It should be observed that this invisible hand paradigm is central to modern analysis in the sense that economists who attempt to justify government intervention feel themselves obliged to start by recognizing the Smithian 'virtues' of the invisible hand, and from then on endeavour to demonstrate some circumstances in which it may be flawed. Economists often argue, for instance, that sometimes the market fails because it takes into account only private costs and private benefits. One classic instance where this calculation is said to be insufficient is the case of the factory that imposes smoke on the neighbourhood, smoke that incurs costs to the residents but not to the factory owners. These social costs, it is contended, call for some correction or compensation by government intervention. While Adam Smith would no doubt be ready to consider the benefits of such programmes, he would demand equal attention to the costs of the intervention itself, costs that involve the setting-up of bureaucracies as well as the costs of tax collection. And Smith would probably urge the same care upon those economists who believe that government has a duty to attempt to counteract the business cycle, or to adopt an anti-trust policy. This is not, of course, to imply a priori that the costs will always outweigh the benefits.

A necessary Smithian condition for overall prosperity, to reiterate, was *limited* government; and this condition was linked to Smith's strong objection to protectionism. The whole mercantile system, in his view, was one of protectionism in foreign trade. In Smith's words: 'Monopoly of one kind or another, indeed, seems to be the sole engine of the mercantile system' (p. 630). The great overseas trading companies such as the English East India Company enjoyed exclusive trading rights that had been bestowed by the sovereign and parliament. Smith pointed to the social costs associated with these companies, costs that servants of the East India Companies (such as the mercantilist writer Thomas Mun) did not dwell upon. The officially protected monopoly trading companies suffered, according to Smith, from marked diseconomies of large scale, including the gross inefficiencies in the overgrown bureaucracies that ran them.

To Smith, however, there was a more important if concealed cost of the colonial system. To maintain that system required a costly defence of the trade routes and resources for maintaining order in the colonies. This expense was born by the general citizens of England through payment of taxes.

> Whatever expense Great Britain has hitherto laid out in maintaining this (colonial) dependency, has really been laid out in order to support this monopoly. (p. 615)

In Chapter 9 we show that Smith's figures suggest that these costs of the monopoly, in the sense of public expenses on defence, came to over five per cent of the average late 18th-century national income as measured, in retrospect, by 20th-century scholars. Smith's emphasis on the condition of limited government implied the need for government to reduce its size by drastically cutting this kind of 'monopoly promotion' expenditure. Over a given range, the smaller the share of government in GNP (to use modern terminology) the greater the expected prosperity. And it is here we have the beginnings of a falsifiable prediction.

The 'grand set of testable propositions' at the core of *The Wealth of Nations* have other key aspects, of course, beyond the share of government in GNP. Of special importance to Smith is the structure of property rights. A country's choice of institutional framework, he urges, has crucial implications for the efficiency of its economy. Consequences will be quite different, for example, where people are allowed the liberty to trade internally and externally and to enjoy full mobility compared to a situation where they are forbidden these freedoms. Smith's own preference for what he called 'natural liberty' could not be more clearly expressed:

> All systems either of preference or of restraint, therefore, being thus completely taken away, the obvious and simple system of natural liberty establishes itself of its own accord. Every man, as long as he does not violate the laws of justice, is left perfectly free to pursue his own interest in his own way, and to bring both his industry and capital into competition with those of any other man, or order of men. The sovereign is completely discharged from a duty, in the attempting to perform which he must always be exposed to innumerable delusions, and for the proper

performance of which no human wisdom or knowledge could ever be sufficient; the duty of superintending the industry of private people, and of directing it towards the employments most suitable to the interest of the society.[12]

To show that these central Smithian propositions are indeed falsifiable it is necessary first to describe some pertinent data that has now become available. Since 1973, Gastil has annually published country rankings of political liberty and civil liberty, type of economic system, and other measures of freedom.[13] Political (civil) rights are ranked by him from one (the highest degree of liberty) to seven (the lowest). The political rights rankings reflect citizen's degree of control over those who govern. For econometric purposes, the continuous variables can be transformed into a set of three dummy variables corresponding to Gastil's categories of high, medium and low levels of freedom. Scully has recently applied these variables to available data on real gross domestic product per capita, population, and the percentage of real gross domestic product devoted to gross domestic investment in 115 countries relating to the years 1960 to 80.[14] All independent variables in his multiple regression study were significant at the one per cent level and of the expected sign. A summary of his findings appears in Table 2.1.

Politically-open societies grew on average at a compound real per capita rate of 2.53 per cent per annum compared to a 1.41 per cent growth rate for politically-closed societies. The table also shows that, on average, societies that subscribe to the rule of law grew at

Table 2.1   *Average growth rates of per capita real gross domestic product by institutional attribute*

Institutional attribute	Per capita growth rate (%)	Institutional attribute	Per capita growth rate (%)	Difference in growth (%)
Politically open	2.53	Politically closed	1.41	1.12
Individual rights	2.75	State rights	1.23	1.52
Free market	2.76	Command	1.10	1.66
Politically open Individual rights, and free market }	2.73	Politically closed State rights and command }	0.91	1.82

Source: Table 1, 'Liberty and Economic Progress' by Gerald W. Scully, *Journal of Economic Growth*, Vol. 3, No. 2, November 1988.

2.75 per cent rate compared to a 1.23 per cent rate in societies in which the rights of the state supersede individual rights.

Remembering Smith's preference for the 'invisible hand' of the market over mercantilist planning, it is interesting that Table 2.1 reports that countries using a market allocation of resources grew at a 2.76 per cent rate compared to a 1.10 per cent rate in nations in which government commands take precedence. Table 2.1 also shows that in countries that have the triple combination of political openness, individual rights and free markets the growth rate is on average 2.73 per cent per annum. Where there is the opposite combination, in contrast, the growth rate is only 0.91 per cent per annum.

The extent of the impact of the growth rate of the capital/labour ratio depends upon how efficiently resources are employed in the economy. For equal rates of capital formation, economies that transform inputs into outputs in a relatively inefficient manner will have slower growth rates than efficient economies. Scully accordingly devised a measure of relative efficiency whose value was a fraction between zero and one. He found that the economies that were politically open, in which individual rights transcend the rights of the state, had, on average, an efficiency level of 0.74 to 0.77, depending on the freedom measure. In contrast, the average economy that was politically closed, in which the rights of the state prevail, or in which private property and the market allocation of resources was circumscribed, had an efficiency level of between 0.34 and 0.36. Such economies, in other words, could produce more than twice as much output using the same resource endowment if they were prepared to introduce liberty.

Such work is obviously an important complement to Smith's economics. It must be conceded, however, that intercountry per capita income figures typically suffer from several statistical problems. Nevertheless the data used by Scully was taken from Robert Summers and Alan Heston (in collaboration with Irving Kravis) and they use a technique that tackles some of these problems and one that is now used by the World Bank.[15] Still richer measures of the institutional framework will no doubt be obtained in the future and more sophisticated models will probably be constructed. But Scully's empirical work as so far accomplished, nearly 200 years after Smith's demise, does at least demonstrate that the core set of propositions in *The Wealth of Nations* lends itself to empirical refutation as required by modern economics. While some may still speak in terms of the *return* of the invisible hand paradigm, others can now argue that it has been in the mainstream all the time, merely waiting for the assembly of appropriate data that permit testing.

With respect to positive microeconomics, Albert Rees has declared Adam Smith's famous Chapter 10 of Book I of *The Wealth of Nations* to contain many ideas that have for a long time stood up to empirical testing.[16] In particular, Rees focused on Smith's idea of what we now call compensating differentials in the wage structure. These operate so as to obtain an equality of what Smith described as the 'natural advantages' between employments. If an occupation has a low pecuniary reward, Smith argued, it would be likely to compensate with non-pecuniary advantages. Unfortunately for modern economics, however, attention has shifted away from the *whole* advantages and disadvantages of an employment because of recent concern with systematic measurement of financial magnitudes. Non-pecuniary advantages or disadvantages have no common denominator whereas money wages do. Again, modern economists focus on the development of supply curves of labour which plot employment against money wages.

It is true that modern writers suspect as untestable the whole 'net advantages argument', the argument that people do not always seek the better paid job even when they know it is there because they are maximizing, not money, but 'net satisfaction'. As Kenneth F. Walker has observed, 'Once the assumption that man maximizes money is replaced by the assumption that he maximizes net satisfactions *which are not specified*, no predictions of his market behaviour can be made'.[17] Rees defends Smith against this charge on the grounds that, whatever the deficiencies of neoclassical economists in failing to specify non-pecuniary components of net advantage, these deficiencies cannot be blamed on Smith. *The Wealth of Nations* specifies in detail the five factors that, in Smith's view, constituted the non-monetary advantages and the disadvantages of employment. Certainly, the concept of net natural advantage does not, by itself, constitute a testable hypothesis. But one can agree with Rees that it provides a framework that leads to the formulation of specific hypotheses. And although we would not expect hypotheses based on the components of net advantage to be exactly the same two centuries later, interestingly enough Rees found that Adam Smith's original list was still relevant!

Consider one non-pecuniary feature of employment (one of the five factors) that Smith called 'agreeableness and disagreeableness', including 'the ease or hardship, the cleanliness or dirtiness, the honourableness or dishonourableness of the employment'. Smith illustrated these attributes as follows:

> ... a journeyman blacksmith, though an artificer, seldom earned so much in twelve hours as a collier, who is only a labourer, does in eight. His work is not quite so dirty, it is less dangerous, and is carried on in daylight and above ground.[18]

It is no longer possible to make the direct comparison because of the lack of wage data for blacksmiths. But Rees found that in 1972 average hourly earnings in coalmining in the US were $5.22 and in fabricated metal products $3.92. And, Rees observes, 'the work of the coalminer is still dark, dirty, and more dangerous than that of most other occupations'. Rees also argues that today there are other arguments explaining why dirty or disagreeable jobs earned low wages. One is demand-deficient unemployment and the second is racial and other discriminations in employment. But Smith did not consider these because they were not obvious in his time.

Smith identified another wage compensation connected with what he called 'the difficulty and expense of learning the business'. His treatment contained rich empirical (refutable) propositions in terms of what we now call 'human capital':

> The work which he learns to perform, it must be expected, over and above the usual wages of common labour will replace to him the whole expense of his education, with at least the ordinary profits of an equally valuable capital. It must do this too in a reasonable time, regard being had to the very uncertain duration of human life, in the same manner as to the more certain duration of the machine.[19]

Rees argues that the revival of interest in the idea of human capital during the 1960s, led by T.W. Schultz and Gary Becker, has provided the impetus for one of the most important subsequent developments in labour economics.

Smith's third special compensation, or differential, related to the 'constancy or inconstancy of employment'. He argued that the work of the mason (bricklayer) was relatively inconstant particularly because of changing weather conditions. The daily wage of a mason or bricklayer must accordingly be higher than that of a journeyman in manufacturing, and that the annual earnings must also be somewhat higher to include a kind of risk premium. Rees argues that not only does this argument remain valid today, but that it still applies to exactly the same trades! Smith's observation that the daily wages of a mason are generally higher than those of a carpenter are true today in most places in the US. In 1969, for instance, the average rate for bricklayers was $6.06 and for carpenters $5.77 an hour.

More examples of Smith's falsifiable propositions will be given in subsequent chapters. Meanwhile, sufficient evidence has already been assembled here to make reasonable the claim that Smith has much more in common with modern economies than was once believed. Later chapters will go further. They will show how much of Smith's work has foreshadowed, if not inspired, many late 20th-century developments.

Notes

1. Blaug (1975).
2. Hollander (1977).
3. O'Brien (1976).
4. Stigler (1976).
5. Blaug (1975).
6. Blaug (1975).
7. Lachman (1977).
8. Gordon (1965).
9. Coats (1969).
10. Hutchison (1988), p. 359.
11. Anderson and Tollison (1982), p. 1240.
12. Smith (1976), p. 687.
13. Gastil (1982).
14. Scully (1988).
15. Summers and Heston (1984).
16. Rees (1975).
17. Walker (1946).
18. Smith (1976), p. 117.
19. Ibid., pp. 118–19.

3. Competition and Free Trade

Smithian versus Neoclassical Competition

It has frequently and correctly been observed that the freedom to compete in *The Wealth of Nations* is a corollary of the principle of natural liberty:

> Every man, as long as he does not violate the laws of justice, is left perfectly free to pursue his own interest in his own way, and to bring both his industry and capital into competition with those of any other man, or order of men.[1]

As several writers point out, however, it is important to distinguish the idea of competition in Smith's work from that of 'perfect competition' in modern neoclassical economics. Smith thought of competition in terms of activity rather than structure. The neoclassical model of perfect competition, in contrast, is based on structure, emphasizing as it does such features as numbers, cross-elasticities, and perfect knowledge. While the neoclassical views perfect competition as an equilibrium state, Smith viewed competition as being activated only when the equilibrium of the market is disturbed, as for instance when it is over-supplied with a good and suppliers have to compete for customers. Smith's competition takes place without perfect foresight and perfect knowledge, that is, in a state of disequilibrium. As Richardson observes:

> Surely it is of the essence of competition that the participants hold uncertain and divergent beliefs about their chances of success; yet, despite this, theorists commonly choose to couple competition with the assumption of perfect foresight.[2]

Richardson's attack on perfect competition in favour of Adam Smith's view is similar to that of F.A. Hayek. Hayek believes that the theory of perfect competition has little claim to be called 'competition'. For the theory 'assumes that state of affairs already to exist which, according to the truer view of the older [Smithian] theory, the process of competition tends to bring about (or to approximate) and that, if the state of affairs assumed by the theory of perfect competition ever existed, it would not only deprive of their scope all the activities which the verb 'to compete' described but would make them virtually impossible'.[3]

Hayek emphasizes that really perfect knowledge and foresight would have a paralysing effect on all action. Nothing is solved when we assume everybody to know everything. The real problem to Hayek is how to bring about the situation wherein as much of the available knowledge as possible is used. The real question in political economy, the question that Smith was considering, is what institutional arrangements are necessary to attract the *unknown* persons who have knowledge to a particular task. We cannot assume perfect knowledge in a model of competition because it is only through competition that the knowledge will be discovered.

As for the pursuit of desirable optima, the target of 'perfect competition' is an impossible one. The real basis for comparison with existing competition is not perfect competition but the situation that would exist if practical competition (in the Smithian sense) were prevented from operating. Moreover, if 'perfect competition' is to be the measuring rod of efficiency in the market, then, symmetrically, we need a similar test of the political apparatus that is to rectify things. That is, existing governments should be compared with governments based on 'perfectly competitive' democracy where there is free entry for any person or group wanting to offer policies 'for sale' in return for votes. Competitors and incumbent governments, meanwhile, must all have perfect knowledge. One has only to cite the political model in these terms to show that Adam Smith worked in a world that was far less abstract and was seeking rather 'the least imperfection' rather than the 'greatest perfection'.

Another way of expressing this is to observe that Smith's approach was not so much that of 'orthodox' or 'pure' economics rather than that of political economy, an approach that tends to be interdisciplinary. This is especially the case with 18th-century Scottish political economy, a body of thought that was clearly problem-oriented and drew upon history, philosophy, political theory, jurisprudence and psychology as well as economics proper in its search for practical solutions.[4]

Richardson views Adam Smith's analysis as a disequilibrium

theory of a world in a state of constant and internally-generated change and sees Smith's division of labour principle simultaneously as a cause and effect of economic progress. Competition in *The Wealth of Nations* explains first the balancing of supply and demand in particular markets, and second the evolution of structural and technological forces. 'Smith offers us, in effect, both a theory of economic equilibrium, and a theory of economic evolution; and in each of these, competition has a key role to play.'[5] Subsequent neoclassical economics in its pursuit of greater analytical rigour has discarded, or ignored, the evolution aspect of competition because of the assumption of constant technology. 'The theorist has come to attend to the things he can most easily handle and in this way, our perception of reality has adapted to the development of our mental machinery.'[6]

Richardson, like Hayek, sees Smithian competition as a dynamic process. More interesting still, he attempts to resolve what some see as a problem in Smith, the problem that if the division of labour is limited by the extent of the market, as Smith tells us, then increasing returns will be so pronounced that monopoly will have to replace competition as an assumption. In Smith's world, Richardson argues, by the time a firm has gained a substantial share in one market, 'it may be time to start looking for others; nothing stands still and there is little point in finally gaining a monopoly when demand for the product starts to turn down'.[7]

It is interesting too to relate this discussion to the paper by Stigler in 1957 in which he derived a set of conditions of competition that were, to him, implicit in *The Wealth of Nations*. One of them is that the number of rivals must be sufficient to eliminate extraordinary gains. On Richardson's view, just described, the number of rivals is not very critical, for monopoly gains are largely a will-o'-the-wisp. Even if there was only one producer, his monopoly gains would hardly be worthwhile, for new products would have come on the scene or existing plants would have become obsolete.

Stigler also found that knowledge of the market was an important condition of competition in *The Wealth of Nations* but, significantly, he described it as the need for economic units to have *tolerable* knowledge of market opportunities not *perfect* knowledge. Certainly there is no mention of perfect foresight in Smith. And there seems to be a world of difference between 'perfect' knowledge and knowledge that is 'tolerable' – whatever the precise meaning of that adjective.

International Trade Theory

If natural liberty leads to free competition and trade at home it also implies the freedom to trade abroad. Until quite recently, however, the analysis of international trade in *The Wealth of Nations* was overshadowed because of the well-known neoclassical observation that Smith failed to discover the principle of comparative costs. Moreover, he dealt with ambiguous doctrines such as the 'vent-for-surplus' theory, and the priority of agriculture as an investment potential. A.I. Bloomfield[8] summarizes these types of criticisms by a series of economists that includes Bastable, Robbins and Viner.

For the uninitiated, or for those who need a reminder, the following simple scenario will quickly illustrate the difference between absolute and comparative advantage theory of trade. Suppose Mr A, born with 'green fingers', has a natural ability in gardening but is not outstanding at anything else. Mr B, in contrast, is a 'natural' at carpentry but is a relative failure at all other things. If this economy is confined to these two persons, we say that Mr A has an absolute advantage in gardening and Mr B in carpentry. It will pay each person to specialize according to his absolute advantage and then trade with his neighbour (for example, vegetables for chairs). Suppose, however, Mr B is a born genius such that anything Mr A can do Mr B can do better. It could still pay Mr B to trade with A and employ him as a gardener even though Mr B could do his own gardening more efficiently. This would be the case where Mr B could earn significantly more by devoting all his time to an alternative occupation in which his *comparative* advantage was greatest. Similarly, Ricardo's law of comparative cost predicts that Mr A will (or should) specialize in that activity in which his comparative *disadvantage* is least. The neoclassical complaint is that Smith failed to recognize this second (comparative cost) case.

A strong defence of Smith's reasoning, however, has recently been offered by Myint.[9] Smith certainly begins with an absolute advantage theory of trade, Myint argues, but he quickly develops this into a dynamic model. Since trade expands the market there is room for further specialization (division of labour). But specialization is positively correlated with learning-by-doing and new opportunities for invention. The situation is thus one of dynamic technological change. In Smith's words:

... the narrowness of the home market does not hinder the division of labour in any particular branch of art of manufacture from being carried to the highest perfection. By opening a more extensive market for whatever part of the produce of their labour that may exceed the home consumption, it encourages them to improve its productive powers, and to augment its annual produce to the utmost and thereby to increase the real revenue and wealth of the society.[10]

The fact is, Myint insists, Smith's theory of foreign trade is closely interwoven with this theory of economic development. Smith's trade analysis is therefore a richer and more realistic model of the domestic economy than would have been possible within the restrictive framework of a comparative cost theory. Smith applied his fundamental principle that 'the division of labour is limited by the extent of the market' to every sphere of economic activity, foreign trade included. His concept of 'vent-for-surplus' is introduced at many points where there is a widening of the market that significantly extends the division of labour.

Two ideas are implicit in Smith's trade theory: (1) by widening the extent of the market there are further divisions of labour so increasing productivity – this may be called the 'productivity' theory; (2) international trade provides a market outlet 'for whatever part of the product of their labour may exceed the home consumption' – this is the essence of the 'vent-for-surplus' theory (which will receive further examination and explanation below).

Some writers have suggested that the 'productivity' and the 'vent-for-surplus' arguments are two aspects of the same theory.[11] Myint argues that the distinction *is* meaningful. In order to widen the market for manufacturers it is necessary to increase the output of agriculture to match the manufacturing output. Optimum development is of the 'balanced-growth' kind. Smith was implying strong possibilities of increasing agricultural output before land is fully utilized, even in the developed 'landed nations' of Europe such as France and England.

The 'vent-for-surplus' theory was, therefore, applied not only to the colonies, but to *most* societies and in terms of the cultivation of underutilized land in *most* places. While the modern economist would foresee a country progressively specializing in manufactures and importing increasing quantities of food, Smith believed that countries like England and France would find it more advantageous to grow the bulk of their food requirements at home 'by the extension of improvement and cultivation'. Myint concludes that one of the major benefits of foreign trade to a country exporting manufactures is the indirect encouragement that it gives to its domestic agriculture. 'The 'vent-for-surplus' mechanism is brought into play through the expansion of *internal* trade between the manufacturing and the agricultural sectors.'

Myint's analysis is a reply to that of Hollander who argues that the 'vent-for-surplus' theory conflicts sharply with the allocative efficiency aspect of Smith's analysis in the context of a fully-employed economy.[12] Myint argues that Smith assumes full employment of labour, but his analysis allows for the possibility of increasing output by recruiting the extra labour for productive uses from the existing pool of 'unproductive' labour. There was fully employed labour but underemployed or surplus land in the Smithian model. When a previously isolated country possessing such a surplus factor becomes a participant in world exchange, the immediate function of trade is not so much to reallocate given resources as to provide a new effective demand for the surplus resource(s) that would have not otherwise have been used. This 'vent-for-surplus' sequence of events contrasts with the static neoclassical comparative cost theory which assumes initial full employment of all resources so that export production can be increased only at the cost of reducing domestic production. The Ohlin version of neoclassical international–trade theory of course assumes that any initial disproportion between land and labour would be resolved by appropriate price adjustments so that relatively land-using commodities would have high prices. A full employment equilibrium would therefore be assured. Myint insists, however, that, in their proper historical setting, genuinely isolated subsistence economies do not have the highly developed price mechanism that the Ohlin theory presumes. Indeed the gradual introduction of a money economy is normally induced by the growth of international trade itself. And this was the thrust of Smith's dynamic theory.

After Smith, and in contrast to him, Ricardo and J.S. Mill increasingly formalized the international trade element of classical economics in terms of the static theory of efficient allocation of given resources in the context of well-established price mechanisms. The analysis of the domestic economy, meanwhile, proceeded on dynamic lines with more stress on the principle of diminishing returns from land. Ricardo and Mill concentrated on the case of an industrially advanced country with a comparative advantage in exporting manufactures and importing 'corn'. Since, in this case, cheaper food imports would lower wages so causing increased profits and economic development, the case for free trade was thought to be conclusively demonstrated.

Myint observes, however, in the case of a country with a comparative advantage in exporting *corn*, free trade would hasten the diminishing returns from land and depress the profit rate. This would have an adverse effect on economic development. While Ricardo and Mill did not squarely face this converse case, Adam Smith obviously did. Smith's more comprehensive analysis nevertheless decided in favour of free trade even in the case of the colonial agricultural countries. For he predicted that the expansion of agricultural exports from the colonies would promote their long-run economic development by widening the size of the home market, an event that would eventually encourage the rise of colonial domestic manufacturing.

Myint seems to view the neoclassical developments of Ricardian theory of international trade as a 'degenerating problem shift' (although he does not use this term from the methodology of Lakatos).[13] For after Smith, foreign trade *and* domestic economy were subsumed as branches of the static general equilibrium analysis. The relationship between international trade and economic development, the great issue that was the focus of Smith's analysis, was suddenly dropped from the agenda. 'And historians of economic thought, looking at Adam Smith through neoclassical spectacles, blame him for his lack of contributions to the neoclassical trade theory.'[14]

Modern international trade theorists are now returning to the issues raised by Smith. Capital accumulation, population growth, and technological change, are all being freshly incorporated into highly-sophisticated formal models of trade and development. The approach adopted in *The Wealth of Nations*, Myint insists, is particularly relevant to the undeveloped countries today, despite the fact that it is in these countries that Adam Smith is regarded with greater suspicion as the arch advocate of *laissez-faire* and free trade. Smith, in fact, comes in between the 'outward-looking' approach that emphasizes the expansion of external trade as the 'engine of growth', and the 'inward-looking' approach which attempts to exclude external economic forces as disrupting factors. On Myint's interpretation Smith saw the importance of 'balanced growth' but believed that the expansion of external trade was complementary, not competitive, with it.

The Return of the Political Economy Approach

Modern trade theorists are now emphasizing the need for what they call a political economy approach, especially in the context of debates about government intervention. They start by pointing to causes of international trade and specialization that are separate from reasons of comparative advantage. In particular, several authors now see economies of scale as an inducement to international trade that is just as fundamental as comparative advantage.[15] And since increasing returns (economies of scale) are so important in the new analysis, so is the imperfect competition that necessarily accompanies them. The earlier or traditional comparative cost theory, in contrast, assumed both constant returns and perfect competition.

Preoccupied with economies of scale, the new vision of international trade tends to converge with that of Adam Smith. As we have seen, one part of Smith's theory is the idea that, by widening the extent of the market, foreign trade produces further divisions of labour and these in turn increase productivity.[16] Correspondingly, the discovery of America was useful because:

> By opening a new and inexhaustible market to all the commodities of Europe, it gave occasion to new divisions of labour and improvements of art, which, in the narrow circle of the ancient commerce, could never have taken place for want of a market to take off the greater part of their produce.[17]

In outlining this kind of dynamic process, however, some of the late 20th-century writing has raised the question whether the imperfect competition that accompanies the unfolding economies of scale argues against widespread free trade and in favour of more government intervention.

One form of potentially useful intervention, it is suggested, is by way of what is called 'the strategic trade policy argument'. It proceeds as follows:[18] Suppose the potential economies of scale expected from a new 'leading edge' industry are so large that, in a world as a whole, there is room for one profitable entrant only. Two 'national' firms, for example, in a world with only two separate countries A and B would involve losses to both. Assume that the surplus or profit is expected to be $100 million. Then if the government of A commits itself in advance to pay a subsidy of say $8 million to a domestic company willing to enter the new industry, then firms in B will be induced to stay out so leaving the field free for A to make a net surplus of $92 million.

A further extension of the argument involves benefits that are external to the firm. In new industries where research and development (R & D) is a large component of the firm's costs, it is likely that the innovative firm will be unable to appropriate fully the new knowledge created. Some of the knowledge, in other words, will be 'dissipated' in the form of free external or spillover benefits to other firms. This argument is relevant in the present context, however, only if the external benefits from R & D occur exclusively (or mainly) at the national level. If the spillovers benefit foreign firms equally there will be no domestic net benefit from a domestic subsidy. The result is that, provided the externalities exist only at the national level, country A in our previous example will generate for its citizens benefits that *exceed* $92 million. The policy of subsidization thus has this additional justification.

According to Paul Krugman, modern international trade specialists are now ready to place strong qualifications around such new arguments for government intervention.[19] And it is here where the 'political economy' approach reasserts itself. First, for a government to carry out a programme of subsidies to selected industries (as in the previous example) it has to have the necessary information about which ones are in the leading edge. Yet it is doubtful whether this could be obtained. If, moreover, government makes an error in selecting its 'winners', as it is in every danger of doing, the country could end up with a serious deficit rather than a surplus. Now Adam Smith pointed all this out two centuries ago, albeit in stronger and more emotive language. The drift of Smith's argument is that the invisible hand mechanism is more reliable than government in the context of 'picking winners' among new industries. To reiterate an earlier quotation:

> The sovereign is completely discharged from a duty, in the attempting to perform which he must always be exposed to innumerable delusions, and for the proper performance of which no human wisdom or knowledge could ever be sufficient; the duty of superintending the industry of private

people, and of directing it towards the employments most suitable to the interest of society.[20]

According to Smith (and later to Hayek) information about which new industries have the greatest promise cannot be accumulated in a political body, let alone in the head of a single government functionary or planner. Such knowledge is dispersed throughout the land, and is often discovered in unexpected quarters.

> What is the species of domestic industry which his capital can employ, and of which the produce is likely to be of the greatest value, every individual, it is evident, can, in his local situation, judge much better than any statesman or lawgiver can do for him. The statesman, who should attempt to direct people in what manner they ought to employ their capitals, would not only load himself with a most unnecessary attention, but assume an authority which could be safely trusted, not only to no single person, but to no council or senate whatever, and which would nowhere be so dangerous as in the hands of a man who had folly and presumption enough to fancy himself fit to exercise it.[21]

Considerations of general equilibrium, according to modern writers, place the biggest information burden upon a government. If it subsidizes one industry it places burdens on others. It therefore has to enter into complex calculation whether the (uncertain) benefits from the subsidy outweigh such burdens. In Krugman's words (1987, p. 140):

> When a particular sector receives a subsidy, this gives firms in that sector a strategic advantage against foreign competitors. However the resulting expansion of that sector will bid up the price of domestic resources to other sectors, putting home firms in these other sectors at a strategic disadvantage. Excess returns gained in the favored sector will thus be offset to at least some extent by returns lost elsewhere.

Now compare the thrust of Adam Smith's analysis of the 18th-century subsidy on British grains, the so-called corn bounty. The bounty, he argued, would cause more grain to leave the home country and so cause domestic grain prices to rise. This, in turn, will raise other prices.

> It [the corn bounty] regulates the money price of all the other parts of the rude produce of land, which, in every period of improvement, must bear a certain proportion to that of corn [wheat], though this proportion is different in different periods. It regulates, for example, the money price

of grass and hay, of butcher's meat, of horses, and the maintenance of horses, of land carriage consequently, or of the greater part of the inland commerce of the country.

By regulating the money price of all other parts of the rude produce of land, it regulates that of the materials of almost all manufactures ...[22]

It was implicit in Smith's argument (which of course, was strongly contested by Ricardo) that it was profoundly difficult to work out in advance the precise magnitude of all the general equilibrium price effects. A correct interventionist policy is thus difficult for these information reasons alone. The fact of such difficulty, nevertheless, is not by itself a defence of free trade. Krugman concludes:

Thus the economic critique of the new interventionism [information difficulty] is only part of the post-new-trade-theory case for free trade. *The other indispensable part rests on considerations of political economy.*[23]

The need for a political economy approach that complements scientific economic analysis stems from the fact that the potential intervention (via subsidies etc.) has income distribution effects. And in politics these usually come to dominate efficiency considerations. The outcome, moreover, is likely to involve inter-country retaliation and intra-country rent-seeking by special interests. When we reconsider the (previous) example of the government of country A subsidizing a leading-edge industry, we must now recognize that such action might simultaneously be matched by country B. The subsequent trade war between A and B (at least under the assumptions of our example) will leave both countries worse off than if a *laissez-faire* approach had been universally adopted. No country will be able to realize economies of scale because each will endeavour to be self-sufficient. If the gains from sophisticated interventionism are in any case small (for reasons given above), then, in Krugman's words, 'there is a reasonable case for continuing to use free trade as a focal point for international agreement to prevent trade war'.

Adam Smith's comments on the subject of international trade wars are very similar. But, on the whole, his analysis of the self-inflicted wounds caused by retaliation are arguably more comprehensive:

The case in which it may sometimes be a matter of deliberation how far it is proper to continue the free importation of certain foreign goods, is, when some foreign nation restrains by high duties or prohibitions the importation of some of our manufactures into their country. Revenge in this case naturally dictates retaliation ... There may be good policy in retaliations of this kind, when there is a probability that they will procure the repeal of the high duties or prohibitions complained of ... To judge whether such retaliations are likely to produce such an effect, does not, perhaps, belong so much to the science of a legislator, whose deliberations ought to be governed by general principles which are always the same, as to the skill of that insidious and crafty animal, vulgarly called a statesman or politician, whose councils are directed by the momentary fluctuations of affairs ...

...When there is no probability that any such repeal can be procured, it seems a bad method of compensating the injury done to certain classes of our people, to do another injury ourselves, not only to those classes, but to almost all the other classes of them. When our neighbours prohibit some manufacture of ours, we generally prohibit, not only the same, for that alone would seldom effect them considerably, but some other manufacture of theirs. This may no doubt give encouragement to some particular class of workmen among ourselves, and by excluding some of their rivals, may enable them to raise their price in the home-market. Those workmen, however, who suffered by our neighbour's prohibition will not be benefited by ours. On the contrary, they and almost all the other classes of our citizens will thereby be obliged to pay dearer than before for certain goods. Every such law, therefore, imposes a real tax upon the whole country, not in favour of that particular class of workmen who were injured by our neighbour's prohibition, but of some other class.[24]

On the subject of rent-seeking, Paul Krugman observes that the kinds of intervention that new trade theory suggests can raise national income will typically raise enormously the welfare of some small groups and impose substantial costs on larger, more diffuse groups. 'The result, as with any microeconomic policy, can easily be that excessive or misguided intervention takes place because the beneficiaries have more knowledge and influence than the losers.' On this criterion the knowledge that will dominate is not, to continue our example, the knowledge of the most profitable leading-edge industry, but the knowledge of which subsidy will score most in terms of relative vote-gaining. This invites political consideration of a wide range of subsidies given to many industries whether leading-edge or not. Such a position is again one that Adam Smith arrived at in 1776, as will be seen in detail in Chapter 9 below.

After weighing all the aspects, Krugman concludes that it is possible to believe that the neoclassical comparative advantage argument is an incomplete model of trade and to believe that free trade is, nevertheless, the right policy. 'In fact, this is the position taken by most of the new trade theorists themselves.' But the considerations that have most swung the balance or judgement appear to derive from a resuscitated 'political economy':

> This is not the old argument that free trade is optimal because markets are efficient. Instead it is a sadder but wider argument for free trade as a rule of thumb in a world whose politics are as imperfect as its markets.[25]

The 'old argument' referred to in the first sentence of this quotation was not that of Adam Smith. It derives from 19th-century neoclassical thinking. But the 'sadder but wiser argument' referred to in the second sentence is, nevertheless, not new either. It appears indeed to be a rediscovery of the 18th-century wisdom, if not sadness, of the author of *The Wealth of Nations*.

Notes

1. Smith (1976), p. 687.
2. Richardson (1975), p. 359.
3. Hayek (1948), p. 115.
4. Dow (1987).
5. Richardson (1975), p. 351.
6. Ibid., p. 353.
7. Ibid., p. 358.
8. Bloomfield (1975).
9. Myint (1977).
10. Smith (1976), p. 447.
11. Haberler (1959), Bloomfield (1975).
12. Hollander (1973).
13. Blaug (1975).
14. Myint (1977), p. 246.
15. Lancaster (1980), and Dixit and Norman (1980).
16. Myint (1977).
17. Smith (1976), p. 448.
18. The example and general discussion draws upon Krugman (1987).
19. Krugman (1987).
20. Smith (1976), p. 687. Modern writers argue that the information problem for government is aggravated by the fact that uncertainty is greater when it is a question of how a policy will affect oligopolistic competition, which they assume to be the typical market structure in international trade. As Krugman points out, economists do not have reliable models of how oligopolists behave.
21. Ibid., p. 456.
22. Ibid., pp. 509–10.
23. Krugman (1987), p. 141, emphasis added.
24. Smith (1976), pp. 467–8.
25. Krugman (1987), p. 141.

4. The Division of Labour Rediscovered

Chapter 3 referred to the important role played by Smith's division of labour theory in his analysis of trade and development and explained how this connection has been rediscovered in modern economics. From the standpoint of the history of economic thought, however, it is necessary, before proceeding further, to acknowledge that the economic usefulness of the division of labour had already been stated by several predecessors of Smith. In this context, the writings of Mandeville and Harris are relevant (they are referred to in the 1976 Oxford University Press Edition of *The Wealth of Nations* edited by Campbell and Skinner). Another previous work worth emphasizing is that of Josiah Tucker.[1] In addition, and perhaps still more important, there is the fascinating account in the anonymously published *Considerations on the East-India Trade*, 1701, the author of which is now believed to have been Henry Martyn.

Despite all the previous work, however, Smith's treatment still remains the most influential with modern economists for three main reasons. First, his pronouncement that 'The division of labour is limited by the extent of the market' brought a new clarity and insight to economic analysis. Indeed, one distinguished writer has described it as 'one of the most illuminating generalizations which can be found anywhere in the whole literature of economics'.[2] Second, as has recently been observed by Rashid, Smith gave the subject a new look 'by his heavy emphasis upon the division of labour as the major reason for increased production'.[3] And such a decisive change of emphasis constitutes an original contribution. Third, Adam Smith's treatment of the division of labour was different in that he did not reproduce the traditional argument (dating from Plato) that productivity is highest when each individual specializes according to his 'natural talent'. Instead, Smith maintained that individual talent was largely the product of education and the environment; it was, in other words, nurture rather than nature that was responsible for productivity differences among workers.

This chapter will demonstrate how the above three important aspects of the reasoning in *The Wealth of Nations* have so inspired research in economics between 1951 and 1990 as to add new confirmation of the clarity, uniqueness and fertility of Smith's classical work.

The Extent of the Market Limitation

The important 1951 paper by Stigler presented Smith's proposition that 'the division of labour is limited by the extent of the market', as 'the core of a theory of the functions of firm and industry, and a good deal more besides'.[4] Smith's theorem implied that some of the many processes within the firm are subject to increasing returns. Stigler creatively used an extended version of the theorem to predict that firms will eventually abandon the functions subject to increasing returns and allow other firms to specialize in them to take full advantage of cost reductions. The original firm is then able to purchase the services of this process at a lower price. Its new supplier, moreover, will not have strong monopoly power because the first firm can always retaliate by reincorporating the process at will. Stigler then distilled from Smith's theorem the empirically falsifiable proposition that 'vertical *disintegration* is the typical development in growing industries, vertical integration in declining industries'.

Smith's extended theorem, according to Stigler, predicts that in the full life of industries they will go from a period of vertical disintegration and back again to integration as the firm or industry declined. Stigler demonstrated this by reference to the cotton textile machinery industry. Its history up to the 1920s was one of progressive specialism, but when the textile market declined in the 1920s, the trend was reversed as firms added new products.

Stigler also used Smith's theorem to shed light on several aspects of the structure and workings of whole economies. In particular, he expected to find some relationship between the functional structure of an industry and its geographical structure – the reductions of transport costs being a major way of increasing the extent of the market. It was consistent with Smith's analysis, he continued, to conclude that, within a market area, geographical dispersion is a luxury that can be afforded by industries only after they have grown large. Stigler conjectured that in highly-localized areas individual plants could specialize in smaller ranges of products. US evidence was accordingly employed and this did indeed show that geographically-concentrated industries usually had fairly small plants.

Stigler could have quoted Smith's own evidence on the significance of transport cost and concentration. In Chapter I of Book III of *The Wealth of Nations*, entitled 'Of the Natural Progress of Opulence', it is argued that the gains of townspeople and country-people, which are mutual and reciprocal, provided a self-generating and growing market. The cultivation of land required artisans such as carpenters, wheelwrights, masons and bricklayers. 'And as their residence is not, like that of the farmer, necessarily tied down to a precise spot, they naturally settle in the neighbourhood of one another.'[5] More precisely,

> an inland country naturally fertile and easily cultivated, produces a great surplus of provisions beyond what is necessary for maintaining the cultivators, and on account of the expense of land carriage, and inconveniency of river navigation, it may frequently be difficult to send this surplus abroad. Abundance, therefore, renders provisions cheap, and encourages a great number of workmen to settle in the neighbourhood, who find that their industry can there procure them more of the necessaries and conveniences of life than in other places.[6]

Smith quoted as evidence the histories of the towns of Leeds, Halifax, Sheffield, Birmingham and Wolverhampton. He also added the important point that transport costs per unit were proportionately much less in the towns than across rural areas. This opened a wider market and the more valuable finished industrial products were gradually sold from the town base to more distant places.

The Positive Effect on Growth

As previously mentioned, the second important aspect of Smith's approach was his strong emphasis on the proposition that the division of labour was a key factor in increased productivity and therefore in economic growth. Scholars today appear to need little persuasion on this score. Thus, Sherwin Rosen is confident in simply asserting that 'The enormous productivity and complexity of modern economies are in good measure attributable to specialization'.[7] But Rosen opens up Smith's theory somewhat in explaining why this should be so and his focus is upon the interaction between specialization and total investment, including investment in human capital or education. The non-specialist worker, Rosen emphasizes, has lesser incentives to invest in each of his several skills than the specialist because of the smaller average return. Worker productivity in each skill is therefore smaller when specialization is not feasible because total investment will be less. It is clear from Smith's work, meanwhile, that a free market results in productivity effects, from the division of labour, that are *cumulative*. Describing this as '*The* Adam Smith proposition', Ippolito recently subjected it to a rigorous test. And his findings were favourable to the Smithian proposition using 20th-century data.[8]

Division of Labour and Increasing Returns

The third previously mentioned aspect of Smith's treatment of the division of labour is his assumption that it was nurture rather than nature that accounted for productivity differences among workers. In Smith's words:

> The difference of natural talents in different men is, in reality, much less than we are aware of; and the very different genius which appears to distinguish men of different professions, when grown up to maturity, is not upon many occasions so much the cause, as the effect of the division of labor. The difference between the most dissimilar characters, between a philosopher and a common street porter, for example, seems to arise not so much from nature, as from habit, custom, and education.[9]

Rashid finds it strange that, unlike others, Smith does not start from the assumption of natural (congenital) differences. 'Why Smith would have chosen to omit this obvious factor is by no means clear.'[10] One potential answer is that Smith was genuinely not convinced that the factor referred to was 'obvious'. Whatever the case, his scenario opened up a new fruitful line of analysis. In particular, he discovered what are now classified as strong tendencies of increasing returns. In Smith's famous pin factory illustration we start with the observation that 'a workman not educated to this business ..., could scarce, perhaps, with his utmost industry, make one pin a day ...'.[11] But after the division of labour is introduced into a real world example of a factory that Smith had seen employing ten men wherein 'one man draws out the wire, another straightens it, a third cuts it' and so on, each of the ten workers made on average 4800 pins in a day! It would surely be stretching common credibility to believe that these results occurred because one man was born with a 'natural talent' for drawing out the wire and another with a similar inborn gift in straightening it! Indeed the 'obvious' factor in this situation is the economy of 'learning by doing'. And if we start with ten homogeneous potential workers it does not matter very much how each individual is subsequently allocated across the different processes. Each and every one will increase his dexterity by concentration on one or two processes, as Smith maintained.[12] And, as will be shown, it is in this context that the process involves what we now call increasing returns.

In Smith's illustration, the isolated and unspecialized individual who by himself could scarce make one pin a day, is described as a workman 'not educated to this business'. In this example which, as Smith concedes, relates to 'a very trifling manufacture', the necessary education would come largely with experience on the job. In 'less trifling' manufactures, education of a more formal and sustained kind would be needed. And it is implicit in Smith that not only would there typically exist a positive pay-off to some quantity of relevant education, but that the total return to the corresponding investment in human capital would depend upon the number of hours it is eventually used (i.e. the utilization rate). This point has been clarified by Barzel and Yu[13] using a numerical example whose essential elements appear in two tables reproduced here as Tables 4.1 and 4.2.

Table 4.1   Division of labour as a function of the utilization rate of human capital

Educ. in A ($)	Working hours in A	Wage in A ($)	Earning in A ($)	Educ. in B ($)	Working hours in B	Wage in B ($)	Earning in B ($)	Total earning ($)
0	4	1.00	4.00	0	4	1.00	4.00	8.00
1000	5	1.20	6.00	1000	5	1.20	6.00	12.00
2000	5	1.30	6.50	0	5	1.00	5.00	11.50
2000	10	1.30	13.00	0	0	1.00	0	13.00

Initially a worker performs two activities, A and B, and obtains the same hourly wage rate, say $1, in each. Since he spends four hours each day in A and four hours in B his total earnings are $8 (first row of Table 4.1). Suppose he now suffers a sudden decline in his personal wealth and wants to compensate by working two more hours. Increased hours imply an increased utilization rate of human capital so that the expected return to education is now higher. If he devotes one extra hour each to activities A and B the worker would increase education in both by the same amount. Since more education raises marginal productivity, the wage rates in both A and B would rise.

Assume the actual wage/education relationship is as shown in Table 4.2. Suppose, given the extension of total working hours to ten, the wealth maximizing level of education expenditure is $1000 for each activity. The hourly wage after the education will increase to $1.20 in both activities. Total earnings will then be $12 (row two in Table 4.1).

The best alternative for the worker, however, is to give up one of the two activities altogether. Suppose he withdraws from B and allocates his total educational expenditures of $2000 to A. The wage rate in A will increase, although at a diminishing rate, to $1.30 (see Table 4.2). The wage rate in B, with zero expenditure on education, will be $1.00. If the worker allocates all hours to A, total earnings become $13 which is the maximum possible (row four in Table 4.1). Notice that the total earnings obtained by spending equal time in A and B (row three in Table 4.1) will result in a total income of only $11.50.

The expectation of a higher utilization rate in a particular activity results therefore in a larger accumulation of human capital specific to that activity. This accumulation leads to a higher wage rate and

Table 4.2   An assumed wage/education relationship

Educational expense ($)	Wage ($)
0	1.00
1000	1.20
2000	1.30
3000	1.35

this in turn feeds back to substituting working hours into that activity.[14]

A second individual, who at the start is identical to the first, will have the same incentives to specialize. The chosen activity in his case, however, could be in B rather than A. Generally, we expect that out of a group of originally homogenous workers some individuals will specialize in A and others in B. At the end of the process there will emerge the *apparent* difference in 'natural talents' to which Adam Smith referred; but the 'talents' are in fact acquired, not natural.

In consequence if, following the above spontaneous market-driven type of specialization, government passes a law decreeing that individuals who engage in activity A must also engage in activity B, the legislation will have a negative effect on the size of the national income. In *The Wealth of Nations* we find just such a criticism in Smith's strong condemnation of laws dating from 1551 that obliged the farmer simultaneously to undertake the trade of a corn merchant, the ostensible aim being to get rid of the 'middleman'. But Smith protested:

> The statute of Edward VI, therefore, by prohibiting as much as possible any middle man from coming in between the grower and the consumer, endeavoured to annihilate a trade, of which the free exercise is not only the best palliative of the inconveniences of a dearth, but the best preventative of that calamity.[15]

The return to investment in a particular skill is increasing in its subsequent rate of utilization, Rosen points out, because educational investment expenses are sunk costs that are independent of how the acquired skills are employed. It is this element of fixed costs that makes it 'advantageous to specialize investment resources to a narrow band of skills and employ them as intensively as possible'.[16] With reference to Table 4.1, by going to a corner solution the worker does not lose any value and reduces costs by eliminating educational investment in one activity (A or B). Non-specialization might occur, Rosen concedes, when costs are non-separable, that is when investment in one skill lowers the cost of investing in the other so that there is economy of scope. But, the interaction has to exceed a given threshold level to overcome the effects of increasing marginal costs of investment. And these latter costs are implicit in Table 4.2.[17]

Observe also that 'the production of comparative advantage

through human capital accumulation is an efficient social use of resources, even if all people are inherently identical and goods production functions exhibit constant returns to scale'.[18] What produces this result is the non-convexity (indivisibility) in human capital investment. The point has generality with respect to virtually all human capital investment even when, like Adam Smith, we minimize the existence of 'natural talents'. Rosen concludes: 'It may be the main reason why trade occurs at all'.

At this point we return briefly to one of the main issues in Chapter 3 where we examined the neoclassical criticism of Smith for not having pioneered the explanation of trade by way of the theory of comparative advantage. It is now arguable that Smith's total analysis is the more comprehensive because it goes well beyond the neoclassical reasoning. For whereas the latter simply takes as a datum an existing structure of comparative advantage, Smith's approach affords opportunities for going behind and beyond it to explain its very foundation. Manufactured instead of 'natural' differences stem from incentives that prompt inherently identical individuals (or countries) to make 'sunk cost' investments in an almost accidental variety of skills. In this light, many comparative advantages are man-made and the incentive for trade is an obvious development *after this fact*.

The experiment using Tables 4.1 and 4.2 was triggered by the assumption of a sudden decline in the worker's personal wealth and his consequent desire to work two more hours. The data, however, could be used in an alternative way to demonstrate a similar incentive to reduce the variety of jobs performed (for example, to select A instead of A and B). Instead of a sudden increase in the utilization rate of human capital, the triggering event now could be an increase in the demand for the activities in question caused, say, by an increase in population. Smith's observation that the division of labour is limited by the extent of the market is of course invoked once more; and here we are assuming a partial relaxation of the market limitation.

The increase in demand for activities A and B means, in the short run, an increase in wages in both cases. Assume that these increases are equal. As a consequence, the returns to education in each grow by the same magnitude. But for reasons parallel to the previous logic, specialization in market time and in education simultaneously in A *or* B is now preferred to the continuance of working half time in each. In the long run, the increased productivity in this competitive world will bring about a new equilibrium in which prices fall somewhat from their short-run levels but much of the new specialization sticks. Smith produces this analytical sequence in the following words:

> The increase of demand ..., though in the beginning it may sometimes raise the price of goods, never fails to lower it in the long run. It encourages production, and thereby increases the competition of the producers, who, in order to undersell one another, have recourse to new divisions of labour and new improvements of art, which might never otherwise have been thought of.[19]

An interesting modern application of specialization analysis has been made by Baumgardner using American data.[20] His systematic evidence supports the conclusion that the degree of the division of labour among physicians increases with local population. In his model, 'specialization' refers to the degree to which a doctor narrows his practice to a small set of patient problems or medical procedures. Another consistent finding of Baumgardner's is that when demand variables such as population are held constant, geographically larger counties exhibit less division of labour.

Once more it seems that Smith was the first to state the relevant hypotheses, while it has been left to subsequent 20th-century economists to test them with an abundance and quality of data not available in the 18th century. One of Smith's several examples of Baumgardner's main proposition is as follows:

> There are some sorts of industry, even of the lowest kind, which can be carried on nowhere but in a great town ... A country carpenter deals in every sort of work that is made of wood: a country smith in every sort of work that is made of iron. The former is not only a carpenter, but a joiner, a cabinet-maker, and even a carver in wood as well as a wheelwright, a plough-wright, a cart and waggon maker.[21]

The discussion, so far, can be further clarified by applying it to conventional modern treatment of scale economies in production. Labour specialization is typically cited in textbooks simply as an explanation of economies of scale but without a clear indication why.[22] The gap in the reasoning results from a failure to state that labour specialization results in increasing returns only through indivisibility (non-convexity) in the use of labour. As has been observed by Edwards and Starr, if labour were fully divisible, Adam Smith's pronouncement that 'division of labour is limited by the extent of the market' would be false.[23] There would be no special reason why the size of the market would hinder the division of production tasks. If, however, labour is indivisible, the statement in *The Wealth of Nations* is correct. Edwards and Starr believe, indeed, that this was in effect Smith's basic message.

Consider, for example, the productive advantage of the division of labour that Smith attributes to the 'saving of the time which is commonly lost in passing from one species of labour to another' (p. 18). In modern terms he is saying that employing the same worker at different tasks involves transition set-up costs. 'Given sufficient scale, it is preferable to allow labour to specialize and avoid this switching cost, that is, to use labour in indivisible increments.'[24] Edwards and Starr conclude, therefore, that:

> the link between specialization (division of labour) and scale economies is indivisibility or other nonconvexity in application of labour. The classic teatment of Smith implicitly recognized this point ... Nevertheless, it is not explicit in the current elementary literature, which thereby obscures the logic of the analysis.[25]

To make the argument from another perspective: even assuming constant returns to scale in technical production, the presence of indivisibilities or set-up costs in the use of labour inputs results in increasing returns to scale overall.

One important qualification to all this analysis, however, remains to be stated. All the above results are sensitive to the assumption that worker motivation and behaviour are independent of utilization. Some limitation may be placed on specialization if, for instance, activity specific fatigue or boredom brings seriously diminishing marginal productivity of time in a given activity.[26]

Division of Labour and Alienation

In this context, it is interesting to consider a recent argument of Frank J. Jones.[27] He contends that because worker alienation can reduce productivity, and because alienation is a function of specialization, the Smithian view that increasing specialization (division of labour) *always* increases productivity, must be severely qualified.

More formerly, where P denotes labour productivity, S specialization, and A worker alienation,

$$P = f(S,A) \tag{4.1}$$

where $A = g(S)$. To the 'Adam Smith proposition' that $\delta P/\delta S > 0$, Jones adds his extra assumption that $\delta P/\delta A < 0$. The total effect of specialization he then shows to be in the total derivative:

$$\frac{dP}{dS} = \frac{\delta P}{\delta S} + \overset{(-)(+)}{\frac{\delta P}{\delta A} \cdot \frac{\delta A}{\delta S}} \tag{4.2}$$

Since the second right-hand term in (4.2) is negative, productivity may eventually decrease with further increases of specialization.

The remainder of this chapter will attempt to demonstrate that: (1) Jones's case is not unambiguously established, and that in any case his 'policy implications' for despecialization are not obvious; (2) much of the issue depends upon definitions of alienation; (3) more variables, especially leisure and job mismatching, need to be specified as arguments in the alienation function; and (4) there are particularly interesting history of thought aspects relating to Adam Smith and Karl Marx.

In his further elaboration of the alienation function, Jones suggests that it can be shifted upwards (diagrammatically) by education (E) and income (Y). Educated offspring with high career aspirations may be 'more alienated by the same assembly line than their fathers were'.[28] The implication is that as income and education increases, the optimal (most profitable) degree of specialization and alienation falls.

One response to Jones is to urge fuller specification of the alienation function so as to include job mismatching (M) and leisure (L). Mismatching is simply defined as the placement of workers in a manner that is not suited to their skills and training (education). The functional relation accordingly become $A = A(S,E,Y,M,L)$. It is arguable that, normally (see our reference below to Adam Smith), education should have *negative* effects on alienation $\frac{\delta A}{\delta E} < 0$. Similarly, leisure can also have a negative effect $\frac{\delta A}{\delta L} < 0$; and leisure is assumed to be an increasing function of (real) income.

Workers are sometimes engaged in duties that underutilize their true abilities and so leave them frustrated. In this sense, the PhD history graduate who finds employment as a bank teller, might be alienated because he has a job that is not matched to his education or training, and not because of the degree of specialization. In this light, despecialization of the working condition, as Jones suggests, may not result in de-alienation of the more educated but misplaced worker; and such attempts may reduce productivity without comparable benefits to labour. Mismatching may result from labour market imperfections preventing an optimal allocation of labour resources. Professional associations, required unionization, or required, but over-rigid, aptitude testing for various employments, to name a few, may be the underlying real causes of alienation. The 'policy' implication here is not to reduce specialization, but to increase competitiveness or information in the labour market.[29]

The above discussion does not require education to be a positive argument in alienation. Consider the case of a highly-educated labourer ideally *matched* to his special scholarly attainments. Such a person enjoys 'fulfillment' in life. Alienation is an inverse function of such education, or,

$$A = g(E)^{-1}.$$

Whereas Jones offers no definition of education, we shall define it as either cultural, of the liberal arts kind for example, or professional and technical, such as the acquisition of vocational skills or on-the-job training. Education of the wide cultural variety may alleviate alienation of the workers especially if it encourages them to find more happiness in their (increasing) leisure hours. Alienation among those who are technically or professionally educated, meanwhile, is likely to be due not to the education but to mismatching. Conversely, and to repeat, the labourer attaining greater skills while on the job, in effect greater technical education, might well find it stimulating and *de-alienating*.

Our reason for including leisure in the alienation function is as follows. Alienation affects work and non-work hours; de-alienation in non-work hours can affect, or compensate for, alienation in work hours. Increased division of labour rewards the worker with more non-work leisure opportunities and income than he would otherwise realize.[30] The more he can look forward to improved leisure aided by increased income, the more reconciled to his job the worker is likely to be; and the smaller the likelihood of absenteeism and turnover.

The rational worker might indeed be willing to trade-off *more* on-the-job alienation for a better quantity and quality of leisure for *total* alienation then falls.

The result of such reasoning changes the productivity function in Jones's equation (4.2) above to:

$$\frac{dP}{dS} = \overset{(+)}{\frac{\delta P}{\delta S}} + \overset{(-)(-)}{\frac{\delta P}{\delta A} \cdot \frac{\delta A}{\delta S}}$$

$$(4.3)$$

This equation contains a *positive* second term on the right-hand side indicating that increased specialization *will* lead to increased productivity as Adam Smith assumes in Book I of *The Wealth of Nations*.

A final comment on Jones's analysis concerns wage adjustments between educated and 'less' educated workers. Suppose mismatching and imperfect labour market problems are intractable. Then, indeed, professionally or technically educated but mismatched persons might continue to be so alienated as to have low productivity. In this case the demand for them, relative to less educated persons, would fall. In this case employers could maintain full specialization but substitute less educated (= less alienated) workers. The reduced wages of highly-educated workers would, consequently, act to discourage that level of education. The problem could thus be resolved in this manner.

The history of thought aspect of this problem concerns the less familiar fact that Adam Smith recognized, not only that specialization increased productivity, but also that it could cause undesirable social effects that look like one form of alienation. He observed:

> The man whose life is spent in performing a few simple operations ... becomes as stupid and ignorant as it is possible for a human creature to become. The torpor of his mind renders him not only incapable of relishing or bearing a part in any rational conversation, but of concerning any generous, noble or tender sentiment, and consequently of forming any just judgement concerning many even of the ordinary duties of private life.[31]

It is not clear from this quotation that Smith envisaged a decline in worker productivity; he was more concerned with a decay of civilized virtues and the danger of turning men into 'work machines'. What is more interesting is that Smith's observation on the dangers of his kind of alienation was a preface to a case for subsidized education. For to Smith, suitable education is an *antidote* to alienation.[32] It would so quicken the mind as to provoke (scientific) curiosity in all environments that individuals found themselves. This is the reverse diagnosis to that of Jones who argues that education will *induce* alienation.

More interesting still, Smith saw increased specialization eventually creating a special class of scientists or philosophers in society whose job it is to speculate about new methods and new products. These highly-educated persons received the fullest satisfaction from their occupations. Here there was obviously no alienation or mismatching. But this begins to take us out of Jones's context of a particular firm and into the realm of the whole society. Nevertheless the connection with our argument (above) and that of Smith's is clear enough.

The other, and more dominant, complaint about alienation in the history of thought comes from Karl Marx. To Marx, alienation in the capitalist system was a symptom of its impending doom. The cause of alienation to him was not just the division of labour but also private property and market exchange.[33] Jones's recommendation, however, that managers should merely adjust existing plants to a less-specialized scale, clearly keeps him within the neoclassical or non-Marxian world. To Marx, neither despecialization nor education in a capitalist world were satisfactory answers to alienation. His prescription, or rather prediction, was the complete abolition of private property and exchange, a 'cure' that, to him, would have made Jones's type of modelling irrelevant.

Notes

1. Tucker (1756).
2. Young (1928).
3. Rashid (1986), p. 295.
4. Stigler (1951).
5. Smith (1976), p. 378.
6. Ibid., p. 408.
7. Rosen (1983).
8. Ippolito (1977).
9. Smith (1976), pp. 28–9.
10. Rashid (1986), p. 296.
11. Smith (1976), p. 14.
12. Smith's full explanation of higher productivity development of course included the saving of time in switching from one process to another and the induced propensity to invent, both of which also accompany the division of labour.

13. Barzel and Yu (1984). The authors make generous reference to Adam Smith.
14. Ibid., p. 19.
15. Smith (1976), p. 532. Although Smith appears to have had the optimal allocation of physical capital rather than human capital primarily in mind, the argument of Barzel and Yu is congenial to his total position. Smith for instance refers to the proverb: 'Jack of all trades will never be rich'. And he concludes 'The law ought always to trust people with the care of their own interest, as in their local situations they must generally be able to judge better of it than the legislator can do'.
16. Rosen (1983), p. 44.
17. In other words, diminishing returns in the wage education function in Table 4.2 can easily be translated into a rising marginal cost of education function.
18. Rosen (1983), p. 47.
19. Smith (1976), p. 748.
20. Baumgardner (1988).
21. Smith (1976), p. 32.
22. See, for example, Mansfield (1976).
23. Edwards and Starr (1987)
24. Ibid., p. 192.
25. Edwards and Starr (1987), p. 194. Rashid (1986) cites Dugald Stewart, Richard Whately, E. G. Wakefield and other 19th-century writers as criticizing Smith for overstressing the argument of the saving of time and for underemphasizing the contribution of inventions and management. The deficiency, however, seems to lay with the critics. They obviously did not appreciate the depth and sophistication of Smith's argument.
26. Rosen (1983), p. 47.
27. Jones (1975). The remainder of this Chapter draws freely from West and Hafer (1979).
28. Jones (1975), p. 19.
29. Kim (1989) points out that the larger the size of the market the more varieties of job requirements are used so that, with positive growth, the average match between a worker and a firm improves through time.
30. The long term trend in US average weekly hours from the middle of the 19th century through the Second World War was continuously and consistently downward (see Zeisel, 1958). Over the same period, of course, specialization and real wages trended upwards.
31. Smith (1976), pp. 781–2.
32. West (1969, 1975).
33. West (1976).

5. Principal/Agent Problems, Moral Hazard and the Theory of the Firm

Most people who know of Adam Smith probably think of him as being concerned exclusively with the invisible hand and allocation by price. This chapter will demonstrate that he was aware of organizational issues also. One such issue comes close to what today is referred to as the principal/agent problem. The problem relates to an economic actor, the principal, purchasing the services of another, the agent. If the principal is an employer he will want to maximize his wealth subject to the opportunity cost of the agent and the latter's incentive to cheat, and he does so by choosing a wage structure that depends on output. The principal, however, soon confronts difficulties in monitoring his agent's performance. In short, it is possible for the agent, upon receipt of payment (or promise thereof), to 'shirk', that is, to provide less effort than is in the principal's interest and expectation.[1] Adam Smith's anticipation of this kind of analysis appears in three main contexts in *The Wealth of Nations*: foreign trade, non-profit organizations and public joint stock companies.

Agency Problems in Foreign Trade

Smith argued that 'upon equal or nearly equal profits' there is a presumption in favour of home trade over foreign trade. The reason is that merchants prefer to invest in domestic rather than foreign enterprises, because they can supervise their agents with less cost.

> Thus upon equal or nearly equal profits, every wholesale merchant naturally prefers the home-trade to the foreign trade ... He can know better the character and situation of the persons whom he trusts, and if

he should happen to be deceived, he knows better the laws of the country from which he must seek redress.[2]

While the principal/agent problem seems implicit in this quotation, the total economic reasoning is not without ambiguity. This is because the preference for the home over the foreign trade is postulated on the assumption of 'equal profits'. Yet, strictly, if expected profits *were* equal per unit of time the merchant should be indifferent between home and foreign trading. The stated preference for the home trade must, in any case, be placed in perspective. If this was all there was to it we would expect to see *no* trade with other countries. Yet in the same chapter and throughout *The Wealth of Nations* Smith accepts that foreign trade has its place, even if it is smaller than the mercantilists would wish. Smith's reasoning makes more sense, therefore, if we interpret it as saying that, because foreign trade involves owners in above-average costs of monitoring their resources, *gross* profit must be correspondingly higher per unit of time in compensation. In final equilibrium marginal net revenues will then be equal across the home and foreign trade for the last dollar invested.

The main ambiguity appears to lay in Smith's precondition: 'upon equal or nearly equal profits'. There is reason to believe that the equality referred to is *not* per unit of time. Thus in his chapter in Book IV *Of Colonies* he argues that the 'monopoly of the colony trade' has in all cases 'forced some part of ... capital from the trade with Europe ... to that with the more distant regions of America ... from which the returns are necessarily less frequent'. In that same chapter also, Smith describes the trade with the more distant parts as being more 'uncertain' and more 'irregular'. But none of these observations detracts from the fact that Smith identified a legitimate cost of trading, the cost of monitoring one's employees, a cost that is described in modern terms as stemming from the principal/agent problem.

Difficulty in supervising one's employees often involves capital costs. An agent's shirking can result in the neglect of the principal's property and sometimes, indeed, in the partial expropriation of it. In the shipping industry the owner's property consists both of the vessel and its freight. Smith correspondingly offers a prediction as to the residential location of such owners.

In the carrying trade, the capital of the merchant is, as it were, divided between two foreign countries, and no part of it is ever necessarily brought home, or placed under his own immediate view and command. The capital which an Amsterdam merchant employs in carrying corn from Konnigsberg to Lisbon, and fruit and wine from Lisbon to Konnigsberg, must generally be the one-half of it at Konnigsberg and the other half at Lisbon. No part of it need ever come to Amsterdam. The natural residence of such a merchant should either be at Konnigsberg or Lisbon, and it can only be some very particular circumstances which can make him prefer the residence of Amsterdam.[3]

In essence this is another example in Smith of a refutable hypothesis. But no doubt the necessary data with which to test it must in this case derive from 18th-or early 19th-century sources.

Agency Problems in Donor Non-profit Organizations

In non-profit organizations such as charities there are no agents with alienable rights in residual cash flows. Such organization indeed appears to be an attempt to avoid agency problems with residual claimants simply by precluding them. The non-profit, however, still faces the danger of indirect expropriation by internal agents (employees). Fama and Jensen argue accordingly that there will be an incentive to appoint boards of directors with tighter than usual control and upon which internal agents will not be allowed to serve.[4] But those who persist further with the self-interest assumption will argue that there is no guarantee that opportunistic behaviour will not recur, and this time among the board members. This danger will be minimized only where the members themselves are substantial donors. In this situation their time served on the board will be consistent with their self-interest as consumers or utility maximizers.

In the case where donations are generated chiefly by bequests, however, it is not possible for the donors to serve on the board since they will no longer be alive. Constraints against agency problems in these instances become especially difficult to construct. Adam Smith dwells in detail upon one particular example: educational institutions in England. As a point of departure he begins with the one circumstance wherein the agency problem is minimal, the case where the agent is paid directly in proportion to results:

In every profession, the exertion of the greater part of those who exercise it, is always in proportion to the necessity they are under of making that exertion. This necessity is greatest with those to whom the emoluments of their profession are the only source from which they expect their fortune.[5] (p. 760)

Smith then proceeds to an example of an opposite situation where the incentives actually encourage the agency problem: the case of English schools and universities financed by endowments (largely accumulated from past bequests).

> The endowments of schools and colleges have necessarily diminished more or less the necessity of application of the teachers. Their subsistence, so far as it arises from their salaries, is evidently derived from a fund altogether independent of their success and reputation in their particular professions.

Smith is arguing that one type of salary fund that varies positively with the teachers' success is one that is accumulated via student fees, that is, direct consumer payments. The higher the proportion of the salary that comes from such a fund, the smaller the agency problem. He observes that in those universities where the total payment to the teacher comes from a mixture of endowment *and* student fees, with fees being the greater source, 'The necessity of application, though always more or less diminished, is not in this case entirely taken away'.[6]

In universities where student fee payments are not allowed and where the teacher's income comes entirely from the endowment fund, his performance will normally be very inferior. In modern terms, shirking will be high. This will especially be the case where the teacher is subject to no authority or monitor.

> His interest is, in this case, set as directly in opposition to his duty as it is possible to set it. It is the interest of every man to live as much at his ease as he can; and if his emoluments are to be precisely the same, whether he does, or does not perform some very laborious duty, it is certainly his interest, at least as interest is vulgarly understood, either to neglect it altogether, or, if he is subject to some authority which will not suffer him to do this, to perform it in as careless and slovenly a manner as that authority will permit. If he is naturally active and a lover of labour, it is his interest to employ that activity in any way from which he can derive some advantage, rather than in the performance of his duty, from which he can derive none. (P. 760)

For-profit corporations continuously face the discipline from the outside takeover market. Non-profits, in contrast, are immune to this pressure because they lack alienable residual claims. Consequently, Fama and Jensen conclude,

> Without the takeover threat or the discipline imposed by residual claimants with the right to remove members of the board, non-profit boards composed of internal agents ... would provide little assurance against collusion and expropriation of donations. Thus, non-profit boards generally include few if any internal agents as voting members ... Moreover, non-profit board members are generally substantial donors who serve without pay.[7]

In Smith's example, however, it is not possible to apply this last Fama and Jensen solution of having boards or committees consisting primarily of the donors, since in this case most of them are deceased. The agency problem therefore is here revealed in all its 'severity'.

> If the authority to which [the teacher] is subject resides in the body corporate, the college, or university, of which he himself is a member, and in which the greater part of the other members are, like himself, persons who either are, or ought to be teachers; they are likely to make a common cause, to be all very indulgent to one another, and every man to consent that his neighbour may neglect his duty, provided he himself is allowed to neglect his own. In the university of Oxford, the greater part of the publick professors have, for these many years, given up altogether even the pretence of teaching.[8]

Agency Problems in Public Companies

In Adolf Berle and Gardiner Means's classic *The Modern Corporation and Private Property*, published in 1932, it was argued that capitalism had by then developed to the point where ownership and control had been largely separated, especially in the newly-evolved big corporations. The main contention was that stock ownership had become so widespread and diffused that shareholders were hostage to a new managerial class that made all the decisions. Managers did sometimes own shares in their companies but where this was so their holdings were very small. Berle and Means announced that the 'managerial revolution' they were depicting marked the birth of a new economic epoch and one that had departed from the classical theory of capitalism. For a description of the latter they quoted Adam Smith.

When Adam Smith talked of 'enterprise' he had in mind as the typical unit the small individual business in which the owner, perhaps with the aid of a few apprentices or workers, labored to produce goods for market or to carry on commerce. Very emphatically he repudiated the stock corporation as a business mechanism, holding that dispersed ownership made efficient operation impossible ... Yet when we speak of business enterprise today, we must have in mind primarily these very units which seemed to Adam Smith not to fit into the principles ... he was laying down for the conduct of economic activity.[9]

The year 1982 being the fiftieth anniversary of the Berle and Means volume, the Hoover Institution hosted a conference to re-evaluate its ideas. Gardiner Means, who was present, stressed that he and his fellow author had not argued that it was impossible for public corporations ever to be efficient. 'We reached no such conclusion. Adam Smith clearly stated this view, and we quoted him. But there are many situations in which corporations can be more efficient than unincorporated enterprise, and we did not subscribe to Smith's view.'[10]

This picture of Smith as an extremist in defence of small unincorporated undertakings, however, has been challenged by Anderson and Tollison. They argue 'Smith did not hold the view that joint-stock firms were inefficient *a priori*. His argument was a posteriori, based on the available empirical evidence.[11] And on this interpretation indeed we have another instance of Smith employing the modern economic practice of framing explicitly a refutable hypothesis and using available evidence to test it.

Before examining the Anderson and Tollison argument further, however, it may be helpful to outline important rejoinders made over the last half century to Berle and Means's general proposition. First, several economists insist that, when sufficiently provoked, shareholders can and will always mobilize themselves for action designed to dismiss ineffective management. The action may, for instance, take the form of a takeover or the acquisition of large stockholdings by one or a few shareholders. And the fact that such events take place in the real world means they are a constant threat to inefficient management. Next, shortcomings of management will lower the price of the company's stock and this will affect unfavourably the terms on which it can obtain capital in the future. If managers' salaries are a function of the company's turnover, the higher price of capital will affect them adversely. The reputation of managers, meanwhile, is itself an asset that is always at stake. They are, after all, keen to see that their expensive investment in human capital maintains its price in the eyes of other firms that may want to employ them in the future. Finally, and perhaps most important, evidence reveals a strong connection between management and owner interests where profit-sharing occurs and when there are significant levels of managers' shareholding in their employer's company.[12]

Berle and Means's portrayal of Adam Smith's version of what they call the 'classical theory of capitalism' is incorrect because Smith recognized the usefulness of some of the constraints on management outlined in the previous paragraph. His vision was one of dynamic change and his concept of competition as a process (discussed in Chapter 2) implies a continual 'weeding out' of inefficient organizations over time. But this occurs, of course, only if there is free entry and exit. Government-granted monopoly powers seriously blunt the process. But provided there is reasonably free entry, at any one time, some organizational forms can be observed that are inefficient and in the process of going under. Efficiency is revealed in terms of long-run survivorship. It is true that Smith believed that joint-stock organizations on average did not have a good survival record, even when they had legal protection. As a conspicious example he quoted the Royal African Company established with an exclusive privilege by charter in the 17th century but which was dissolved in 1733 because it could not compete against 'private adventurers'. Similarly, the notorious South Sea Company could not compete against foreign competition despite its monopoly charter.

It is wrong, nevertheless, to assume that Smith was opposed to joint-stock organizations on principle. His examination of them was discriminating and perceptive and he referred to examples of successful operations such as the Hudson Bay Company. What interested him was a search for explanations of the differences in recorded performance and survival. He started by recognizing one advantage pertaining to all joint-stock organizations. They allowed greater direct investment by individuals since they facilitated portfolio diversification so that the risks associated with a given level of investment were reduced.

> The trade of a joint stock company is always managed by a court of directors. This court, indeed, is frequently subject, in many respects, to the control of a general court of proprietors. But the greater part of those

proprietors seldom pretend to understand any thing of the business of the company; and when the spirit of faction happens not to prevail among them, give themselves no trouble about it, but receive contentedly such half yearly or yearly dividend, as the directors think proper to make to them. This total exemption from trouble and from risk, beyond a limited sum, encourages many people to become adventurers in joint stock companies, who would, upon no account, hazard their fortunes in any private copartnery. Such companies, therefore, commonly draw to themselves much greater stocks than any private copartnary can boast of.[13]

Smith's diagnosis of the main disadvantage of joint-stock firms is the recognition once more of the principal/agent problem:

The directors of such companies, however, being the managers rather of other people's money than of their own, it cannot well be expected that they should watch over it with the same anxious vigilance with which the partners in a private copartnery frequently watch over their own. Like the stewards of a rich man, they are apt to consider attention to small matters as not for their master's honour, and very easily give themselves a dispensation from having it. Negligence and profusion therefore, must always prevail, more or less, in the management of the affairs of such a company. It is upon this account that joint stock companies for foreign trade have seldom been able to maintain the competition against private adventurers. They have, accordingly, very seldom succeeded without an exclusive privilege; and frequently have not succeeded with one.[14]

It seems to have been this passage that encouraged Berle and Means and others to believe that Smith was dismissing joint-stock enterprise altogether. Yet, as Anderson and Tollison observe, Smith is not in fact committing himself 'to any a prioristic assessment of the degree of managerial inefficiency necessarily associated with the joint-stock company. He is pointing out an economic problem involving the structure of incentives which are inherent in this organizational form.'[15] Negligence and profusion, Smith argues, 'must always prevail *more or less*'. To get them to prevail *less* called for special circumstances and incentives. And it was possible, within limits, that these could be arranged.

The Need for Special Incentive Structures

It is pertinent that in the previous quotation Smith is explicitly referring to 'joint stock companies for foreign trade'. His opinion of such companies in domestic activities is much more favourable. His whole discussion of the need for 'public works' at home, for instance, lead to recommendations for joint-stock enterprise in banking, canals, water supply, roads and bridges. But even in the case of companies in foreign trade, Smith recognized the usefulness of one form of incentive that has become common in the 20th century, namely profit-sharing arrangements.

> The directors of a joint stock company, on the contrary, having only their share in the profits which are made upon the common stock committed to their management, have no private trade of their own, of which the interest can be separated from that of the general trade of the company. Their private interest is connected with the prosperity of the general trade of the company.[16]

The implication of such reasoning is that ownership and control need not be as separate as the Berle and Means type critics tend to think. More important, Smith's argument amounts to another testable hypothesis, this time to the effect that the survivorship rate among unprotected public joint-stock companies is positively correlated with the degree of managers' shareholdings in them. Relevant evidence for the US in the 20th century has recently been offered by Demsetz. He reports that an examination of an average of 20 firms, ten in the middle and ten at the bottom in the Fortune 500, reveals that corporate managers owned about 20 per cent of outstanding shares in 1975.[17] The agency problem is, of course, one that varies in intensity or, in Smith's words, one that occurs 'more or less'. It follows that if the costs of agency can be reduced sufficiently by appropriate incentives, the advantages of joint-stock enterprise recognized in *The Wealth of Nations* can outweigh the agency problem. Smith, in fact, quotes examples of such incentive structures and of the survivorship of joint-stock companies that practised them.

Agency costs will vary with the nature of the firm's activity. The more 'severe' they are the more likely we can expect the concentration of ownership. In general, variations in the structure of corporate ownership can be in direct response to variations in the agency costs. Where, for instance, markets experience fairly stable prices, stable technology and stable market shares, we can expect relatively low costs of monitoring managerial performance. Where, in contrast, prices and technology change frequently there is a greater need for managerial decisions (discretion) concerning the best response to the instability. But in these situations it is difficult to disentangle the positive contribution of managers from the exogenous changes going on.[18] The prediction or hypothesis that emerges, therefore, is that the more unstable the environment the greater the incentive of owners to maintain tighter control and therefore to ensure more concentrated ownership. Using modern US data, Demsetz and Lehn report systematic evidence consistent with this hypothesis.[19] What is more they quote Adam Smith as having presented the following variant of it:

> The only trades which it seems possible for a joint stock company to carry on successfully, without an exclusive privilege, are those, of which all the operations are capable of being reduced to what is called a routine or to such a uniformity of method as admits of little or no variation.[20]

The particular illustrations of this 'rule' that Smith quotes are debatable as will be shown when they are re-examined in Chapter 7. For the moment, however, one can accept as reasonably persuasive Smith's general theoretical point.

The Theory of the Firm and Organization

McNulty has observed that it is rather paradoxical that the theory of economic organization, and in particular the role of the firm, does not get more attention in *The Wealth of Nations* despite the fact that, in his opening discussion on the division of labour, this is precisely where Smith's analysis begins.[21]

Williamson, however, gives credit to Smith for giving more attention to the firm than does much of modern neoclassical economics.[22] The neoclassical firm, he argues, is characterized merely as a production function and the main focus is on the issue of the efficient choice of factor proportions. Problems relating to the organization of work, which involves economizing on transaction costs, are typically unaddressed. In contrast, Williamson describes a minimum of six different methods of organization both in ownership and in contracting terms. These include entrepreneurial modes, wherein each work station is owned and operated by a specialist, collective ownership where the stations are owned in common by the entire group of workers, and capitalist modes wherein a single party owns the plant equipment and stocks of all kinds. Beyond this the alternative arrangements vary in terms of their degree of reliance on contractual detail to co-ordinate the production. The entrepreneurial and putting-out systems, for instance, rely extensively on contracting. The same is true of what Williamson calls the 'federated work stations'. These are located side-by-side in a common facility wherein intermediate product is transferred across stages by each worker. Because each individual works at his own pace, buffer inventories play an important role, but of course involve their own special costs.

Perhaps a more important way of differentiating the methods of organization is by examining the degree of hierarchy. The degree is obviously low where decisions are subject to collective approval and high in the case of factory organization. Williamson observes that the most hierarchical decision-making mode is a capitalist arrangement although he also finds that there is a considerable degree of hierarchy under collective ownership also.

It seems clear that Smith's pin factory example, unlike neoclassical analysis does involve some minimum examination of the ways in which costs of organization can be economized. Hence the observation on such things as the saving in set-up time costs in the factory division of labour. Smith's example can also be described as the full hierarchical capitalist mode of organization (in Williamson's terms). McNulty's criticism presumably involves the question of why Smith did not make a comparative study of many more alternative modes of organization so as to determine which of them was the most efficient. The only alternative that Smith considered was each man being his own entrepreneur and working 'separately and independently', one pin being produced at a time, start to finish, before work on the next is begun. As Williamson suggests, 'Intentionally or not, the comparison is thereby rigged in favour of factory modes of organization'.[23] Williamson's study is interesting because, after careful analysis of a wide variety of organizational modes, he concludes that the capitalist hierarchical mode usually scores highly in terms of efficiency, a conclusion which seems to imply that Smith's instincts on this subject were in the right direction after all.

Consider next the doubts of Marglin concerning the efficiency justification for hierarchy. Bearing in mind that the division of labour in enterprises such as Smith's pin factory is supervised by capitalist bosses, Marglin raises the question 'What do bosses do?' His reply is simply that they exploit workers via the device of hierarchy. Marglin agrees with Smith that the separate production of each individual pin is grossly inefficient. The division of labour is necessary and Smith is correct in pointing out set-up time economies and gains in dexterity. Hierarchy, however, is not required. A family business, for instance, could undertake batch processing and could proceed from task to task 'first drawing out enough wire for hundreds or thousands of pins, then straightening it, then cutting it and so on ...'[24] The capitalist division of labour in Smith's pin factory, however, according to Marglin, was the result of a search not for *technologically* superior organization of work, but for an *organization* 'which guaranteed to the entrepreneur an essential *role* in the production process, as integrator of the separate efforts of his workers into a marketable product'.[25]

From the point of view of Anderson and Tollison, Smith has an implicit answer to such a conclusion (although they make no reference to Marglin). The answer is that so long as there is free entry, and this was the most important condition for competition in Smith, *all* kinds of organizational modes can be tried at any time. Only the most efficient, however, will survive. The fact that Marglin's batch processing family organization embodying the division of labour is not typical in modern Western economies, suggests that it is not the most efficient in competition with other modes. The same is presumably true of worker co-operatives which, according to Williamson, have repeatedly failed in competition with other forms of organization. Marglin argues that hierarchy is to be understood in power terms and power is exercised by a property-owning capitalist class. Williamson's analysis indicates, however, that hierarchy has redeeming efficiency properties *independent of ownership*, and these explain its prevalence in production.

Moral Hazard

While Williamson's analysis is an answer to the question: 'Why do hierarchies exist?' Marglin's central question is strictly the different one: 'Why does capital hire labour?' Some work of Alchian and Demsetz[26] appears, at first sight, to get close to a reasonable answer to the second question. They observe that because workers usually operate in a team, each one of them has an incentive to 'free ride' on the others: the so-called 'moral hazard problem'. The result is that costs of the firm's operation will increase and the demand for labour will fall. It is in the interests of all employees therefore to appoint a monitor to maintain each and every worker's performance. The monitor selected is the residual claimant because he has an incentive to self-monitor. His profit income is a function of the success of the whole operation and this implies his inducement to keep costs (including the costs of moral hazard) to a minimum.

But if we accept the Alchian and Demsetz scenario what is to prevent an appointed monitor coming from the ranks of labour? Could he not borrow the necessary capital and become the boss? In other words, why should moral hazard in team operation prevent labour hiring capital rather than the other way round?

A recent attempt to answer the last question[27] proceeds as follows: Consider production under uncertainty so that there exists a finite probability of bankruptcy. Where the capital employed is borrowed, bankruptcy implies a default on the loan. But because of legally limited liability the expected costs of capital are lower than under full liability. This means that the employer will consume more leisure than he would under full liability, especially since his effort is unobservable. The creditors' expected losses from bankruptcy are thus higher than need be. And it is *this* reason why the owner of capital has an incentive to become the boss.

Eswaran and Kotwal focus next on Marglin's argument that the division of labour was an effect rather than a cause of the capitalist mode of production. The capitalists, Marglin insists, simply wanted to 'divide and conquer'. Having done this they created a role for themselves as co-ordinators. Eswaran and Kotwal, observe however that Marglin's argument: 'does not explain how the capitalists could sustain an inessential role. Why did not individual craftsmen, engaged in batch processing, compete away to zero the returns to the unnecessary service of a coordinator?' They offer the following as a possible explanation.

For a given output, batch processing as described by Marglin has the disadvantage of requiring larger amounts of working capital than does the division of labour. This is because Marglin's individual craftsman (or family) needs to carry stocks of intermediate products for longer periods of time than does a production process that uses the division of labour. To continue their business the craftsman could perhaps borrow the extra working capital required. But this brings us again to the moral hazard problem: the craftman's price of leisure on the job is relatively low since he is protected by limited liability. The capitalists themselves therefore enter directly into the production activity.

> But why did they hire outside labour? Because by introducing the specialisation of labour, the amount of capital tied up in inventories of intermediate products was greatly reduced. This was probably the origin of team production. The introduction of team production, in its turn, necessitated labour supervision a la Alchian and Demsetz. The capitalists thus become the bosses.[28]

This argument seems consistent with the spirit of the reasoning in *The Wealth of Nations* in the following sense. With competition viewed as a process (the Smithian definition), various experimental organizational models are constantly trying themselves out over time. Only those that are proved to be least costly survive. With widespread limited liability laws the costs of moral hazard is a handicap to owners of capital who lend to independent craftsmen borrowers undertaking batch production. Competition therefore, leads to the preponderant survival of the capitalist/boss organizations.

Smith certainly reported such a preponderance:

> It sometimes happens, indeed, that a single independent workman has stock sufficient both to purchase the materials of his work, and to maintain himself till it be completed. He is both master and workman, and enjoys the whole produce of his own labour, or the whole value which it adds to the materials upon which it is bestowed. It includes what are usually two distinct revenues, belonging to two distinct persons, the profits of stock, and the wages of labour.
> Such cases, however, are not very frequent, and in every part of Europe, twenty workmen serve under a master for one that is independent; and the wages of labour are every where understood to be, what they usually are, when the labourer is one person, and the owner of the stock which employs him another.[29]

The argument of Eswaran and Kotwal reported so far, however, still does not easily explain the dominance of the capitalist/boss-type organization in Smith because, in his particular time, limited liability was severely restricted to the very few joint-stock enterprises that the law allowed. In the absence of limited liability over the bulk of manufacturing business, loanable funds would have been severely rationed and the workers' possibility of borrowing would have been a function of the collateral they were willing to put up. But in a contest over who could raise the greatest collateral (to mitigate the moral hazard problem) the rich must always be the winners. And Eswaran and Kotwal's additional (concluding) reasoning fits this case effectively.

> Wealthier borrowers will thus obtain a disproportionate share of the rationed credit, which would enable them to become the bosses; the poorer agents, due to their inability to offer collateral, will either work for the rich in widget production or will continue in their subsistence activity. We conclude that even when borrowers have assets of their own, the rich among them get to become the bosses.[30]

This part of the discussion of recent literature suggests again, therefore, that Smith's treatment is more comprehensive than that of the neoclassical writing that succeeded him. For even though it is of an embryonic kind, there *is* a theory of organization in *The Wealth of Nations*, and rudiments of the modern concepts of transaction costs, principal/agent problems and moral hazard can also be found in the same classic work.

Notes

1. Ross (1972), Demsetz (1983).
2. Smith (1976), p. 454.
3. Ibid., p. 454.
4. Fama and Jensen (1983).
5. Smith (1976), p. 759.
6. Ibid., p. 760.
7. Fama and Jensen (1983), p. 319.
8. Smith (1976) p. 761.
9. Berle and Means (1932), pp. 345–6.
10. *Journal of Law and Economics*, XXVI(2), June 1983, p. 299.
11. Anderson and Tollison (1982), p. 1240.
12. Demsetz (1983), pp. 388–9.
13. Smith (1976), p. 741.
14. Ibid.
15. Anderson and Tollison (1982), p. 1242.
16. Smith (1976), p. 737.
17. Demsetz (1983), p. 388.
18. Demsetz and Lehn (1985).
19. Ibid.
20. Smith (1976), p. 756. Anderson and Tollison (1982) observe that Smith's 'most extreme' remarks concerning abuses of the corporate form were reserved for the East India Company and it is these that have encouraged the view that Smith was opposed to joint-stock enterprises in principle. In fact, the East India

example was presented correctly by Smith as one of a company that had been granted governmental status in India. Smith was not diagnosing *market* failure; he was diagnosing *government* failure.

21. McNulty (1984).
22. Williamson (1980).
23. Ibid., p. 9.
24. Marglin (1974), p. 38.
25. Ibid.
26. Alchian and Demsetz (1972).
27. Eswaran and Kotwal (1989).
28. Ibid., p. 175.
29. Smith (1976), p. 83.
30. Eswaran and Kotwal (1989), pp. 175–6.

6. Money, Banking and the Rate of Interest

As is well known, the mercantilists' concern over the adequacy and stability of the money supply was heavily criticized by Adam Smith as irrational and obsessive. A country with no gold mines can acquire gold, Smith insisted, simply by exchanging exports for it. The higher the national income (output), the higher the country's ability to obtain the precious metal and to augment its money supply adequately. In this way prices could be kept reasonably stable. But it is true too that *The Wealth of Nations* argues that the simultaneous use of paper money could also make a useful contribution. Hutchison has recently suggested that Smith was too simplistic in believing that paper currency would automatically be created to the appropriate amount, 'without giving rise to any serious problems of central regulation'.[1] The words in quotation could be ambiguous. Smith's mechanism could *not* have been associated with problems of central regulation because it was not intended by him to be regulated. Another possible meaning of Hutchison's words is that the creation of paper currency in the appropriate quantity could be achieved only via central regulation, difficult though this may be. This interpretation is more probable judging from Hutchison's supporting quotation from Checkland:

> The banking expression of Smith's system of natural liberty was a set of institutions composed of many enterprises, none capable of monopolistic power or even leadership, each guided by prudential rules, and all trading in an environment of law provided by the state. Acting in aggregate they would, Smith implied, provide an optimal money supply or an effective approximation of it.[2]

The reference in this quotation to the absence of 'monopoly power' or 'leadership' suggests the implication that a 'monopoly leader' is ultimately necessary if we are *effectively* to provide the nationally desirable quantity of currency. In other words, it could be a statement of a 'believer' in politically-appointed central banks. Seen in this light, Smith is not necessarily wrong. The situation may be one of difference of judgement between him and others. But it so happens that, today, two hundred years after Smith's demise, a vigorous debate has arisen concerning whether or not to privatize the money supply after all. And the current advocates of privatization are clearly in the Smithian mould.

Free Banking

The new controversy appears to have started with a work by Hayek in 1978 entitled *Denationalization of Money: The Argument Refined.*[3] Challenging the assumptions that generations of economists have been making, he offered a proposal to remove the government's monopoly of money and to permit domestic currencies to compete. Among received opinion, meanwhile, has been the belief that government has to control money variables via a central bank monopoly in order to stabilize the economy. Hayek, in contrast, is convinced that the best achievable level of monetary stability is available via the same system of competing note-issuing banks that prevailed in Scotland in Smith's time.

Hutchison, no doubt, would readily agree that the different positions of this debate are testable (refutable) by reference to the evidence. It so happens that a note-clearing system arose during the free banking period in Scotland in the early 19th-century and that this seems to have led to a relatively stable system of note issue.[4] In contrast, acute crises occurred in England in the early 19th-century and these have been attributed by many observers to over-issues of notes by the Bank of England. In general, historical evidence from 18th- and 19th-century Scotland, Canada during much of the 19th century and pre-Civil War USA shows that free banking has experienced relatively more stability than regulated banking systems.[5]

Regulated banking systems usually imply government protection. And this is provided because of the frequent claim that without it there might be a run on one bank that could, like a contagion, spread to the banking system as a whole. But again the historical evidence offers no substantial support. And especially relevant to our subject is the record of stability of the free banking system in Scotland in Smith's own time. In the words of a modern specialist,

'During the free banking period of Scotland (1728–1845) there was not one case in which the banking system as a whole was seriously threatened by a run on a particular bank'.[6]

It is now arguable that the government protection afforded in a regulated banking system is indeed itself a potential source of serious instability. In the opinion of some, for instance, much of the current world debt crisis has arisen because some banks have taken excessive risks because of the perceived assurance that their own central banks, or the IMF, would rescue them from any subsequent difficulty. Recent US bank failures, meanwhile, have similarly been attributed to special protection, this time from subsidized state-managed deposit insurance that guarantees banks' deposits, and again with the aim of preventing runs on banks by their individual depositors. The policy of attempting to prevent runs is challenged by Dowd as follows:

> runs perform a useful role in closing down insolvent institutions, and the *threat* of a bank run is a major factor serving to discourage a bank's management from pursuing excessively risky policies. Remove these and insolvent banks will continue in operation possibly long after they should, and managements will be encouraged to take risks they would otherwise have avoided. Banks will therefore adopt policies more likely to lead to failure, and this will aggravate banking instability rather than reduce it. Bank runs are therefore best regarded as a *symptom* of banking instability rather than a major cause of it, and attempts to cure the symptom by discouraging runs are more likely than not to aggravate the underlying disease.[7]

A Stable and Optimal Money Supply

Return again to Hutchison's suggestion that Smith was not sufficiently aware of the difficulties of relying on a free banking system to create automatically the appropriate aggregate quantity of money in circulation. A close reading of the relevant parts of *The Wealth of Nations* suggests the contrary interpretation since Smith shows thoughtful awareness of the dangers of overextension of credit by the banks. Notice first that, besides the division of labour, he emphasizes and re-emphasizes throughout his book the additional importance of capital creation in encouraging the increase of a nation's wealth. But capital creation can arise only in proportion to voluntary abstention from consumption (i.e. saving).

Whatever a person saves from his revenue he adds to his capital and either employs it himself in maintaining an additional number of productive hands, or enables some other person to do so, by lending it to him for an interest, that is, for a share of the profits. As the capital of an individual can be increased only by what he saves from his annual revenue or his annual gains so the capital of society ... can be increased only in the same manner.[8]

The question now arises, however, whether the loans made in monetary form by banks correspond exactly to decreases in consumption so that savings matches new investment as indicated in the last quotation. Any excessive lending, after all, will result in damaging inflation. Perlman argues that Smith was fully aware of this problem[9] and focuses first on the following quotation from *The Wealth of Nations* that compares English banking with, what Smith believed to be the more efficient system in Scotland.

The London merchant must always keep by him a considerable sum of money ... in order to answer the demand continually coming upon him for payment. By being obliged to keep so great a sum unemployed ... the [annual] number of people employed in preparing his goods for market must be less by all those that [this amount] of stock could have employed. The merchant in Edinburgh, on the other hand, keeps no money unemployed for answering such occasional demands. When they actually come upon him, he satisfies them from his cash account [overdrafts] with the bank ... With the same stock, therefore, he can, without imprudence, have at all times in his warehouse a larger quantity of goods than the London merchant; and can thereby make a greater profit himself, and give constant employment to a greater number of industrious people. (p.300)

With the help of their banks, therefore, the Edinburgh merchants are able to increase their investment relative to their English counterparts. But no one has reduced consumption. The next question obviously concerns the origin of the resources that keep the Edinburgh merchants' warehouses better stocked than the English. Smith's answer is that Scottish bank lending substitutes for the stock of gold and silver previously required by the merchant to meet his suppliers' continual demands for payments. The gold is released and exchanged abroad for stocks of real materials. The bank lending in Scotland was in the form of overdrafts (called 'cash accounts') and/ or the discounting of bills of exchange.

One question remains. Will there be an incentive for any given bank to lend *in excess of* the level corresponding with the reduction in previously idle gold stocks of the merchants. Smith insists that ordinary prudence will normally prevent such excess.

> What a bank can prudently with propriety advance to a merchant or undertaker of any kind is not *either the whole capital with which he trades, or even a considerable part of that capital;* but that part of it only, which he would otherwise be obliged to keep by him unemployed and in ready money for answering occasional demands.[10]

If more credit, or paper money, than the prudent quantity indicated by Smith was created 'There would, ... immediately, ... be a run upon the banks to the whole extent of the superfluous paper'.[11]

One automatic mechanism constraining the tendency to inflation is thus implicit; it is the very threat of a run on any bank that is on the borderline of self-control. Beyond this Smith speaks of a prudent rule that banks will automatically be encouraged to adopt: the timing of repayments on a loan such that they are continual, relatively short-term and as coincident as possible with the flow of payments to the merchant by his customers.

> The banking companies of Scotland, accordingly, were for a long time very careful to require frequent and regular repayments from all their customers, and did not care to deal with any person, whatever might be his fortune or credit, who did not make, what they called, frequent and regular operations with them. By this attention, besides saving almost entirely the extraordinary expense of replenishing their coffers, they gained two other very considerable advantages.
>
> First, by this attention they were enabled to make some tolerable judgement concerning the thriving or declining circumstances of their debtors, without being obliged to look out for any other evidence besides what their own books afforded them; men being for the most part either regular or irregular in their repayments, according as their circumstances are either thriving or declining. A private man who lends out his money to perhaps half a dozen or a dozen of debtors, may, either by himself or his agents, observe and enquire both constantly and carefully into the conduct and situation of each of them. But a banking company, which lends money to perhaps five hundred different people, and of which the attention is continually occupied by objects of a very different kind, can have no regular information concerning the conduct and circumstances of the greater part of its debtors beyond what its own books afford it. In requiring frequent and regular repayments from all their customers, the banking companies of Scotland had probably this advantage in view.[12]

Central Bank Performance

The impression given by all such quotations is that Smith had detailed reasons to believe that his invisible hand theorem of flexible decentralized decision-making could approximate an aggregate quantity of money that was appropriate to the current national income. And critics seem to focus on the absence of an explicit guarantee by Smith that the mechanism would act perfectly at all times so as to produce *the* optimal money supply. The same critics usually imply that only a regulated system with an official central bank could effect this task. If Smith returned today he would undoubtedly ask for evidence that this alternative arrangement that was initiated in the 19th century, did prove, in fact, to be superior. And he would be interested in the verdict of one current writer who concludes that when government sets up a central bank with unique privileges and subjects the rest of the banking system to its authority, the most significant consequence is that it 'destabilizes the banking system by suppressing some of the automatic stabilizing that would arise spontaneously in the free market'.[13]

The rigidity of a bureaucratically-operated central bank system, with its somewhat mechanical rules concerning the 'proper' supply of currency, has certainly led to bank panics in the past. The 1844 Bank Charter Act in England, for example, which gave the Bank of England a monopoly of the note supply and imposed 100 per cent marginal reserve ratio, was unable to accommodate sudden increases in the public's demand for notes 'and their awareness of this weakness made the customers of the banking system extremely nervous'.[14] And the history of the central bank since then is far from flattering to the system.

Barro and Gordon indeed now produce one line of reasoning that suggests that the benefits to a government from generating inflation via its central bank outweigh the costs. Shughart and Tollison have a separate, but complementary, explanation.[15] It is obvious, for example, that the greater the size of a government's debt the more it has to gain by (unanticipated) inflation. Barro and Gordon's conclusion is that a fiat monetary authority will encourage a regime of unpredictable bouts of inflation. Prices will certainly *not* be kept stable.

It appears, therefore, that it is clearly insufficient to criticize Smith's world of free banking simply by concluding that it was unlikely to achieve perfect stability. The question is: Compared with what? For government regulated monetary regimes since Smith's time have themselves failed, and are continuing to fail, in this task.

Smith and Predecessors

Another long prevailing complaint against Smith has been that he treated money simply as a veil or, in modern terms, as being neutral. He failed to employ, or develop, the non-neutral monetary dynamics of predecessors such as Locke, Cantillon, Hume and Steuart, so causing them to languish for over a century. Smith's preoccupation, Vickers has complained, was with real variables and with the long term. What short-term analysis there was ignored the distinction between the price-forming and the activity-forming effects of an increase in the quantity of money, a distinction that Cantillon and Hume had recognized. Any increase in the quantity of silver, Smith simply observed, 'could have no other effect than to diminish the value of that metal'.[16]

In reply to Vickers, Laidler maintains that Smith's role in driving the inflationists' doctrines into the background 'was an important one' while 'their re-emergence in the last forty years has hardly been an unmixed blessing'. The difference of opinion here primarily concerns the relative merits of alternative traditions in monetary economics rather than questions of accuracy in textual reporting. The monetary economics of *The Wealth of Nations*, Laidler insists, had their own dynamics but they concerned the supply side rather than the demand side. First, by overcoming the many hindrances of the barter system, money was socially productive. This effect, moreover, was cumulative because it led to a widening of markets, more developed divisions of labour, and, as a result, continual changes in technology. Second, Laidler refers to the point previously explored in this chapter, namely Smith's argument that the introduction of paper money released resources to be transferred to the stock of circulating capital. The use of paper money at home would release gold reserves for purchases abroad. These, in turn, resulted in an increased domestic wage fund, or, in other words, in a permanent contribution to the stock of circulating capital. Laidler concludes that such Smithian argument 'amounts to a major contribution to monetary economics, since there is nothing akin to this analysis to be found in the writings of Hume'.[17]

Hume, of course, pioneered a major attack on the theory of mercantilism, the theory that each country could (and should) endeavour to have a perpetually favourable balance of trade. Such a balance, Hume argued, would cause gold to flow into a country. This, in turn, would raise domestic prices relative to foreign prices. In consequence, imports would expand and gold would move abroad in payment. By this 'price-specie flow' argument, Hume contended that in the long run the mercantilists could never succeed in their stated (foreign balance) objective.

Laidler argues that Smith's failure to incorporate Hume's price-specie-flow mechanism into his analysis, while regrettable, amounts only to an omission (or incompletion) rather than to the fatal flaw that others have attributed to him. Humphrey, on the other hand, emphasizes that Smith's reasoning was an early example of what in modern economics has come to be called the monetary approach to the balance of payments (MABP), an approach that denies the validity both of the quantity theory of money and the price-specie-flow mechanism.[18] MABP assumes, as did Smith, a small open economy (like Scotland) operating under fixed exchange rates. The latter fixity in Smith is guaranteed by his firm assumption of convertibility of paper currency into gold. An excess money supply in this economy cannot result in price level changes since these are determined on world markets, i.e. they are given exogenously. Adjustment has to take place through balance of payments as citizens export the excess money and import goods. The mechanism is that of direct spending effects instead of Hume's relative price effects. The latter are ruled out because commodity arbitrage ensures that the prices of traded goods are everywhere the same. An excess supply of money is thus resolved by a direct real balance effect running from the increase in money to the demand for imported (traded) goods.

Humphrey's conclusion is that 'Smith may be said to have laid the groundwork for the modern monetary approach to the balance of payments'. Laidler acknowledges that such a line of defence for Smith is possible but questions whether there is any real reference in *The Wealth* to the crucial component of commodity arbitrage. Humphrey, meanwhile, appears to argue as if this component is implicit in Smith.[19]

Humphrey also claims to have resolved the question why Smith did not incorporate the quantity theory of money into his analysis of the small open economy. The reason is that the MAPB approach predicts that causality runs from prices to money, not the other way round as in the quantity theory. Of course Smith recognized that, in the case of the world as a whole (the closed aggregate economy), the quantity of money does have positive relationship with (world) prices. This is clear from our earlier quotation of his observation that an increase in silver in the world 'could have no other effect than to diminish the value of that metal'. It is only in Smith's small open economy where the quantity of money is treated as an endogenous variable.

The Real Bills Doctrine

A remaining issue returns us to the discussion in *The Wealth of Nations* of the Scottish banks' ability to avoid over-issue of paper money. Mints has argued that Smith was 'the first thoroughgoing exponent of the real bills doctrine' in its modern form.[20] Certainly a clear statement of it appears in *The Wealth of Nations*. Thus it is asserted that paper money varies appropriately with the needs of trade when each bank 'discounts to a merchant a real bill of exchange drawn by a real creditor upon a real debtor, and which, as soon as it becomes due, is really paid by that debtor'.[21]

Since the publication of Henry Thornton's *Paper Credit* (1802) two major problems with the real bills doctrine have been widely accepted. The first is that the market value of the real bills contain a price component and this is determined by the money supply itself which, in turn, is determined by the number of real bills. A two-way inflationary interaction can thus occur between money and prices in which both can rise without limit. But the attempts by Mints to level this particular criticism against *The Wealth of Nations* has now been convincingly attacked by Laidler on the grounds that Smith advocated and assumed that paper money was convertible into specie. Indeed, he recommended that banks be required by law to convert their paper notes into specie so as to avoid over-issue.

The second problem with the real bills doctrine is that any number of bills can be raised on the security of the same real goods. In Thornton's words:

Suppose that A sells one [dollar's] worth of goods to B at six months credit, and takes a bill at six months for it; that B, within a month after, sells the same goods, at a like credit, to C, taking a like bill; and again, that C, after another month, sells them to D, taking a like bill, and so on.

On the expiry of six months although only $1 worth of goods had been produced there would be $6 worth of bills outstanding. In general, an extension of the turnover rate of the goods (or of the maturity of the bills) would lead to a quantity of money well beyond 'the needs of trade'.

Laidler believes that this particular critique may validly be applied to Smith because he expressed the belief that, if only banks would manage their loans to merchants so as to ensure that 'in the course of some short period ... the sum of the repayments which it commonly receives from them, is ..., fully equal to that of the advances which it commonly makes to them,' they would tend not to over-issue. In this particular quotation, however, Smith is referring to bank advances when the borrower 'has no bills to discount'. These advances were intended to match only that part of the entrepreneur's capital 'which he would otherwise be obliged to keep by him unemployed, and in ready money for answering occasional demands'. According to Dowd, Smith is simply stating, although in a roundabout way, that each bank could tell whether it was over-issuing or not simply by looking at the state of its individual reserves.[22] Banks could prevent over-issue merely by maintaining adequate reserves in each individual case.

Thornton's criticism that the same goods could generate more than one bill amounts to the failure to make a distinction between real and fictitious bills. Yet, Dowd maintains, this same point is eventually made in *The Wealth of Nations*.

> When two people, who are continually drawing and re-drawing upon one another, discount their bills with *the same banker*, he must immediately discover what they are about ... But this discovery is not altogether easy when they discount their bills sometimes with one banker, and sometimes with another, and when the same two persons do not constantly draw and redraw upon one another, but occasionally run the round of a great circle of projectors, who find it in their interest to assist one another in this method of raising money, and to render it, upon that account, *as difficult as possible to distinguish between a real and a fictitious bill of exchange* ... When a banker had even made this discovery, he might sometimes make it too late, and might find that he had already discounted [so many bills] that by refusing to discount more [he might ruin everyone, including himself].[23]

Such argument reveals Smith in the role of opponent, not advocate, of the real bills doctrine. The point has been developed further by Perlman. He finds it most significant that Smith makes repeated emphasis on the need for the frequency and regularity of bank repayments by the merchant borrowers. It is evident, Perlman concludes, that Smith considers this point much more significant than the realness of the bill.

> But nothing in the Real Bill doctrine requires such frequency of repayment ... If the bill is real, the loan will be in proportion to trade, and the frequency of the repayment will presumably be in proportion to the velocity of circulation of the trade. On the other hand a fictitious bill may be repaid with monotonous regularity.[24]

Perlman returns repeatedly to Smith's central argument that the bank lending should provide merchants, not with the whole of their circulating capital (as the real bills advocate assumed), but only with a sum sufficient to cover what would otherwise be their idle money balances (see again the quotation pertaining to note 10). Such balances involved stocking up gold, and this was wasteful since gold could be exchanged abroad for useful real resources. Smith's high frequency of repayment rule was accordingly aimed at restricting bank advances in paper money to this part of the merchant's capital only. To the 'hard line' real bills advocate, Smith's rule was quite incomprehensible.[25]

Perlman concludes unambiguously that the attribution of the Real Bills doctrine to Adam Smith is wrong. Dowd, meanwhile, appears to go further by suggesting that Smith was, if anything, in advance of his time in being the first major *critic* of the doctrine. 'It is John Law and not Adam Smith who deserves to be known as the author of the "real bills" doctrine'.[26]

The Rate of Interest

Smith has so far been presented as being in favour of banks undertaking commercial loans within the conditions and qualifications mentioned. He was very critical, however, of loans for consumption purposes. When a person borrows simply to increase his immediate consumption: 'He acts the part of a prodigal, and dissipates in the maintenance of the idle, what was destined for the support of the industrious'.[27] Smith was convinced that loans for consumption purposes involved the highest risk of all: 'The man who borrows in order to spend [on consumption] will soon be ruined, and he who lends to him will generally have occasion to repent his folly'.[28]

Because of the higher risk involved in consumption loans they incurred much higher interest rates than those for the most secure loans to commercial businesses. If, therefore, the law disallowed high interest rates it would also curtail loans for consumption purposes. And it was partly because Smith wanted to stop consumption loans he was willing to advocate a legally fixed interest-rate ceiling. This rate: 'ought always to be somewhat above the lowest market price, or the price which is commonly paid for the use of money by those who can give the most undoubted security'.[29] The rate, nevertheless, should not be *much* above the lowest in the market. At the time of writing the legal rate of interest in Great Britain was five per cent. Smith described this as, perhaps, 'as proper as any' bearing in mind that money was lent to private people upon good security at four per cent.

Smith's argument was based on another consideration besides that of the need to discourage consumer loans. Society needed to be protected from investors in very risky or speculative ventures, investors who Smith described as 'projectors'. He was aware that different loans had different degrees of risk attached to them and that risk premiums were demanded according to the degree of risk. Fixing the ceiling only slightly above the rate for the safest loans therefore would usefully crowd out *this* undesirable type of lender. If, on the contrary, the legal rate ceiling was set high, Smith predicted, 'the greater part of the money which was to be lent, would be lent to prodigals and projectors, who alone would be willing to give this higher interest'.[30]

Smith's whole position on interest-rate regulation has been something of an enigma to readers as far back as the 18th century. It was, for instance, subjected to what Hutchison (1988) calls a logical rebuke by Jeremy Bentham in the latter's work *Defense of Usury*. Bentham objected that the regulation was a violation of Smith's own principle of natural liberty. This kind of criticism has now been developed further by Garrison who maintains that *The Wealth of Nations* contains an intertemporal bias. Smith's anxiety to see substantial capital growth implied that he had a standard of zero time preference that he wanted to impose on society. Moreover, just as the mercantilists were mistaken in believing their plans for interspatial reallocation of resources (to obtain a favourable trade balance) would work, so was Smith in error for believing in the potential success of his intertemporal reallocation via credit controls.

> In reality credit controls serve only to reduce the gains from intertemporal exchange. Individuals may prefer, say, one unit of a consumption good now to two or even five units of the good next year. If this preference is not allowed to be expressed in the market, then the wealth of the nation, reckoned in terms of present value, i.e., discounted at a rate corresponding to the individuals' true time preferences will actually decrease. Wealth, correctly conceived, will be maximized in a system that restrains neither the international nor the intertemporal allocation of resource.[31]

Other writers interpret Smith as arguing in terms of what we would now call external benefits.[32] Without interest-rate regulation too much of society's capital would be diverted from those 'likely to make a profitable and advantageous use of it' to 'those which were most likely to waste and destroy it'.[33]

> Where the legal rate of interest, on the contrary, is fixed but a very little above the lowest market rate, sober people are universally preferred, as borrowers, to prodigals and projectors. The person who lends money gets nearly as much interest from the former as he dares take from the latter, and his money is much safer in the hands of the one set of people, than those of the other. A great part of the capital of the country is thus thrown into the hands in which it is most likely to be employed with advantage.[34]

Smith appears, once more, to be presenting a refutable hypothesis: the use of funds by low-risk borrowers tends to promote external capital formation economies. It is pertinent, meanwhile, that one modern writer has developed a theoretical model which suggests that loans in high-risk credit markets may indeed generate external diseconomies.[35]

Buchanan (1976) explains that in a fully competitive world and within a given institutional setting, there may be no relevant external economy exerted by private decisions at the margins of adjustment. Nevertheless, useful infra-marginal changes in behaviour might be produced by modifying the institutions themselves.[36] Infra-marginal external economies from investment and capital formation are especially likely in a world where collectivities claim increasing shares of national incomes so causing capital shortages. Few modern economists, however, would follow Smith in seeking to correct for these by establishing interest ceilings, 'but the widespread introduction of subsidies to investment reflects the basic thrust of his argument'.[37]

In so far as these external economies' arguments are persuasive they offer one answer for Bentham in the 18th century and for Garrison in the 20th century. In Jadlow's opinion:

> Smith does seem to have been in tune with today's modern welfare economist in that he distinguished between what are now called techno-logical and pecuniary externalities. He supported interferences with the 'natural liberty' of individuals when significant technological spillovers were involved, but he opposed restrictions on individual market choices when only pecuniary externalities were exhibited.[38]

Jadlow, nevertheless, points out an important remaining problem with Smith's argument. If ceilings are imposed on *legal* markets then traders will resort to illegal markets. Smith himself clearly explains the potential for this behaviour. He observed that:

> the complete prohibition of interest instead of preventing, has been found from experience to increase the evil of usury; the debtor being obliged to pay, not only for the use of the money, but for the risk which his creditor runs by accepting a compensation for that use. He is obliged, if one may say so, to insure his creditor from the penalties of usury.[39]

Because, however, Smith's proposed legal interest-rate ceiling would lead to a prohibition of high-risk borrowing and lending, the traders involved would again resort to illegal markets. Since, on Smith's own logic, these underground markets would then charge a premium to cover potential legal penalties, the real interest rates on risky loans would climb further and lenders would still find willing customers among the high-risk borrowers.

It is interesting, finally, that a current leader in the new field of economic theory known as 'market signalling' is now claiming affinity with Smith's argument about the need for defences against 'prodigals and projectors'. Joseph Stiglitz's recent article 'The Causes and Consequences of the Dependence of Quality on Price' is prefaced by quotations from *The Wealth of Nations* and opens with the observation that price often serves a function in addition to that usually ascribed to it in economics. In such instances, firms are not

Figure 6.1   The efficiency rate of interest

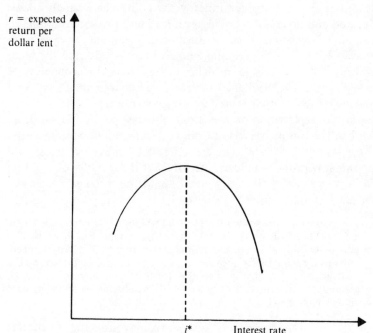

simple price takers. A bank may assume, for example, that as it increases the interest rate, the 'quality' of those who apply decreases. In other words, the bank may have observed that those who apply for loans at a high interest rate have, on average, a higher probability of defaulting. The safest borrowers in the meantime are unwilling to borrow at high interest rates. The expected return on a loan, r, may actually decrease as the interest rate, i, increases.[40]

This situation is shown in Figure 6.1. What Stiglitz calls 'the efficiency interest rate' is shown as i^*. If at this rate there is an excess demand for loans, i^* is still an equilibrium. Anyone offering to borrow at a higher rate will be refused by the bank because the expected return, r, would be lower than what it obtains by lending at i^*. The position at i^* is known as a credit rationing equilibrium. In conventional market analysis, in contrast, price (in this case the interest rate) does all the rationing. If credit rationing temporarily appears, those who are willing to borrow at the given interest rate but are denied credit will offer the bank a higher rate. As the interest rate is thus bid up, the supply of credit increases and demand contracts. The process continues to the point where supply equals demand and no credit rationing occurs. Smith's story, according to the Stiglitz version, is set in the non-conventional analysis of a market with a credit rationing equilibrium. In this case the bank realizes that, if it charges a higher interest rate, the probability of default increases. No banks therefore will charge an interest rate above i^*. Interest itself is used as a screening device.

On this explanation of events one obvious question arises: If *no bank* will charge an interest rate above i^* why should there be a need for a legally-fixed rate? The self-interest of individual banks will presumably provide sufficient incentive for the socially optimal rate to be generated. Smith's argument about the 'prodigals' appears, indeed, to admit as much:

> The man who borrows in order to spend will soon be ruined and he who lends to him will generally have occasion to repent of his folly. To borrow or to lend for such a purpose, therefore, is *in all cases*, where gross usury is out of the question, contrary to the interest of *both* parties ... from the regard that all men have for their own interest, we may be assured, that it cannot happen so very frequently as we are sometimes apt to imagine.[41]

In the case of the 'projectors' or high-risk investors the situation is less clear. Smith's wording does not suggest the unambiguous conclusion in this instance that lending to the high-risk entrepreneurs is in *all* cases contrary to the interest of both parties. This leaves open the possibility of a situation of a high-risk project, promising a high return with some finite probability distribution, but where the probability is less than that associated with the lower-risk project. Where a bank has to choose exclusively between two projects, one high and the other low risk, so long as there is some positive probability of success in the former there is a possible trade-off between the lower probability success and a higher interest rate. It is possibly quite rational, therefore, for a bank sometimes to lend to borrowers with the higher-risk project.

Stiglitz and Weiss construct just such an example and point out that although the bank's choice maximizes its expected private returns these could be less than expected *social* returns. 'In this case a usury law forbidding interest rates in excess of [a given level] will increase net national output'.[42] If Smith's reasoning was, indeed, probing towards this more technical explanation of events, he deserves credit once more for producing inspirational analysis and for anticipating today's modern welfare economist.

We are, nevertheless, still left with serious problems. First, it is necessary to reiterate that Smith leaves open the use of illegal capital markets so that his legally-fixed rate policy will be largely undermined. The same objection would seem to apply also to the Stiglitz and Weiss argument for the possibility of pursuing Pareto optimal improvement with the aid of a usury law. Expressed in other words, although Stiglitz and Weiss have constructed one theoretical case where such a law could increase wealth via improved capital allocation, it is incomplete because of a missing variable: the costs of policing the legislation. If these costs more than outweigh the gross wealth benefits (which is very plausible) the argument for the usury law collapses.

Second, the information requirements of a government wishing to conduct the usury rate regulation policy would apparently be considerable if not overwhelming. It would, for instance, have to know from day-to-day the expected rates of return and success probability distributions of thousands of new projects coming on to the market. It is highly questionable whether government administrators have this capability and whether their own subjective biases would not interpose themselves.

Third, and finally, it is curious why, in this case, Smith failed to analyse legal restrictions on interest rates in the context of his usual economics of politics approach, an approach that is fully explored in Chapter 9. Since he recognized special mercantilist interests at work in the context, for instance, of particular legal restraints on imports, why did he not search for the individual beneficiaries of usury laws? In the absence of further enquiry on these lines we are left with the impression that, on this issue, Smith is presuming, uncharacteristically, a government that is fully informed and willing to pursue indifferentiated (public) benefits as distinct from differentiated (private) benefits.

Notes

1. Hutchison (1988), p. 367.
2. Quoted in Hutchison (1988), p. 368.
3. Institute of Economic Affairs (1978), Hobart Paper No. 70.
4. White (1984).

5. Dowd (1988).
6. Ibid., p. 34.
7. Ibid., p. 43.
8. Smith (1976), p. 337.
9. Perlman (1989), p. 79.
10. Smith (1976), p. 304.
11. Ibid., p. 301.
12. Ibid., pp. 305–6.
13. Dowd (1988), p. 38.
14. Ibid. Dowd quotes similar evidence from the US in the 19th century.
15. Barro and Gordon (1983), pp. 101–21. Shughart and Tollison (1983) give an economics of bureaucracy explanation of why the US Fed has apparently been more willing to engage in expansionary than contractionary monetary policies. The objective function of most bureaucracies is the expansion of their own particular budgets. Since the Fed's budget is size correlated with the monetary base, this appears to guarantee an inflationary bias.
16. Vickers (1975), p. 503.
17. Laidler (1981), p. 195.
18. Humphrey (1983).
19. Humphrey's position is obviously in contrast with that of Petrella (1968) who argues that there has been overemphasis on *The Wealth of Nations* as a theoretical work and a lack of appreciation of its polemical qualities. It was the polemical intent of Smith, according to Petrella, to omit reference to Hume's price-specie-flow mechanism because of some of its implications about the non-neutrality of money.
20. Mints (1945).
21. Smith (1976), p. 304.
22. Dowd (1985).
23. Smith (1976), pp. 311–12.
24. Perlman (1989), p. 86.
25. Ibid., p. 86.
26. Dowd (1985), p. 15.
27. Smith (1976), p. 350.
28. Ibid.
29. Ibid., p. 356.
30. Smith (1976), p. 357.
31. Garrison (1985), p. 292.
32. Jadlow (1977), Buchanan (1976).
33. Smith (1976), p. 357.
34. Ibid.
35. Avio (1973), quoted in Jadlow (1977).
36. Buchanan (1976), p. 283.
37. Ibid.
38. Jadlow (1977), p. 1198.
39. Smith (1976), p. 356.
40. Stiglitz (1987), see also Stiglitz and Weiss (1981).
41. Smith (1976), p. 350, emphasis added.
42. Stiglitz and Weiss (1981), p. 408.

7. Adam Smith's Public Economics

Twentieth-century literature on Adam Smith contains two major accepted interpretations of his public economics, both of which challenge the popular view of him as the leading champion of the unqualified or vulgar doctrine of *Harmonielehre*, the spontaneous harmony of interests. The first, or older approach is to compile a catalogue of extracts from *The Wealth of Nations* showing that its author apparently recognizes distinct comparative advantage in government participation in business to obtain *calculated* (non-spontaneous) harmony in certain areas. The major example of this tradition is Jacob Viner (1928). Supporting his argument with such a list of Smithian *pragmatic* exceptions to spontaneous harmony, a list that included education, the post office, the public mints, roads, and canals, Viner concluded: 'The modern advocate of laissez faire who objects to government participation in business on the ground that it is an encroachment upon a field reserved by nature for private enterprise cannot find support for this argument in *The Wealth of Nations*'.[1]

The second approach is to play down the improvised, or piecemeal, nature of Smith's policy presumptions and to focus upon consistency in his formal theory, especially upon his implied theory of market failure. In this perspective, Smith's arguments for public works are really propositions about what modern economic theory classifies as public goods; that is, they concern those goods characterized by pronounced jointness efficiencies and exclusion problems, goods that in the hands of J.S. Mill became symbolized in the example of the lighthouse.

This chapter produces quite different, if not opposite, findings. First, Viner's catalogue of Smithian recommendations for government intervention will be shown to be unsystematic and his treatment of individual items to be ambiguous. More important, he failed to appreciate that the thrust of most of Smith's prescription for new public works was the extension of private provision by way of public companies enjoying new privileges of joint stock and limited liability. Second, the more recent interpretation that Smith's analysis of public works foreshadowed modern public goods theory will also be rejected. In all examples of Smith's public works (aside from provision of defence and justice), exclusion problems and jointness efficiencies will be shown to be minimal. This does not mean that there is here no linkage at all with modern developments in economic analysis. On the contrary, Smith's reasoning in this area foreshadows much current 'public choice' literature, especially that dealing with the new constitutional economics (the subject of Chapter 8).

Section 1 of the chapter discusses Smith's first and second duties of the sovereign. Section 2 begins the examination of his prescription for 'public works' in the introduction of his third duty of the sovereign. Section 3 examines the historical attitude to joint-stock operation and limited liability. Section 4 presents a detailed analysis of Smith's public works via public companies. Section 5 reviews Smith on toll roads; section 6 deals with coinage and the post office. Section 7 re-examines Smith on education. Finally, section 8 attempts to demonstrate a consistency in Smith's total position that resolves much of the difficulty in previous interpretations. These have presented Smith as the paradoxical writer who championed the invisible hand over mercantilist state planning yet (absent-mindedly?) finished his book with his own considerable agenda for government intervention.

Smith's First and Second Duty of the Sovereign

Smith divided the functions of the state generally into 'protective' and 'productive'.[2] The protective state was charged with the first and second duties of the sovereign, namely, justice and defence. The productive state undertook the third duty, that of establishing responsibility for public works. Smith urged the full separation of powers between these two departments of state because the productive state (government) had a propensity to exceed its proper bounds in a quest for excessive power and revenue.

One example of unhealthy concentration of power is provided in Smith's comment on the use of the judges by King Henry II. They were, Smith alleged, little more than 'itinerant factors' sent round the country for the purpose of levying certain branches of the king's revenue. 'This scheme of making the administration of justice sub-servient to the purposes of revenue, could scarce fail to be pro-ductive of several very gross abuses. The person, who applied for justice with a large present in his hand, was likely to get something more than justice.'[3]

Much of this section 'The Expense of Justice' in *The Wealth of Nations* is accordingly devoted to a search for a system that would give to judges and lawyers efficient rewards. These should not be paid by governments, yet should be designed to avoid corruption; at the same time the rewards should respect the guiding principle that 'public services are never better performed than when their reward comes only in consequence of their being performed, and is propor-tionate to the diligence employed in performing them'.[4] As will now be shown, the same guiding principle informed Smith's prescriptions for public works.

The Third Duty of the Sovereign

The third section of Book V of *The Wealth of Nations*, entitled 'Of the Expense of Public Works and Public Institutions', begins:

> The third and last duty of the sovereign or commonwealth is that of erecting and maintaining those public institutions and those public works, which, though they may be in the highest degree advantageous to a great society, are, however, of such a nature, that the profit could never repay the expense to any individual or small number of individuals, and which it therefore cannot be expected that any individual or small number of individuals would erect or maintain.[5]

Several modern economists seem to have interpreted this quotation to foreshadow the 20th-century idea of 'market failure', either in the sense of Pigou's concept of the excess of social marginal benefits over private marginal benefits, or in the sense of the extreme joint-ness in supply characteristic of Samuelsonian public goods.[6] The price system 'breaks down' for two reasons. First, there is no mecha-nism for excluding individuals from the benefits of a good that a single individual, separately, might be willing to contribute payment for; in which case each person waits for his neighbour to pay the price. Second, because of jointness in supply each person will con-ceal his true preferences or 'dissemble'. For both reasons we would not expect to see a system of prices, tolls, or fees operating, because the revenues generated therefrom would not be sufficient to cover the costs of the suppliers.

Smith proceeds to give examples of those 'public works' which 'facilitate the commerce' of any country, 'such as good roads, bridges, navigable canals, harbours etc.' The first evidence that Smith's reasoning is *not* parallel with the modern pure-public-good model appears when he comes to discuss the methods of financing the public works:

> it does not seem necessary that the expense of those public works should be defrayed from that public revenue, as it is commonly called, of which the collection and application are in most countries assigned to the executive power. The greater part of such public works may easily be so managed, as to afford a particular revenue sufficient for defraying their own expense, without bringing any burden upon the general revenue of the society.[7]

Some exclusion therefore *is* possible; and future revenues from the users *are* expected to cover total costs. The essence of this part of Smith's argument seems to be very similar to that in Ronald Coase's (1974) analysis of lighthouses. Coase demonstrates that, historically, the 'public good' of the lighthouse was financed, not by the general taxpayer, but by that portion of the population that enjoyed most of its benefits. These were primarily the owners of ocean-going and coastal vessels; and they financed the lighthouse through specific fees that were collected at the same time as the port and harbour dues. Thus exclusion, although 'imperfect', was possible, and so was some approximation of preferences. Smith developed the same line of reasoning. He reminds us, for instance, that customs duties paid by merchants originated from the need to finance the 'public good' of protection of those same merchants, for 'the protection of trade in general, from pirates and freebooter'. Generally he emphasized that where public works generated only local benefits they were better financed by the local beneficiaries:

> Were the streets of London to be lighted and paved at the expense of the [national] treasury, is there any probability that they would be so well lighted and paved as they are at present, or even at so small an expense. The expense, besides, instead of being raised by a local tax upon the inhabitants of each particular street, parish, or district in London would, in this case, be defrayed out of the general revenue of the state, and would consequently be raised by a tax upon all the inhabitants of the

kingdom, of whom the greater part derived no sort of benefit from the lighting and paving of the streets of London.[8]

This principle of payment by 'local beneficiaries' was considerably sharpened in Smith's general analysis of public works, where the local beneficiaries became defined as the individual users. His major example of public works, namely roads, bridges, and canals, he eventually tells us, can be financed by prices, tolls, or user taxes: 'A highway, a bridge, a navigable canal, for example, *may in most cases be both made and maintained* by a small toll upon the carriages which makes use of them; a harbour, by a moderate port-duty upon the tunnage of the shipping which load or unload in it'.[9] The conventional modern concept of public goods seems here to dissolve altogether; for in this case there is no serious problem of preference revelation or of exclusion. Each separate and individual purchaser (user) of the road or bridge pays for his private benefits in full; otherwise, he is excluded from its use. And no relevant externalities seem to be involved.

Why then did Smith see this area as a legitimate one for public intervention? And did he really imply that the market had failed here? If individual prices and tolls can finance the whole of a project, why, to use Smith's words again, should it never yield a profit that could 'repay the expense to any individual or small number of individuals?' If we speculate that he was impressed not with the public goods, but with the 'natural monopoly' aspect of the case of roads and canals, this will not get us very far. For then the monopoly profits of a turnpike company or canal company would more than repay its expenses.

A much stronger case can be made that Smith was impressed with what we would now call capital market 'imperfection'. Where the private capital market has a very low pooling facility it is most likely that the profit from the public 'could never repay the expense to any individual *or small number* of individuals' (emphasis added). Smith implicitly agrees, however, that it could repay a large number of individuals because, as will be shown in the next section, the sequence of his argument leads to a discussion of the need for joint-stock enterprise. Much of Smith's argument about the intervention of the sovereign was in fact in terms of adjusting the legal framework and sets of property rights so that new larger-scale markets were possible; this was typically not the case of existing market failure, for markets that were not allowed to operate cannot fail.

The key historical fact is that in Smith's time, large groups of individuals were so hindered by the absence of an appropriate variety of legal instruments with limited liability that much needed capital markets were blocked. With one or two exceptions, to be examined later, Smith was generally arguing about the need for the introduction of such legal instruments as the most direct way of using new types of *private* enterprises for 'facilitating commerce in general'. The introduction of these new instruments, moreover, had as much to do with constitutional change as with the day-to-day business of government; that is, it concerned the 'protective state' as much as the 'productive state'.

Smith's Caution on Joint-stock and Limited-Liability Companies

Before examining in detail Smith's plans for public works through public companies, it will be helpful to give an historical outline of the growing need and pressure for these organizations in his time, despite the popular suspicion of them, a suspicion that Smith himself shared.

Up to 1776 a private company or corporation was instituted largely by way of the special vehicle or sovereign edict. There was a growing need for instrumentality for carrying on a large business. To merchants and entrepreneurs the commercial advantages from incorporation were becoming obvious: continuity of existence and management independent of that of members, ease of suit against third parties or against members, transferable shares, unlimited divisibility of the equities, and the distinct limitation of liability for a company's debts and for those of its shareholders.[10]

Traditionally, the major ways that a corporation (company) was created were by judicial interpretations of the common law or by the king's charter. This area of royal (and later parliamentary) discretion to create new property rights substantially explains Smith's discussion of public works under the head of the 'third duty of the sovereign'; for indeed it was traditionally the sovereign's responsibility long before that of legislatures. Most of the corporations formed from 1485 to 1700 were created exclusively by royal charter. The

Russia Company (1555), the East India Company (1600), the Hudson's Bay Company (1670) were originally chartered directly by the crown without benefit of Parliament. Charters, or equivalent letters patent, were granted by the crown in pursuance of special statutory authority, as for the Bank of England (1694) and the London Assurance Company (1720).

Later on, and especially after the Revolution of 1688, the additional sanction of the legislature was increasingly demanded to accompany privileges created by the crown. In the latter half of the 18th century, incorporation by special Act became increasingly common for 'utilities' such as the canal (and water) companies. Charters and private Acts of incorporation usually included special provisions regulating the activities of the particular organization. It is arguable that the nature of the complex procedure necessary to secure incorporation, and the rather peculiar history of some of the companies that had existed, would have made it difficult for Adam Smith to have envisioned the emergence of the modern corporation (with easier procedures and routine obligations) as the typical business unit. Certainly the formation of joint-stock companies with limited liability by the processes we now take for granted, such as simple registration under general statutes, did not become a matter of general right until after the middle of the 19th century. Incorporation, which is essential to modern business organization, was in the late 18th- and early 19th-centuries either a dispensation (favour) within the special gift of Parliament or a carefully guarded bureaucratic concession.[11]

In view of all these inhibitions it was believed in the late 18th-century that special deliberation was called for in deciding how to satisfy the needs of new projects that required large sums of capital. It was in such a context that Smith examined 'the third duty of the sovereign'. The fulfilment of that duty was a delicate matter calling for shrewd judgement, especially at a time when the joint-stock organization was very widely suspect after the calamity of the South Sea crash of 1720. We now know that the great shortcoming in that period lay not so much in the joint-stock system itself as in the way it was then applied and the need for more experience with it. Before 1720 there was insufficient appreciation of the dangers of ambitiously selling new bonds to raise financial capital beyond the amount necessary for the operation of any given undertaking. The collapse of the South Sea Boom and the restrictive Bubble Act of

1720 were the immediate consequence. Joint-stock companies fell into indiscriminate disrepute, and Smith's treatment reflects this.[12]

Smith discusses the limited-liability principle when comparing joint-stock companies with private partnerships ('co-partneries' in Smithian language). Apart from the non-transferability of shares in a partnership, Smith explains, it differed from the joint-stock company in that 'each partner is bound for the debts contracted by the company to the whole extent of his fortune. In a joint-stock company on the contrary, each partner is bound only to the extent of his share.[13]

The facts possessed by Smith suggest indeed that the pooling facilities of some of the largest trading companies exceeded those of governments.[14] Smith also acknowledged the principle of limited liability in his observation that the greater part of the proprietors of the joint-stock companies received annual dividends and enjoyed 'total exemption from trouble and from risk, beyond a limited sum'. This facility encouraged many people to become adventurers in joint-stock companies who would never hazard their fortunes in a private partnership. 'Such companies, therefore, commonly draw to themselves much greater stocks than any private co-partnery can boast of.'

Despite the advantages, Smith was circumspect towards joint-stock companies for two main reasons: first, because incorporation often gave them exclusive privileges of trade; second, because such large organizations eventually became rigidly bureaucratic and supervised by managers of other people's money. It could not be expected, Smith argued, 'that they should watch over it with the same anxious vigilance with which the partners in a private copartnery frequently watch over their own. Like the stewards of a rich man, they are apt to consider attention to small matters as not for their master's honour, and very easily give themselves a dispensation from having it'.[15] With respect to the first ground, Smith believed that large chartered joint-stock foreign traders, despite their exclusive privileges, 'have seldom been able to maintain the competition against private adventurers'; and this because of the 'negligence and profusion that usually prevails in such large enterprises'. Smith's judgement, however, was not based on the most reliable source, despite his reference to it as 'that sober and judicious writer Mr. Anderson'. It has subsequently been observed by Scott that Anderson's attempts at separate histories of the several companies were in fact unscientific and controversial.[16]

Had Smith studied the facts more carefully, he might have more readily acknowledged the economic significance and wide usefulness of the large capital accumulation that joint-stock and limited-liability principles allowed. But he conceded the need for forts in the East India and Africa trades, and also that these could not have been successfully created and maintained by *regulated* companies. The latter were defined as those companies that did not trade upon a joint-stock 'but are obliged to admit any person, properly qualified, upon paying a certain fine, and agreeing to submit to the regulations of a company, each member trading upon his own stock, and at his own risk'. Smith argued that the directors of such concerns soon managed 'to confine the greater part of the trade to themselves and their particular friends'. Moreover, Smith believed they had no desire to maintain forts and garrisons because they had no particular interest in the prosperity of the general trade of the company. More important, unlike joint-stock companies, they had little common capital to manage, but only 'the causal revenue arising from the admission fines, and from the corporation duties, imposed upon the trade of the company'.

The joint-stock monopolist of foreign trade, such as the East India Company, certainly had an incentive to maintain forts and garrisons, but this advantage was usually offset in Smith's eyes by what he believed to be excessive monopolizing behaviour, which caused the prices of their products to be higher than they otherwise would be. On the other hand, and Smith recognized this, without the monopoly the products would not be forthcoming at all – at *any* price. The monopoly grant was, like a patent, a special 'reward' that was instrumental to economic development. And just as patents can be licensed, would-be adventurers could purchase licences for one or more 'permission ships'.[17] Certainly the monopoly element might be reflected in the price of the licence, but it could still be regarded as a contribution towards the 'public good' – the fortifications and garrisons. Furthermore, illegal interloping was always a possibility, and it is interesting that those interlopers who did meet with moderate success were not, as Smith's theory would predict, individual concerns or partnerships, but small joint-stock companies. Finally, such companies could arrange to be amalgamated with the dominant chartered company and so achieve proper legal status and increased economic security.[18]

Public Works via Public Companies: Smith's Final Agenda

Despite his general antagonism to joint-stock companies with exclusive privileges, Smith nevertheless proceeded to show that the third duty of the sovereign frequently involved an obligation to allow a variety of such companies that did not enjoy such privileges. Generally, such form of enterprise was best applied to undertakings whose operations were capable of being reduced to fairly uniform methods. Two other circumstances qualified the granting of joint-stock status. It should be shown, first, that the undertaking 'is of greater and more general utility than the greater part of common trades' and, secondly, that it 'requires a greater capital than can easily be collected into a private co-partnery'.[19]

The businesses that Smith considered to pass these tests are of special interest. First, insurance was a public work that he was almost forced by historical circumstances to allow joint-stock status, circumstances that must have also influenced the sovereign's decision. The need for accumulation of capital was paramount. Observing that the trade of fire and marine insurance gave great security to the fortunes of private people, Smith continues: 'In order to give this security, however, it is necessary that the insurers should have a very large capital. Before the establishment of the two joint-stock companies for insurance in London, a list, it is said, was laid before the attorney general, of one hundred and fifty private insurers who had failed in the course of a few years.'[20]

Second, the public work of banking required a special form of contract and was also worthy of the sovereign's attention. A bank expected to support public credit and sometimes to lend to governments millions of pounds pending their annual tax collections, 'requires a greater capital than can easily be collected into any private co-partnery'.

Third, among those public works which facilitate 'commerce in general'[21] canals and water supplies qualified. Again there is emphasis on the large capital requirement: 'That navigable cuts and canals, and the works which are sometimes necessary for supplying a great city with water, are of great and general utility; while at the same time they frequently require a greater expense than suits the fortunes of private people, is sufficiently obvious'.[22] On such grounds, Smith concluded that joint-stock organization was appropriate for the four 'public works' mentioned, banks, insurance, canals, and water supply.

The logic of events must have influenced Smith's judgement on canals and water companies as well as on banking and insurance. In the instance of canals there was a strong demonstration effect in the laborious but ultimately successful efforts of the Duke of Bridgewater to get his Bill through Parliament in 1766.[23] Scores of private canal Acts establishing companies were receiving assent during the time Smith was writing his book. Private Acts were also establishing water companies. The first petition for a bill to incorporate a body of adventurers to supply Westminster with water from the Thames came before the House of Commons in 1721. A charter was eventually granted, the trustees were incorporated by the king under the Great Seal, and they received the title of Governor and Company of Chelsea Waterworks. There were no restrictions on water rates, but the corporation was obliged by its Charter to provide at its own charge 'pipes standing upright, in the likeness of pumps, to be ready on all occasions for better conveying water into engines for extinguishing accidental fires' (Clifford, 1885). The Charter authorized the corporation to raise by subscription jointstock not exceeding forty thousand pounds.[24]

We have already seen that Smith approved his cases for joint-stock incorporation on three grounds: first, that they could be reduced to 'such uniformity of method that admits of little variation'; second, that they were of greater and more general utility than usual; third, that they required greater capital than could easily be collected otherwise.

The third ground was surely the most important of the three. Indeed, the first does not stand up. The industries of banking and insurance were by no means routine. They were in a constant state of experiment and flux and process of creating new forms of organization. The water-supply undertakings were characterized by strong competition and continual technological innovation. In many dynamic (non-routine) industries, moreover, where surprises and new invention were the order of the day, a strong capital base was the prime requirement for survival as well as progress.

On the second ground, great utility, Smith is not very precise. But he does observe that 'if a moderate capital were sufficient, the great utility of the undertaking would not be a sufficient reason for establishing a joint-stock company; because in this case, the demand for what it was to produce, would readily and easily be supplied by private adventurers'.[25] Clearly, the instruments of joint stock and limited liability were the means to be adopted to overcome the capital restriction in other cases. Smith is still not arguing that if an activity has unusual utility it should be 'nationalized'; his discussion relates exclusively to the duty of the sovereign to observe proper methods for screening joint-stock or public-company concessions.

Roads as Public Works

Apart from the public mint, the post office, and education, to which further references will be made below, the major remaining example of a public work that Smith included in his list was the system of high roads. Here he does begin to make an exception to his general rule of non-government (public company) provision, but for reasons that are somewhat obscure. His exception, however, is still not based on modern public goods or collective goods reasoning, for he concedes that tolls can successfully finance the building and maintenance of high roads. What is interesting is his argument that the same tolls cannot 'with any safety be made the property of private persons'. Whereas he argues that a canal, when neglected, becomes altogether impassable and therefore proprietors can collect no tolls, a high road was different, since 'though entirely neglected [it] does not become altogether impassable'. Therefore the proprietors of tolls on high roads might neglect altogether the repair of the road and continue to levy 'very nearly the same toll'.

The modern economist will consider several arguments for governmental road provision, but Smith's appears strange. Where there is free (and cheap) entry into road-building and road assets are transferable for a capital sum on the market, the incentives to maintain roads in good repair, contrary to Smith's opinion, should be fully effective. If reasonably free entry and market transferability of assets were not typical, it would have been more consistent with the usual Smithian approach for him to have urged solutions whereby these conditions *could* prevail. Instead he settled for putting tolls under the management of public, albeit local, trustees. Now even if private owners would be discouraged from keeping the privately-held road systems in good repair, for instance because of monopoly enjoyment, why should individual employees in the public sector not also be equally prone to enjoy monopoly rents?

Smith's public choice argument here is surely inadequate, and in this instance one is inclined to agree with George Stigler's (1971) conclusion that Smith was, on occasion, politically naïve.[26] Smith even admits that there were many justified complaints against the publicly-appointed trustees of the tolls: 'At many turnpikes, it has been said, the money levied is more than double of what is necessary for executing, in the completest manner, the work which is often executed in a very slovenly manner, and sometimes not executed at all'.[27]

Monopoly rents are obtained by charging the same price for reduced quality, as in Smith's complaint of private owners, by raising the price, or both. Smith accused the public operators of both. The user is 'exploited' in both cases, and it is not clear which is the lesser of the evils. Smith, however, made two unexpected arguments. First, the system of operating the high roads under public trustee supervision was not of very long standing and would probably improve in the future and, second, that 'mean and improper persons are frequently appointed trustees'. He complained that proper courts of inspection and account had not yet been established for controlling their conduct and 'for reducing the tolls to what is barely sufficient for executing the work to be done by them'.

Smith does not further define 'mean and improper persons' in the public road enterprise. If they are simply self-interested, this characteristic is not immoral elsewhere in Smith. If he was drawing attention to a special need for 'trust', he might have been implying uneconomically low salaries; for in Chapter 10 of Book I of *The Wealth of Nations* 'trust' has to be purchased for a higher wage. If this was the case, publicly-operated roads could not much hope to reduce costs even with trustworthy commissioners; for they too would enjoy the higher wage. Finally, we are not assured in this instance why public commissioners would not suffer from the same defects as managers of joint-stock enterprises, who, according to Smith, being agents of other people's money, would be 'negligent' and profuse in spending it.

Whatever the weight of Smith's argument on high roads it must be re-emphasized that it is far different from the modern public good type of argument that his introduction to his section on public works originally seemed to promise. With respect to canals, the revenue could repay the expense to an individual or small number of individuals provided there was an efficient set of property rights. In the case of roads, the argument of the superiority of public provision or trusteeship over private provision (in joint-stock form) had clearly not been empirically demonstrated, as Smith admits. But even if it had, the appropriate modern category is that of the 'private good publicly supplied'.[28]

We must be clear, however, that Smith's discussion was initially addressed to interlinking high roads and not to the multiple-access roads, common to towns and villages. Public provision of the latter is today justified on grounds of the high transaction costs of private operation, that is, the overwhelmingly large costs of exclusion of non-payers from multiple side roads. Perhaps, indeed, Smith eventually confused the two cases (witness his reference, cited above, to London streets and the need to finance them by taxes on parishes). It is certainly pertinent that the earliest road legislation in England was prompted by responses to faulty or inadequate common law. In early times, parishes were liable to maintain their local roads, but there was insufficient incentive upon particular parishioners. Indeed the long evolution of road legislation can be seen as a stumbling attempt to solve the 'free-rider' problem partly by creating new forms of private property rights (as in the other cases of public works we have examined) and partly by some form of collective local provision or control.

By Smith's time the turnpike systems were peculiar combinations of public and private provision and control. The public aspects centred on the detailed regulations, especially of prices. The first Turnpike Act had appeared in 1663 (in the private Act roll). This allowed toll payments to augment road finance in a very heavily used road network in the Cambridge area. It was explained: 'Neither are the inhabitants through which the road doth lie of ability to repair the same without some other provision of moneys'. There were powers to levy: 'for every horse one penny; for every coach, sixpence; for every waggon one shilling; for every score of sheep, one half-penny; for every score of cattle five-pence.[29] Surveyors were authorized to mortgage the tolls and eventually trustees were enabled to lease them, but they retained the right to fix their levels up to the maximum imposed by their special Act.

Coinage and the Post Office

Jacob Viner argued that Smith dealt with the issue of the propriety of government participation in commerce 'solely from the viewpoint: Can government make a net revenue of it?'[30] In Book V, as has been shown, Smith was largely concerned, not with government participation in business, but with the sovereign's duty of providing an improved legal framework for private participation. But in this particular quotation, Viner refers to two rather exceptional or unexpected Smithian cases of government participation, coinage and the post office. He presumes that Smith 'takes coinage for granted as a government function without considering any possible alternative'. Smith, moreover, 'apparently approves of government operation of the post office, but if so, the only ground given is the ability of the government to manage it with successful financial results'.

It is important, however, to read Smith in the precise context. His almost incidental references to coinage and the post office come at the beginning of his discussion of public works, where Smith is illustrating a general principle. Whatever the public works in question, he asserts, it does not seem necessary that the expense of them should be defrayed from the general revenue, for they can usually 'be so managed as to afford a particular revenue sufficient for defraying their own expense'.[31] After illustrating the point by references to tolls on highways, bridges, and canals, Smith adds: 'The coinage, another institution for facilitating commerce, in many countries, not only defrays its own expense, but affords a small revenue or seignorage to the Sovereign. The post-office, another institution for the same purpose, over and above defraying its own expense, affords in almost all countries a very considerable revenue to the Sovereign.' Smith, it seems, was not raising the question of comparative efficiency between government and private provision of these enterprises. He was simply observing that they can pay for themselves whoever runs them, without help from general revenue. The fact that they can also usually earn a surplus for the government only drives home his major principle.

Again, the modern reader should notice that because self-financing charges can be made, there is no question of these enterprises having public-good qualities. Smith, it appears, was pragmatically taking the world as he found it; but in the instance of coinage and the post-office the world was set in its ways. In the case of banking, insurance, and canals, novel organizations based on joint-stock principles were newly *emerging*, and this fact probably prompted Smith to say more on the subject of comparative organization, because in this case his arguments might have a better chance of influencing events.

Education

Smith's verdict on 'The Education of Youth', his remaining illustration of the need for 'public institutions or works', follows his treatment of canals and roads. Such institutions can again finance themselves from their own revenue: 'The fee or honorary which the scholar pays to the master naturally constitutes a revenue of this kind'.[32] Acknowledging the public benefits of education, Smith then argues that that is not always a reason for government finance. But even when it is, it is not necessary to finance it from that general revenue that is assigned to the 'executive power'. The public beneficiaries, being largely local, can themselves be expected to finance, to some extent, the local provision of education. Here, however, Smith recognizes more characteristically the likelihood of public servants enjoying rents from local endowments when these are paid to them independently of their diligence.

If education was seen at all by Smith in terms of what we call public goods, it was in the nature of a mixed good; that is, it featured what we now call Pareto-relevant externalities. But if 'collective' finance was thus called for, it was in the form of partial finance or cost-sharing. This point is exemplified in Smith's championship of the Scottish system of parochial schools. The fees in that system were paid by families to cover the teacher's salary, whereas local property-owners financed the school buildings. Smith was ultimately so heavily critical of the way in which *any* element of 'subsidy' was in danger of being squandered, that one often gets the impression he believed they were typically non-productive, if not counter-productive.

The penultimate paragraph of Smith's long section on public

works deserves more attention than it usually receives. It shows a final balancing of all the arguments reviewed earlier in the same chapter. Although expenditure on institutions for education and religious instruction is no doubt beneficial to the whole society, he concludes, and while it may be defrayed by the general contribution of the whole society, it 'might perhaps with *equal propriety, and even with some advantage, be defrayed altogether* by those who receive the immediate benefit of such education and instruction, or by the *voluntary contribution* of those who think they have occasion for either one or the other. In modern terms, Smith is making one of two arguments. First, although external benefits may be recognized, they are Pareto-irrelevant, or, in other words, of no significance at the margin. Average external benefits in other words are positive, but marginal external benefits are zero.[33] Second, any public benefits would accrue in very localized areas, and individual beneficiaries therein can be left to provide subsidies to augment family education and expenditure. It must be acknowledged that the free-rider problem might arise even locally; but the smaller the locality, or the more we approach the small-numbers case, the less will this objection apply; and it is relevant that Smith relies on *voluntary* contributions from the 'neighbours'. This is *not* therefore an argument in favour of elaborate provision of universal education by the state.

The Final Assessment

The general content of Smith's third duty to the sovereign was, with few exceptions, the search for new forms of property rights that would better enable private organization to produce public works. These new rights related especially to capital markets at a time when there was a growing need to mobilize funds on a large scale. Smith's analysis in this part of his classic work was not the most comprehensive. Frequently it is misinformed, as in the case of foreign trading companies, and the economic judgement is often not well explained, as in Smith's belief that joint-stock incorporation was suitable only for 'routine trades'. The sequence of analysis often seems a grudging endorsement of historical events, and certainly Smith's argument cannot be fully appreciated without substantial acquaintance with such history.

Nevertheless there is much more consistency in this part of *The*

Wealth of Nations than its author has been given credit for. Woven into the whole argument is the particular principle that there is little justification in most cases for reliance on the general revenue to support 'public' works. They should and could be financed on the 'benefit principle', that is, by the direct beneficiaries of each separate project. Ultimately the market is the most efficient respecter of the benefit principle, and it should therefore be relied on wherever possible. Usually this was possible, provided the sovereign had done his duty of legally arranging for suitably modified or created property rights; and where it was not quite possible the next best thing was a quasi-price system that employed 'user-taxes'.

The important point about Viner's 'modern advocate of laissez-faire' is that he has placed himself by definition in a non-Smithian world. Such an advocate believes that business is 'a field reserved by *nature* for private enterprise'.[34] Smith's private enterprise, in contrast, presupposes some previous conscious act of will that, influenced by cool reason, has established a rational legal framework in which property rights and contract rules are specified and upheld by the 'protective' state within the constitution.

The term 'laissez faire' is not in *The Wealth of Nations*; and indeed, in Viner's sense, it would have been almost meaningless to Adam Smith. For he believed that the world of 'nature' was a Hobbesian jungle wherein man himself, let alone private business, could hardly survive. So Viner's discussion of *The Wealth of Nations* in terms of *laissez faire* versus public intervention dichotomy is largely beside the point. More relevant is the question to what extent Smith's 'intervention' was rooted in the protective state (the whole legal framework) and to what extent in the productive state (government). The view here is that, on balance, it was predominantly in the former. Smith's 'sovereign', moreover, was certainly not identical with 'government' in the 20th-century sense. And just as we do not today identify primarily with the government sector the whole field of public corporations (companies), including for example modern banking and insurance corporations, so it would be erroneous to make a similar classification of Smith's joint-stock enterprises in banking and insurance. Smith's analysis of the latter, under the heading 'public works' or 'public institutions', is apt to mislead a 20th-century reader.

At the same time there remains a need for some deeper treatment of those legal instruments that are specially complex. While the simplest of legal instruments require little supervision or administration by official departments, a whole continuum of contracts exists, ranging up to agreements that almost have their own complicated 'constitutions'.[35] Contracts dealing with patents require some minimum 'intervention' or 'participation', at least in the form of a patent office. Smith agreed with patents on principle, and treated foreign trading monopolies on analogous reasoning; his acquiescence to 'intervention' of this type is therefore implicit. And although Smith wanted to grant to private companies, such as water supply enterprises, the duty of producing public works that we now call 'utilities', there is no evidence that he objected to the more sophisticated (restrictive) nature of the charters of incorporation that have been shown to have been emerging in these cases, charters that called for more continuous official supervision ('partnership'). It is also true that Smith was in some exceptional areas favourable to regulation, such as with currency and building standards to prevent fire.[36]

The fact remains that where public works were concerned Smith relied on finance by the *users* of each project in turn. His opening observation that such projects would not be forthcoming in his time because they would not profit a small number of venturers prefaced his review of the need for concession of joint-stock and limited liability that would allow large numbers of (private) ventures to take advantage of a wider (private) capital market. The degrees of intervention necessary were proportional to the complexity of each new contract in turn.

Meanwhile, the law and its concomitant administration was always a 'partner' in Smithian private enterprise, whatever its form and however 'routine'. Indeed, administration of the law fulfilled a necessary condition for existence of the market. The real question is: What level of complexity did the law have to reach before significant degrees of supervision and discretion appeared in its administration, the level at which we begin to approach 'intervention' in the strong sense? When does Smith's sovereign change from being a 'stage manager' to become a 'leading actor'? This question no doubt calls for further reflection and research, but our own opinion of where the balance lies has been made clear.

Finally, when we seek any element of modern public good reasoning in Smith, it does not appear in the usual context of 'market failure'. Rather it manifests itself mainly in the 'public goodness' of a total system of property rights protected by the law. In so far as

Smith's public works discussion is rooted in the joint-stock/limited liability facets of the total legal structure, we certainly begin indirectly to connect with the public good reasoning; but then Smith's 'non-public' works have the same connection.

Notes

1. See also Robbins (1952), p. 38; Crouch (1967); Hutchison (1988).
2. This terminology is borrowed from Buchanan (1975).
3. Smith (1976), p. 716.
4. Ibid., p. 719.
5. Ibid., p. 723.
6. Writers who explicitly associate Smith's argument with modern 'public goods' thinking include Ekelund and Hebert (1990), Herber (1971), and Skinner (1974). Blaug (1985) links Smith with Pigou's distinction between private and social costs but also emphasizes the importance to Smith of the design and pattern of the legal framework in allowing markets to work.
7. Smith (1976), p. 724.
8. Ibid., p. 730–1.
9. Ibid, p. 724, emphasis added. Jacob Viner (1928), concludes that Smith 'completely ignores the criterion he had laid down at the beginning of his discussion' when it came to particular public works – the argument that they would not pay as private enterprises. As I shall now show, the issue is much more complex than this, and Smith is *not* inconsistent in most cases.
10. Hunt (1968), p. 3.
11. Ibid., p. 5.
12. Scott (1912), p. 460. Scott has criticized Smith for 'failing to take account of the gradations between the true partnership and the overgrown company'. Yet, as will be shown in the next section, Smith's writing on public works was a survey of those few areas where he believed, not that 'nationalized', or even municipalized, organization was typically called for, but that 'public joint-stock companies, that is, special large-scale *private* enterprise institutions with special legal property rights, might, after all, have their role'.
13. Smith (1976), p. 740.
14. Ibid., p. 232. It is certainly interesting to learn from him that in his time the South Sea Company had a trading stock three times as large as the capital of the Bank of England.
15. Smith (1976), p. 741.
16. See Anderson (1964) and Scott (1912), p. 445. The main example of 'negligence and profusion' that Smith had in mind was that of the East India undertaking. He argued that from the end of the reign of Charles II to the beginning of that of William III the company was 'reduced to great distress'. Yet even from the references in Anderson, the company made on average 50 per cent dividend per annum over this period! Certainly there was a presumption that private interlopers traded at an advantage over the chartered company. The latter obtained its exclusive privileges on the grounds that it was obliged to build forts and other defensive appliances. From a statement compiled from the East India Company about 1685, such expenditures amounted to between one-fifth and one-quarter of the whole. Interlopers, therefore, in escaping such expenses, acted as free-riders enjoying public (collective) goods for which they were not obliged to pay.

Yet despite these advantages the interlopers had been almost driven out towards the end of the 17th century, not because of successful policing by the chartered company, but because of the large risks involved.

17. Scott (1912), p. 454.
18. Thus, the Scottish Whale Fishing enterprise was purchased by the Joint Committee of the Russian and East India Companies during the reign of James I. The interloping India Company at the time of Charles I was eventually amalgamated with the chartered body.
19. Smith (1976), p. 757.
20. Ibid. Smith does not mention life assurance, which would qualify for joint-stock status on his grounds. Such business had not yet been much developed, although the Equitable Society (1756) was between a mutual society and a joint-stock company.
21. Smith separated his public works into those that facilitated commerce in general and those that facilitated commerce in particular. He treated banks and insurance as pertaining to commerce in particular, although there seems no clear reason why they would not also be classified under commerce in general. Smith discussed canals under both headings.
22. Ibid., pp. 757–8.
23. The cumbrous procedure of Bridgewater's legislation (which started with a petition in 1761) is detailed in Clifford (1885), pp. 34–8.
24. As another example, in 1748 an Act was obtained by George Montgomerie and others authorizing them to supply the Stratford and West Ham area with water from the River Lea. Provision of fire hydrants was again obligatory. Later in the century came the Lambeth Water Works Company (1785), the South London Water Works Company (1805), and the Kent Water Works Company (1808). One of the largest companies to emerge was the Grand Junction Water Works Company, under an Act of 1811 and with powers to raise £150 000 to supply water to 'the Parish of Paddington and parishes and streets adjacent'. This act contained a larger variety of restrictions, including several that will interest modern students of the economics of pollution and 'externalities'. One provided that every furnace should be constructed as to 'consume its own smoke', that every chimney should have its shaft at least 130 feet above ground level, and 'that the smoke issuing there from shall not at any one time exceed the quantity of smoke usually issuing from chimneys of twenty-four fires for domestic use' (Clifford, 1885, p. 107). That the consent was required of a Mr Edward Berkely Portman, his heirs or assigns, might suggest an early instance of disproportionate use of political power or influence in obtaining stakes in the newly-emerging property rights in clean air.
25. Smith (1976), p. 757.
26. Generally, however, a challenge to Stigler's verdict is contained in Chapter 8 below.
27. Smith (1976), p. 726.
28. For one formal definition of the 'private good publicly supplied' see Stiglitz (1974). His definition, however, does not quite cover the present case. He argues: 'A pure publicly provided private good is a private good (a good for which there is a substantial marginal cost of an additional person consuming it) which is provided in *equal quantities* to all individuals (within a given class) without charge'. The words in (my) italics show the main difference. Stiglitz offers roads (probably he means multiple access roads) and in some circumstances education, as examples that fit his definition. Notice that there can be some public good quality in a monopoly (licensed) highway that is operated below capacity – in which case the costs of an additional user is zero. Smith appears to have been

thinking of full capacity roads and assuming reasonably free entry to the toll-road industry in the long run.

29. Clifford (1885), p. 8.
30. Viner (1928), p. 148.
31. Smith (1976), p.724.
32. Ibid., pp. 758–9.
33. Viner again makes no reference to Smith's basic principle – let the private beneficiaries pay wherever possible – but simply asserts that Smith 'supports the participation of the government' and outlines the types of public benefits that occur without apparently understanding Smith's argument that the existence of such benefits was not a sufficient argument for government participation.
34. Viner (1928), p. 149, emphasis added.
35. Goldberg (1976).
36. Robbins (1952), p. 31.

8. Adam Smith and Public Choice

Public choice or the economics of politics is a new branch of economics that began in Virginia under the leadership of James Buchanan and Gordon Tullock. Its original professional journal was called *Papers on Non-market Decision Making* but in 1968 the journal changed its name to *Public Choice*. Gordon Tullock continues to serve as the senior editor. In the US there is a Public Choice Society which conducts annual meetings and since the early 1970s this has been matched by an active European Public Choice Society which also meets once a year. A public choice group also exists in Japan.

The amount of literature on public choice has grown so rapidly that in the opinion of Robert Tollison, the most important current research is published not in *Public Choice* but in the major journals of economics and political science. The subject, moreover, has now attained a place in the *Journal of Economic Literature*'s classification system for economic writing. (The classification falls under 'general economic theory' and is listed as '025 Social choice; bureaucratic performance'.) As Tollison observes: 'the fact that the profession provides a convenient means to keep up with current research in the area is an impressive sign of the general scientific acceptance of public choice'.[1] Finally, the award of the 1986 Nobel Prize for Economic Science to Professor James M. Buchanan has been another measure of worldwide recognition of the new subdiscipline.

Buchanan has always emphasized that there are three dimensions in the study of public choice: the economics of the pre-constitutional stage of society, the economics of constitution making, and the economics of post-constitutional politics.[2] The pre-constitutional dimension, or the state of anarchy, re-emerged in the 1970s as a topic for considerable re-examination and discussion. At the same time, new interest in the second dimension, constitution making, was stimulated among others by philosopher John Rawls, as well as by economists James Buchanan and Gordon Tullock. The third, post-constitutional dimension, which up to the early seventies was the one typically assumed in the 20th-century economics, is concerned with legislative tactics within *given* majority rules, *given* 'property' rights and *given* electorates. The pioneering work in the economics of politics as understood in this third dimension originated with Anthony Downs.[3]

It will be argued in this chapter that Adam Smith's economics of politics centres largely, but not entirely, on the second dimension, constitution making, and that several modern critics might have lost perspective because they have concentrated excessively on the third level. This is not to say that this level is without interest. Indeed the whole of the next chapter will be devoted to the economics of post-constitutional politics in Smiths' work and especially to our retrospective application of the modern economic concept of 'rent seeking'.

It is not the intention to argue that Smith's writings contain an explicitly coherent analysis of political behaviour. Nevertheless, he did inform us that he had conceived a book on law and government, and it is a challenging task to attempt a partial assembly of the numerous insights on this subject that lie scattered through his published works. The exercise is worthwhile since it promises a better understanding of Smith's strengths and weaknesses and a possibility of bringing other writers, new and old, into sharper relief.

Among 'new' writers, for instance, this chapter will make a brief comparison with Rawls, and will bring further to the surface a difference between the modern Virginian School associated with James Buchanan and the Chicago School of George Stigler, the former focusing upon the first two dimensions of politics (above) and the latter upon the third dimension. Among 'old' writers, the investigation will bring some new significance especially to Joseph Schumpeter's fear that capitalism and democracy are incompatible.

The sequence of the examination of Smith will be arranged according to the order of the three dimensions of politics already outlined. While the main focus of this book is still upon modern economics and Smith's inspiration for it, discussion of the first dimension, anarchy, will require more than usual reference to older writers in order to provide an appropriate background to the enquiry.

Anarchy

The foremost classical views here are those of Proudhon, Godwin, and Hobbes.[4] Proudhon pictures anarchy as a natural harmony in which each person freely pursues happiness and develops his own talents. His view, however, is not supported by systematic evidence. Its most serious deficiency is that it does not face up to the need for reconciliation of tastes among heterogeneous individuals in social interaction. Godwin believed that there would be so much abundance that conflict would not be provoked. The Hobbesian view of anarchy, of course, is opposite and non-romantic. It does recognize heterogeneity and assumes there will always be *some* individuals in the state of nature who would take by force the goods produced by others.

It is with the Hobbesian view that most economists, from Adam Smith onwards, have begun. What has impressed them most is the sheer waste involved in a state of anarchy – waste by those who undertake the effort of stealing and by others who use more resources for their own defence. In terms of modern game theory these writers have recognized the imperatives of the 'prisoner's dilemma' and the nonzero-sum, noncooperative game. This reasoning then proceeds to the rationale of attempts to resolve the dilemma via a constitution that collectively protects private-property rights. The collective protection then becomes a public good from which 'free riders' are excluded.[5] Three corollaries should be stressed. First, the establishment of the legal framework can be predicted on the simple assumption of self-interest; second, the larger the potential wealth, the larger the incentives to establish the framework; third, once established, a succeeding economic prosperity, *provided it is not too unequally or unjustly distributed,* will for all members dramatically increase the opportunity costs of abandoning it and reverting to anarchy.

In Part II of Chapter I in Book V of *The Wealth of Nations,* Smith argues that among nations of hunters there is no incentive to establish 'a permanent magistrate' or any regular administration of justice. This is because there is very little in the way of potential property, or at least 'none that exceeds the value of two or three days' labour'. In these circumstances conflict between *propertyless* individuals is a negative-sum game. In Smith's words: 'Though he to whom the injury is done suffers, he who does it receives no benefit'. Personal violence in this setting is prompted by malice and resentment; but most men, Smith observes, 'are not very frequently under those passions'. Other passions that are 'much more steady in their operation' are brought into play where, in contrast, there is much property. These passions are 'avarice and ambition in the rich' and, in the poor, 'hatred of labour and the love of present ease and enjoyment'. It is these that 'prompt to invade property'. Extensive property accumulation can therefore succeed only under 'the powerful arm of the civil magistrate'. But while the law is needed to protect the rich against the poor, prior to its establishment the latter were poorer still. In *The Wealth of Nations*, capital accumulation is a necessary condition for economic growth: but since Smith explicitly argues that growth benefits 'all ranks of society', so must the property-rights system.

These initial quotations might suggest very sweeping judgements by Adam Smith about his fellow men. He believed, however, that there was a high probability in *most* men of developing refined moral sensibilities and respect for others, but only after a system of law had been established. In the first instance, this system would, or could, emerge from the narrowest self-interest. In Adam Smith's words:

> Society may subsist among different men as among different merchants, from a sense of its utility, without any mutual love or affection; and though no man in it should owe any obligation, or be bound in gratitude to any other, it may still be upheld by a mercenary exchange of good offices according to an agreed valuation. ... If there is any society among robbers and murderers, they must at least, according to the trite observations, abstain from robbing and murdering one another.[6]

Smith's friend David Hume was even more vigorous in maintaining that self-interest was the basis of the constitution. In his *Treatise of Human Nature*, Hume argued that a convention or contract was inevitable. 'By this means every one knows what he may safely possess; and the passions are restrained in their partial and contradictory motions.'[7] By abstaining from the possessions of others, we promote not only their interests but ours too. By such means 'we maintain society, which is so necessary to their well-being and subsistence, as well as to our own'.[8] The characteristics of the human mind, according to Hume, were *selfishness* and limited generosity. It was from these characteristics that the constitution, or 'justice', originated.[9]

With such reasoning, Hume and Smith were able to meet a problem associated with the Lockean and Hobbesian theories. The historical social contract of the latter could not easily be the foundation of political obligation for new generations who were not a party to it. Hume and Smith argued accordingly that the self-interest of succeeding generations usually dictates a *tacit* consent to conventional rules in existence. Each generation would thus behave 'as if' it had signed the social contract anew. In his Glasgow lectures of 1762 Smith deals explicitly with these points. There were no grounds, he asserted, for believing in any social contract (in the historical sense): 'Ask a common porter or day-labourer why he obeys the civil magistrate, he will tell you that it is right to do so, that he sees others do it, that he would be punished if he refused to do it.' Men are induced, Smith argued, to enter into and remain in civil society by the two principles, 'authority and utility or obedience and the instinct of self preservation'.[10]

It is not so well known that Adam Smith had considerable respect for Jean-Jacques Rousseau's work *The Social Contract*. It is reported that in his later life Smith spoke of Rousseau 'with a kind of religious respect' and expressed the belief that his *Social Contract* 'will one day avenge all the persecutions he suffered'.[11] Interestingly enough, in the recently developing interest in public choice Rousseau has been rediscovered.[12] The new focus of interest is Rousseau's treatment of the *obstacle* of egoism in the constitution – the problem that each individual may place his private interest before that of the public and so become a free-riding consumer of a public good, each to the detriment of himself in the long run. Rousseau had only one public good in mind, that of the constitution or system of law itself.

Adam Smith and Rousseau shared a characteristic that distinguished them from Hume. The latter was mainly concerned with predicting a long-run system that suited individuals who were characterized by 'selfishness and limited generosity'. Smith and Rousseau, in contrast, emphasized that the balance of these characteristics or passions is changed by the very experience of living in a stable society: men cannot be virtuous in a state of nature; only in a society based upon law do they become virtuous, and the non-selfish virtues can increase with time. In Rousseau's proposals, such virtue should be furthered by the development of what he calls a 'civil religion' that could be inculcated by the sovereign.[13] The religion would consist of a few simple dogmas expressed as categorical imperatives. They would include tolerance, the sanctity of the social contract, and respect for law.

By inculcating social morals, the adoption of the 'civil religion' was one attempt at resolving what we now call the free-rider problem.[14] If successful, it could indeed be a more efficient method than conventional policing, since less resources would be needed. Such a solution is recognized in some degree in the modern economics of trust and altruism. And to some it might offer a partial answer to the major question concerning the Hobbesian model: if formal rules exist, these must be enforced – and how is the enforcer himself to be controlled?

In Adam Smith's writings, the word 'civilization' is used almost interchangeably with 'commerce'; and this of course implies a system of property rights. But for Smith, just as for Rousseau, a constitution drawn up by merchants merely in the spirit of a mercenary exchange was only a beginning. Eventually people can become more conscious of their *long-term* self-interest and readier to adopt civilizing virtues. This development is associated by Smith with wisdom, temperance, prudence, and fellow feeling, qualities that he favours and explores in *The Theory of Moral Sentiments* (1759).

Moral improvement is fostered in Smith by each individual's consultation with the 'Impartial Spectator'. This agency can be an imagined or a real person who has sympathy with each 'actor' and with others. Continual consultation or checking with the Spectator by each individual in turn serves as a social mirror for his own individual action. Since each party seeks the sympathy of the Spectator, there is ultimately a moderation of passions and a development of fellow feeling.

The shaping of the constitution requires the most sensitive understanding of men and presents the Impartial Spectator with the most difficult task of all. But implicitly for Smith, as for Rousseau, the development of morals reduces the policing problems of the state. Yet whereas Rousseau desired a complete 'transformation of human identity'[15] in which self-interest finally disappears, Smith certainly did not go this far. Smith's individual should maintain his identity, but at the same time he should be developing a proper regard for others. And it was not from civil religion but from Christian religion that Smith reached this judgement. In his words: 'As to love our neighbour as we love ourselves is the great law of Christianity, so it is the great precept of nature to love ourselves only as we love our neighbour, or, what comes to the same thing, as our neighbour is capable of loving us'.[16]

Some form of constitution was imperative for Smith, and he did not spend long in establishing such a fairly obvious point. What was more complex was the remaining technical question of selecting the appropriate constitutional model for each set of historical circumstances. The predominant choices available were from aristocracies, monarchies, democracies, and republics. It is this second dimension of politics indeed with which Smith seems to have been especially occupied and on which he offered his most considered 'public choice' judgements.

The Constitution-making Dimension

Rousseau had distinguished carefully between the legislative sovereign body and the executive or government. He believed it was an empirical fact that all governments everywhere had a tendency to encroach upon the territory of the sovereign rights of the people; there was in other words a tendency to overgovernment, where particular private interests will usurp those of the general community. The checks and balances of a republican system based on the separation of powers were, Rousseau argued, the best delay to this eventual corruption of the law.[17] While the democratic form of government of the small city-state came nearest to perfection, Rousseau believed it to be the most liable to change to another form, largely because of the growth of population. Where vast multitudes had to be governed, he preferred what he called 'elective aristocracy'. This – unlike monarchy, the other alternative – had the advantage of distinguishing more clearly between the sovereign and the government. Provided the law carefully regulated the procedure of elections, wise government could be fairly guaranteed and a strong republican constitution would emerge.

Table 8.1 Comparative systems and constitutions in Smithian literature

	Reference
Hobbes's social contract	Lectures, p12
Nations of savages, shepherds, clans, aristocrats, 'little republics'	Lectures, pp. 14–28
Shepherd nations: Arab and Tartar nations, North American Indians	*Wealth of Nations** 690–1, 705, 712–13
Greek republics, agrarian states, European monarchies	WN 696–708
Feudal governments	WN 696
Standing armies and the constitution: the best security to peace is when the sovereign is the general	WN 706
China: opulent but stationary because of constitutional laws and institutions unfavourable to commerce	WN 111–12
Governments and constitutions of mercantile companies in the East Indies compared with 'the genius of the British constitution', which protects and governs North America	WN 91
The constitutional distinction between Greek and Roman colonies	WN 556–8
Circumstances leading to the constitutions of European colonies in the East Indies and America	WN 558
Political institutions and English colonies are more favourable to land cultivation than the French, Spanish, and Portuguese	WN 572
The constitution of North American establishments, 'an ever-memorable example of how small an expense three millions of people may not only be governed, but well-governed'	WN 574
British control over American colonies compared with the King of France's authority over French provinces	WN 620
The Roman republic's decline due to refusal of citizenship rights to its allies	WN 622
The need for taxation and parliamentary representation of the American colonies	WN 622–3
The British constitution would be successfully completed by union with colonies	WN 624
The Church's relationship to the State: religious persecution is politically unwise for the sovereign. Fear is a 'wretched instrument of government'	WN 798

The constitution of the Church of Rome in the 10th to 13th centuries: the 'most formidable combination that ever was formed against the authority and security of civil government' WN 802

The inverse relationship between the size of bene- fices and the influences of the church upon the common people. Only in Presbyterian countries are the people successfully converted to the established church WN 804, 807

Economic invention and commercial development destroyed the temporal constitutional power of the clergy. It destroyed also that of the great barons WN 810

---

*Smith (1976), hereafter WN

Adam Smith seems to have reached a very similar position and after an extensive, although not exhaustive, survey of historical evidence. This survey, illustrated here in Table 8.1, suggests that Smith's public choice pronouncements were not uninformed conjectures. While he was more pragmatic than Rousseau, he assigned the same weight to the general need for checks and balances. One of the most important tasks of the constitution in Smith, as in Rousseau, was to secure individual liberty. In the Glasgow lectures, Smith wanted what he called 'a happy mixture of all the different forms of government properly restrained, and a perfect security to liberty and property'. One had to proceed by trial and error and to retain what experience shows to be valuable. For instance, Smith believed the element of some separation of powers that had developed in the British Constitution and thought it to be a welcome feature. Monetary affairs had to be dealt with in the Commons: the judges were independent of the king; the Habeas Corpus Act was further security to individual freedom. The jury system was also a 'friend of liberty'. It is well known that Smith speaks of an 'obvious and simple system of natural liberty' which often leads, in the private market, to the reconciling of private with social interests. When, however, he examines the 'political market', he shows the same apprehension as Rousseau. For here liberty seemed to risk being in unstable equilibrium. Smith repeatedly examines outcomes serving the self-interest of members of established oligarchies, entrenched aristocracies, oppressive religious establishments, and cunning political lobbies.

It is interesting to contrast Smith's theory of justice with that of

John Rawls, the leader of the contractarian revival in the 1970s. Advancing the notion of 'justice as fairness', and that just principles would emerge from the unanimous agreement of men, each of whom was behind a veil of ignorance concerning his own position in the post-contractual world, Rawls, like Smith, establishes individual liberty as the supreme principle. The conspicuous difference is that Rawls produces a *second* principle of justice, the 'difference principle': economic inequalities are to be arrayed so that they are to the advantage of the poorest in society. No such principle is to be found anywhere in Smith. His system of natural liberty was sufficient and was directed to the release of men's energies. Smith was more interested in the *pursuit of income* than in its size, and in the process of contracting than in its actual outcome. One can find no social-welfare functions in Smith calculated to guide some 'distributive branch' of government. Indeed there *is* no such branch. Smith's Impartial Spectator is emphatically not (as Rawls seems to believe) ultimately some supreme utilitarian planner.[18] 'Every man,' Smith argues, 'is, no doubt by nature, first and principally recommended to his own care; and as he is fitter to take care of himself, than of any other person, it is fit and right that it should be.'

From Smith's point of view, indeed, Rawls's scheme seriously compromises liberty. For in it liberty is a luxury good. In Rawls's words: 'As the conditions of civilization improve, the marginal significance for our good of further economic and social advantages diminishes relative to the interests of liberty, which become stronger as the conditions for the exercise of the equal freedoms are more fully realized'.[19] In Smith's eyes, liberty was a means as well as an end; the liberties of the person, of trade, and of contract were essential to the very economic progress that Rawls believes to be a prior condition for liberty; and Smithian liberty is best secured when protected in the highest degree from the coercion of government. Coercion was to be confined to the substantive general rule of law. Such a rule, with the aid of the principle of separation of powers, keeps all parties, including *governments* and legislatures, under the law.

Rawls's second principle suffers in the Smithian scheme of things because all economic changes have to be monitored in an attempt to maximize the total income of the least advantaged, and the chief monitor is *government*. Modern democratic governments are based on simple majority voting. Rousseau and Smith were enamoured neither of government nor of such voting rules. Rawls's attempt at redistribution would not, in their eyes, have much chance of success anyway; for, in such systems, self-interest groups will use their votes to foster their interests and not those of the poor. Similarly, for an increasing number of people today it is too much to believe that a sense of justice will even marginally restrain the self-interest demands of the majority. As Hayek argues, 'In any group it is soon believed that what is desired by the group is just'.[20] Some economists maintain that simple majority voting in practice tends to result in social expenditures that hurt both the rich and the poor for the benefit of the middle class.[21]

Among the classical contractarians, Rousseau was the most explicit on the disadvantages of simple majority voting. In *The Social Contract* he recommended varying the majority rule to require a ratio much nearer unanimity (say 80 per cent) 'the more important and serious the matter be'! Wicksell later advocated the near-unanimity rule in public finance. It was advocated along with simultaneous tax and expenditure budgets as an efficient expression of the benefit principle. Buchanan and Tullock acknowledge direct inspiration from Wicksell in the writings of their classic work in public choice, *The Calculus of Consent*. In it they argue that the optimal majority rule ratio would be chosen by an individual (in something like Rawls's original position) only after he had determined the minimum costs of voting to be expected. Decision-making costs will increase with the size of the majority demanded because costly strategic bargaining is required to persuade the last few voters whose interest may be to hold out. The 'external' costs of other voters' actions on to the individual will decrease with the increase of the number required to take collective action. The summed decision-making and external costs produce a U-shaped average cost function, and the optimum majority rule is determined at its lowest point. In many decisions the rule is likely to be well above 50 per cent.[22]

In Smith's theory of justice most weight is placed on *general* laws. And the basic function of these was to protect property. This was not, moreover, the reflection of an upper-class propertied interest, for, to Smith, the 'most sacred and inviolable' property was 'the property which every man has in his own labour'. It was for this reason, indeed, that he condemned the statutes requiring long apprenticeship laws; such laws were, to him, a violation of property.

Smith indeed saw them as a source of inequality. If government could enact such obstacles, presumably it would be an even more dubious agent to be entrusted with a general redistribution of income. And while many writers argue as if Smith had quite an extensive agenda for government, the detailed examination of it in Chapter 7 shows this belief to be incorrect. Smith's discussion of the need for public works and institutions, to reiterate, is largely an enquiry about the desirability of the sovereign altering the constitution to allow new legal instruments such as joint-stock enterprise and limited liability into certain areas. Smith's use of the word 'public' is predominantly in the context of the desirability of *public companies*, i.e. private, not 'nationalized', concerns.

Democratic governments are usually based on simple majority voting. In Smith's view, the use of this whole apparatus was more conducive to monopoly than any other. It was one key to statutory protectionism. Implicitly the vote was a property right that, to Smith, violates other, more legitimate, property rights. The evidence for this view is his reference to statutory regulations that enable members of the same trade to tax themselves to provide sickness and welfare funds. By giving them a common interest to manage, Smith observed, the regulation 'renders such assemblies necessary'. After that, a simple majority vote is given statutory respect, and this in turn is followed by a severe setback to the Smithian system. In his words:

> An incorporation not only renders them [the assemblies] necessary, but makes the act of the majority binding upon the whole. In a free trade an effectual combination cannot last longer than every single trader continues of the same mind. The majority of a corporation can enact a by-law with proper penalties, which will limit the competition more effectually and more durably than any voluntary combination whatever.[23]

Notice that the statute itself need not be based on democratic majority voting; Smith's system was aristocratic and he was complaining here about an unwise area in its legislation. Nevertheless, the implication is that in a full democracy, with active governments operating on simple majority rules, one can predict group-interested legislation such as tariffs, bounties, and price-fixing laws. Organized pressure for legislation itself will become a commercial undertaking.[24]

As Jacob Viner once detected, Smith believed in some degree of representation in the law-making authority, but his criteria of representation were not fully democratic ones.[25] It is arguable, moreover, that Smith was not disturbed by this implication because, as Schumpeter was later to argue, capitalism and full democracy are not compatible. Not that Smith was opposed to constitutional democracy altogether, but he was more concerned with the establishment of general laws of procedures that laid down the permanent limits to the coercive powers of government than with the precise voting rules within it. He was convinced that arbitrary monarchical despotism had to be ruled out since it was not a satisfactory answer to the petty domination of smaller coalitions in democracies. The despot, after all, is only a smaller coalition still. Smith in fact seems to have had much in common with the Founding Fathers of the American Constitution, which was a blend of republicanism and democracy. In a 'full democracy' the will of the people, or 'popular passion', as 18th-century writers like Smith were apt to call it, reigns supreme. In a republic it is not the will of the people that predominates but a *rational consensus* – which is implicit in the term 'consent'. And such a republic, if ruled by wise men, can enjoy a liberty that is not threatened by tyrannical majorities. As Smith's politician friend, Edmund Burke, told his constituents, he owed them only his *judgement*; and he was not going to sacrifice this universally to their opinion. We confront here of course the most vulnerable part of the political philosophy of Smith and Rousseau. Both writers ultimately leaned heavily upon the guidance of the wise lawgiver, that is upon 'good' natural leaders.

Although it is still arguable that the chances of receiving laws that originate behind some Rawlsian 'veil of ignorance' are greater when a legislator is qualified more by wisdom and other-regarding virtues than by simple lobby support, in any real world we must 'start from here' with imperfection, unequal endowment, and inadequate communication and knowledge. As has been argued, 'Rules for social order ... will [always] reflect the struggle among interests, and will rarely if ever qualify as 'just' in accordance with any idealized criteria'.[26] Adam Smith expresses the same realism in the following words:

> The man whose public spirit is prompted altogether by humanity and benevolence, will respect the established powers and privileges even of individuals, and still more those of the great orders and societies into which the state is divided. Though he should consider some of them as in some measure abusive, he will content himself with moderating what he

cannot annihilate without great violence. When he cannot conquer the rooted prejudices of the people by reason and persuasion, he will not attempt to subdue them by force. ... He will accommodate, as well as he can, his public arrangements to the confirmed habits and prejudices of the people, and will remedy, as well as he can, the inconveniences which may flow from the want of those regulations which the people are adverse to submit to. When he cannot establish the best system of laws, he will endeavour to establish the best that the people can bear.[27]

This judgement of Smith is repeated in *The Wealth of Nations*. Referring to some welcome modification of the corn export bounty, Smith observes: 'With all its imperfections, however, we may perhaps say of it what was said of the laws of Solon, that, though not the best in itself, it is the best which the interests, prejudices, and temper of the times would admit of'.[28]

Thus it was the especially complex and arduous task of the legislator of constitutions that was the central focus of the economics of politics that are scattered in *The Wealth of Nations*. Smith was more occupied with finding workable improvements in the rules of the game than with the tactics of the games played within the existing imperfect rules by 'that insidious and crafty animal vulgarly called a stateman or politician whose councils are directed by the momentary fluctuations of affairs'. And if Smith was not optimistic about the chances of free trade ever being adopted, he was even less so concerning the supply of wise statesmen. Indeed their useful influence on affairs was usually fortuitous; but when it did occur, it did so at the constitutional level:

> The leader of the successful party, however, if he has authority enough to prevail upon his own friends to act with proper temper and moderation (which he frequently does not), may sometimes render to his country a service much more essential and important than the greatest victories and the most extensive conquests. *He may re-establish and improve the constitution*, and from the very doubtful and ambiguous character of the leader of a party, he may assume the noblest of all characters, that of the reformer and legislator of a great state; and, by the wisdom of his institutions, secure the internal tranquility and happiness of his fellow-citizens for many succeeding generations.[29]

It should be re-emphasized that Smith's wise legislator was not directly appointed by a majority of citizens, for they did not yet have the franchise. The noble object of Smith's efforts was not the expedient, incremental legislation that satisfies some particular lobby demanding specific reform proposals, but the non-incremental shift in, or development of, the fundamental laws that underpin the basic structure of the constitution. Such a change is the outcome of a systematic, philosophic, and long-term consideration of the fabric of the social order itself. Similarly, Adam Smith's economics of politics were typically concerned, not with pragmatic legislation dealing with particular programmes, but with a shift in basic paradigms that shape and inform all serious legislation. He sought to dislodge the whole system of mercantilist thought that had been modifying, if not weakening, the basic constitution for centuries. Smith's was the *general* principle that the removal of effective government restrictions on trade would produce long-term results that would be preferred by all concerned. It was a principle of ordered anarchy; and it was based on well-defined individual rights and respect for voluntary contracts relating to them.

The Post-constitutional State

In the third category of this study, political activity is set in the post-constitutional state. There a typically pragmatic (incremental) legislative activity takes place within some form of constitution, however perfectly or imperfectly constructed. Modern progress in the economics of parliamentary politics based on such fixed rules started with the work of Arrow, Black and Downs in the forties and fifties.[30] It brought to light what is believed to be a curious dichotomy in economic analysis. Economists had expended considerable energy in making sophisticated demonstrations of 'market failure' in private-exchange processes, processes that were analysed upon a hypothesis of individual 'self-interest'. When turning to the government sector, however, the sector that was often implicitly or explicitly looked to for improvement, they had replaced the reference to such 'profit-maximizing' behaviour by more obscure goals such as 'the public interest' or to the attainment of theoretical 'optimality conditions'. In basing themselves on the hypothesis of individual self-interest in *all* spheres, the new analyses of the forties and fifties paved the way for the emergence of theories of *government* failure. Many of these theories were implicit in Smith's *The Wealth of Nations* two centuries earlier.

Numerous empirical studies over the last few years have indeed produced systematic evidence to support the proposition that in a weakening political constitution, self-interest rather than 'public interest' is a more explanatory behavioural rule in politics. Individuals attempt to maximize their wealth through political activity, especially through allegiance groups who purchase from the sellers of 'political power for wealth', the political parties. It has been shown, for example, that in America employees, managers, or shareholders of a given private industry are well aware that they will all profit if they can share the major resource of the state. And as George Stigler has reminded us, the essence of the resource of the state is coercion.[31] Such power of compulsion can be used, for instance, in the form of statutorily encouraged industry regulation. This, as Adam Smith recognized (see p.136), is in the interests of a majority of existing operators and against those of (i) potential new entrants and (ii) the industry's customers. It is, in other words, in the same mercantilist world that Smith was challenging. Meanwhile, the industry purchases the legislation with two things needed most by the party: votes and resources.[32]

In the political process the rewards of individual political effort are usually only indirect. Stigler suggests, for instance, that legislative leaders probably enjoy extra political payments by way of unusual customer loyalty to a congressman's legal firm, bank, or insurance company.[33] Economists, he seems to argue, must adjust themselves to the fact that a government agency that operates openly to foster special interest is not a passing 'imperfection'; it is characteristic of and predictable in the system. To advise a representative merely that it is the 'public interest' that requires his support for policy, is quixotic. In Stigler's words:

> A representative cannot win or keep office with the support of the sum of those who are opposed to: oil import quotas, farm subsidies, airport subsidies, hospital subsidies, unnecessary navy shipyards, an inequitable public housing program, and rural electrification subsidies.[34]

> And the frequent complaint of economists that the I.C.C. conducts prorailroad policies is as appropriate as a criticism of the Great Atlantic and Pacific Tea Company for selling groceries.[35]

After such trenchant criticism of *modern* economic analysis it is only to be expected that similar scrutiny will be made of the works of the classical economists. Criticizing with hindsight is easy, of course, and the history of thought is especially conducive to it. What is surprising, however, is that the classical writer who has been chosen by George Stigler for especial criticism is Adam Smith.[36] More surprising still is his conclusion that because Smith 'failed to see the self-interest written upon the faces of politicians and constituencies' his ship of state was, in effect, a ghost ship. Stigler's basic question appears to be 'Downsian' and is certainly rooted in our third dimension of the economics of politics. Why didn't Smith ask: 'If self-interest dominates the majority of men in all commercial undertakings, why not also in all their political undertakings?'[37] One answer is that Smith didn't have to ask; he knew better than anybody, but his economics of politics were not primarily preoccupied with the third dimension – the post-constitutional stage. Only two per cent of the population yet had the vote. Smith was concerned to stop Stigler's spoils system from developing further. To do this required that errors in the emerging constitution should be anticipated and checked by those in a position to do so. This is a normative position no doubt, but an unavoidable one.

Stigler's criticism is prefaced with the following quotation from *The Wealth of Nations*:

> The natural effort of every individual to better his own condition, when suffered to exert itself with freedom and security, is so powerful a principle, that it is alone, and without any assistance, not only capable of carrying on the society to wealth and prosperity, but of surmounting a hundred impertinent obstructions with which the folly of human laws too often incumbers its operations; though the effect of these obstructions is always more or less either to encroach upon its freedom, or to diminish its security.[38]

Stigler's point is that Smith should have been more consistent and should have shown, without surprise, and presumably with resignation, that the 'hundred impertinent obstructions' erected by legislators were the product of the same self-interest that led men to seek, and achieve, prosperity. Stigler amply demonstrates that Smith was indeed aware that self-interest groups were behind much legislation. Smith recognized, for instance, that the beneficiaries of the Statute of Apprentices were the owners of corporations; the beneficiaries of wage-fixing laws were the employers; and the beneficiaries of laws restricting tobacco planting were the tobacco farmers. Stigler's major criticism is that when Adam Smith came to prescribe policy he apparently forgot these lobbies and addressed himself to some ideal government. He failed to remember that party governments need votes and the spoils of office. Consider, for example, Smith's famous canons of taxation. These recommended convenience (to each subject), certainty, minimum exaction, and ability to pay. Such canons, Stigler argues, are straight from the armchair of a professor of moral philosophy. According to George Stigler's Chicago School approach there are only two canons appropriate to the self-interest of real-world governments; and neither of them is mentioned by Smith. These are (i) that taxes should not unduly lose votes, and (ii) that they should produce revenue.

In defence it could be argued (i) that Smith was operating predominantly at the constitutional level (the second dimension of the economics of politics), (ii) he was *not* addressing himself to some ideal government, and (iii) there was something in Smith that *could* lead to the public interest, and that was a wise constitution and a firm rule of law. Re-examine Stigler's opening quotation from Smith, to the effect that individual self-interest will enable people to surmount 'a hundred impertinent obstructions with which the folly of human laws too often encumbers its operations'. A more balanced view is given when we include the Smithian sentence that precedes the passage in Stigler's quotation: 'That security which the *laws* in Great Britain give to every man that he shall enjoy the fruits of his own labour is alone sufficient to make any country flourish, *notwithstanding these and twenty other absurd regulations of commerce*' (emphasis added). This quotation more than any other shows that Smith had the vision of law that was common in the 18th century but is today almost forgotten. The law meant general rules of just conduct; it did not mean 'every expression of the will of the duly authorized representative body',[39] and it was the latter that was responsible for the absurdities.

It is this emphasis upon the basic laws that suggests the view that it is the constitutional dimension that dominates the work of Smith. For those recognizing this in *The Wealth of Nations* it is easier to answer Stigler's question: Why should Smith tell the sovereign that free trade is desirable, if he had no method of disarming the merchants and manufacturers who have obtained the protectionist measures?[40] Arguably, however, it is fair to interpret Smith as believing that he *had* some method of disarming the merchants; he was addressing (or thought he was addressing) himself to a change in the rules, in the constitution. His clients were the custodians, the draftsmen, and the innovators of a constitution, not a passing government that is intimidated by the mob.

Smith's proposals with respect to *existing* monopolies were expressed with extreme caution. Changes should be very gradual. The sovereign had unwisely granted (sold) the monopoly in the first place in pursuit of a short-term gain. The sovereign should at least learn one lesson: existing monopolies were already potential cancers in the constitution; the development of others, monopoly escalation, should be prevented by every means. In this advice, Smith largely escapes Stigler's criticism. As Smith puts it:

> This [manufacturer's] monopoly has so much increased the number of some particular tribes of them, that, like an overgrown standing army, they have become formidable to the government, and upon many occasions intimidate the legislature.
>
> The legislature, were it possible that its deliberations could be always directed, not by the clamorous importunity of partial interests, but by an extensive view of the general good, ought upon this very account, perhaps, to be particularly careful neither to establish any new monopolies of this kind, nor to extend further those which are already established. *Every such regulation introduces some degree of real disorder into the constitution of the state, which it will be difficult afterwards to cure without occasioning another disorder.*[41]

The above advice is clearly conditional upon the 'possibility' of a lawgiver directed to an extensive view of the general good rather than to 'partial interests'. It is difficult to believe that Smith would have gone to such trouble in formulating his advice if he thought there was no possibility at all of implementing it. While there may have been romantic elements in his thinking, it would be difficult to describe Smith's advice to avoid new monopolies as entirely unworkable or academic, even though he was not very explicit. For legislation since his time has demonstrated its practicality. Antitrust, at least since Senator Sherman's day, *has* been grafted on to the constitution of the state, and for all its imperfections it is still arguable whether there would be any net advantage in removing it. Moreover, experience under monopolies legislation shows that merger control of potential monopolists is normally easier than dismemberment of mature ones.[42] Furthermore, the Chicago School's habit of classifying behaviour as either self-interested or romantic can easily mislead. The 'self' in Smith's idea of self-interest *can* extend to an identification with one's country. Smith and Rousseau drew from history to show crucial acts of 'patriotism' by individuals who gave their country wise laws.

Rousseau observed that 'a people does not become famous until its constitution begins to decline. We do not know for how many centuries the constitution of Lycurgus gave happiness to the Spartans before there was talk about them in the rest of Greece.'[43] After two centuries, the relevant question in America today is whether *its* constitution is in disarray. If he could return, Smith would probably ask *this* question rather than Stigler's question. Smith, like Rousseau, concluded from the study of history that an efficient constitution called for the most judicious balance of diffusion of power. This should accommodate the sovereign's interests at one end and those of his subjects at the other. The bulk of the revenue of the sovereign, Smith is insistent on reminding his readers, has to be drawn from the masses of the people. It is always in the sovereign's interest, therefore, to increase as much as possible 'the annual produce'. This is especially so if his revenue comes chiefly from land rent. Consequently, there was need for the most extensive market and 'the most perfect freedom of commerce in order to increase as much as possible the number and the competition of buyers; and upon that account to abolish, not only all monopolies, but all restraints upon the transportation of the home produce.'[44]

Smith therefore did certainly appeal to self-interest. In the first instance it was the self-interest of the sovereign. The sovereign could and should preserve the constitution and prevent it from being rewritten by, and in the interest of, special groups. At a time well before universal franchise, Smith's advice was of course easier to follow than it would be today. Nevertheless, he appealed to the self-interest of the rest of the population; but in all cases it was long-term, not short-term, self-interest. In the long run, rich and poor alike would prosper under order and liberty protected by law.

Stigler's several illustrations of Smith's 'naïvete' take on a different light when examined in this perspective. One example will be selected that is particularly striking. It relates to Smith's fiscal advice to the French government. 'Why tell the French sovereign,' Stigler demands of Smith, 'to abandon the *taille* and capitations and increase the *vingtièmes*, when only a revolution can dislodge the tax-favoured classes?'[45]

The first thing to notice is that Smith did in fact warn that the interest and opposition of the favoured subjects would be an 'obstacle'.[46] Next and more important, we should remember that a few years after Smith's advice a revolution *did* dislodge the tax-favoured classes. And in retrospect, considering what happened to the sovereign, it is arguable that Smith was not such a bad adviser after all!

This argument does not necessarily lean on the benefit of hindsight or a special coincidence of events. Smith's advice was probably based on much more profound reasons than the dictates of short-term parliamentary politics. In the France that Smith visited in 1764 there were, according to modern estimates, about 22 million peasants out of a total population of 30 million. The peasant class was thus a significant political constituency on any definition of a constitution. It was a time when peasant revolts were endemic throughout Europe. The central concern of the French economy at all times was the price of bread. After poor harvests many individuals retrogressed to that very lawless state of nature about which Smith was so apprehensive, but which he predicted in societies where the mass of the people enjoy very little property. The unemployed and the starving formed marauding bands of 'half-beggars'.[47] In the words of historian C.B.A. Behrens: 'Illiterate and brutalized by misery ... they were always a potential menace to law, and property'.[48]

Adam Smith saw glaring official errors that aggravated the problem. These included price fixing which produced entirely the wrong incentives and aggravated the shortage.[49] Also the average output of corn per year was too low because there was insufficient investment in agriculture. This insufficiency in turn was due to the mercantilist policy which favoured manufacturers, commerce, and the colonial trade.

The supreme error as Smith saw it, however, was the French system of taxes which were crippling the poor peasants. The severity of these taxes in fact was the last straw. The *taille* to which the peasants were subject (and the taxes levied in conjunction with it) yielded the bulk of the revenue. In origin it was a servile obligation; indeed it was hated for this reason alone. It involved high transaction costs and serious excess burden. It was arbitrary and varying. It made the country people hostile to the towns (where its severity was escaped); it forced the privileged (tax-exempt) to defend themselves against the unprivileged.

The total sums to be collected were never adjusted to the capacity of the taxpayers; and the militarily ambitious monarchies were failing to trim their projects to their resources. The total burden was distributed arbitrarily between the generalities and in these each *intendant* divided it, again arbitrarily, between parishes. The responsibility for paying the *taille* in each parish was a collective one. Even peasants of substance had an incentive to move to the town, an event which increased the per capita burden in the country. The jails filled with collectors who had been caught absconding with money or who had failed to raise their quota.[50]

In this historical context, more than any other, the constitutional adoption of Smith's famous canons of taxation appears as good political advice in all senses. Similarly, Adam Smith's immediate counsel to switch the tax burden from the *taille* and on to the *vingtième was by no means the advice of an uninformed political amateur*. It was possible in *some* degree to attack the nobles' tax privileges. The successful establishment of the *vingtième* (a tax of 5 per cent) in 1750, was testimony in itself. Turgot emphasized this point in 1775: 'C'est donc un fait que la prétention de la noblesse de n'être sujet à aucun impôt est actuellement vaincu'.[51]

What was quite impossible politically was to spread the tax burden by imposing the *taille* on the nobles. The social stigma of this tax would have been insufferable to them. The government, moreover, was itself becoming increasingly persuaded of the superiority of the *vingtième* over the *taille*. The former was a tax on the individual, not on the community. It was, therefore, more compatible with the ideas of distributive justice 'to which the French Government become increasingly addicted'.[52] Again it was easier administratively because in practice it came to fall mainly on landholdings, and these could be more accurately and less arbitrarily assessed.

While it is true that the nobility usually resisted attempts to increase the *vingtième*, it had been successfully doubled in 1756; and in 1760 it had been tripled.[53] When Adam Smith was writing the notes for *The Wealth of Nations* in France four years later, it is understandable if he considered further increases in the *vingtième* to be politically wise – especially considering the possible alternative costs of a total uprising. As argued earlier, a return to the first dimension of politics (anarchy) would be unlikely where the constitution was based on laws that encourage stable expectations and the distribution of gains was not unjust. Because these circumstances did not exist in France, the relapse into anarchy was clearly threatened.

Smith's advice was directed to the interest of everybody concerned, and not least to that of Stigler's 'tax-favoured classes'. As Buchanan argues, where the relative positions of persons cannot, by any stretch of the imagination, reflect the relative positions that might be attainable after a detour into anarchy and out again into a new constitutional contract 'it should be rational for those who seem differentially favoured in the status quo to accept reductions in the measured value of their assigned rights'.[54] In the Glasgow lectures, Smith had concluded: 'Exorbitant taxes no doubt justify resistance, *for no people will allow the half of their property to be taken from them*; but though the highest propriety be not observed, if they have any degree of moderation people will not complain'.[55] Adam Smith was still in France in 1776 when his friend Turgot, the *intendant* in Limousin, found that in his district the proportion of the net income of the peasant proprietors taken by the government was about 80 per cent![56] On Smith's views, therefore, the time for uprising was more than ripe.

Smith argued that if his advice was taken and the *taille* abolished, whilst an increase was made in the *vingtième*, 'the superior ranks might not be more burdened than the greater part of them are at present'. One implicit reason was that more stability and justice would lead to an increase in the national income. Another explicit reason was that the expense of average tax collection would be diminished. In this Smith is supported by subsequent historians. Under the prevailing unjust tax system, large sums had to be spent on maintaining garrisons to catch the defaulters and rebels 'and the sums expended on lawsuits over the taxes were sometimes even larger than the taxes themselves'.[57]

When Louis XVI came to the throne there was unusual pressure for reform of these grossly inefficient institutions. Turgot, who had been appointed controller-general in 1774, was indeed by 1776 beginning to implement some 'Smithian' changes. He had just introduced reforms into the collection of the *taille* and had re-established a free internal market in corn when Smith's *The Wealth of Nations* was published. Turgot certainly aroused the antagonism of vested interests (Stigler's 'tax-favoured classes') and was ousted from office in May 1776. The antagonism was one reason; but another was that the character of the King's chief advisor Maurepas, and that of the King himself, were both weak.[58]

What else should Turgot have done? What else should Smith have advised? Stigler's argument is that 'unless the basic logic of political life is developed, reformers will be ill-equipped to use the state for their reforms, and victims of the pervasive use of the state's support of special groups will be helpless to protect themselves'.[59] One must agree. But Smith and Turgot *were* fully aware of the basic logic of current French political life. Short of revolution, there was no other way of attempting to protect the long-suffering peasant victims of the entrenched political interests; and a revolution that throws people back to the state of nature is supremely costly to all. As long as his influence lasted, Turgot continually urged the King to stand firm and register the necessary constitutional edicts. Like his business counterpart, the political entrepreneur operates under all the pressures of uncertainty and the threat of bankruptcy. Turgot made a calculated risk. But it was his misfortune that he had to work with a constitution that was already too decayed and with a king who had lost his nerve.

Stigler questions several Smithian references to what he calls 'the failure of self-interest' in *The Wealth of Nations*. He suspects that in each case Smith had misconstrued because people, in ways unnoticed by Smith, were indeed 'doing their job' of pursuing self-interest. 'The High Priest or self-interest,' Stigler observes 'like all other high priests, has a strong demand for sinners. But if, as Adam Smith believed, each successful constitution is sustained by a large base of self-interest, the failure of constitutions to survive is a real, not an imagined, 'sin'. Is the Chicago high priest's heaven lacking in this (constitutional) dimension?

Conclusion

While one could counter Stigler's attack on Smith's 'naïveté' in other examples that he quotes, and could give counter-examples, especially in Smith's treatment of the American crisis, the Irish problem, and the politics of the East India Company administration, it is necessary to conclude an already lengthy chapter. It has been argued that, of the three dimensions of politics, preconstitutional, constitution-making, and post-constitutional, Smith was predominantly concerned with the second. The wealth of nations to Smith is substantially correlated with the wealth of wisdom in their political constitutions. It is also dependent on the degree of 'civilized' behaviour that true law protects and encourages. Smith was evidently one of those sages of the 18th century who received a rare vision of constitutional democracy, a vision that has since been almost lost. The 'Downsian' economics of politics which concerns itself with the third dimension of our subject, does not address itself to these higher questions. Nevertheless, knowledge of it is still important in its own right if we are to have a comprehensive grasp of the real world. Smith's knowledge and grasp will be examined in the next chapter.

Notes

1. Tollison in Buchanan and Tollison (1984).
2. See especially Buchanan, (1975).
3. Downs (1957).
4. Buchanan (1975), Bush (1972).
5. Buchanan (1975), Chapter 7, 'Law as public capital'. For game theory concepts see Ordeshook, (1986).
6. Smith (1969). John Rawls in his *A Theory of Justice* (1971), p. 126, emphasizes that the theory must begin by assuming that a system of justice is based on rational choice; and to be robust, it must provide for the contingency that people take no interest in one another's interests. In these circumstances there must be gains for every individual if he is to subscribe to the constitution. In Rawls's words, 'Social co-operation makes possible a better life for all than any would have if each were to try to live solely by his own efforts'.
7. Quoted in Watkins (1951), p. 39.
8. Ibid.
9. 'It is only from the selfishness and confined generosity of men along with the scanty provision nature has made for his wants, that justice derives its origin.' Ibid., p. 45.
10. Cannan (1896), pp. 11–12.
11. West (1969), p. 123.
12. Runciman and Sen (1965). Elliot M. Zashin, 'The Logic of Collective Action: Rousseau's *Social Contract* Revisited'; and James A. Roumasset, 'Institutions, Social Contracts and Second Best Pareto Optimality' – the last two being papers presented at the Public Choice Society Meetings, 21 March 1974.
13. Rousseau (1968), Chapter 8.
14. Roumasset (1974) argues, 'Rousseau's Social Contract, an implicit agreement to abide by government authority, can be thought of as a social more similar to trust'. He quotes Kenneth Arrow: 'citizens obey the law to a much greater extent than can be explained on the basis of control mechanisms'.
15. Zashin (1974).
16. Smith (1969), p. 28.
17. The word 'law' in Rousseau had a very special meaning. It was the expression of the General Will, that is, the will of the body of the people. 'A people, since it is subject to laws, ought to be the author of them.' Not only individuals but the

government too is subordinate to the law. Government is a body charged with the execution of the laws and the maintenance of freedom. But there is a necessary division of labour; though the people are fitted to be the source of legislation, they will fail if they try simultaneously to act as the executive. Rousseau (1968), p. 83.

18. Rawls (1971), p. 22, n. 9.
19. Ibid., p. 542.
20. Hayek (1973).
21. Stigler (1969).
22. Other writers who have recently argued for more inclusive majority rules include Niskanen (1971), Chapter 20, and Hayek (1973).
23. Smith (1976), p. 145.
24. Rawls (1971) himself argues (p. 356, n. 15) that majority rule violates liberty.
25. Viner (1965), p. 85.
26. Buchanans' (1972), p. 123.
27. Smith (1969), p. 340.
28. Smith (1976), p. 543. This sentence did not appear in the first edition, and its addition has been attributed (by Viner (1965), p. 26) to the influence of Edmund Burke. Burke was certainly rather critical of Smith's free-trade prescriptions in the light of various factions. Recent work, however, shows the quotation to be consistent with other (earlier) arguments in *The Wealth of Nations*. See Hollander (1973), p. 270.
29. Smith (1969), p. 340, emphasis added.
30. Arrow (1951), Black (1958), Downs (1957).
31. Stigler (1971). Most of the present paragraph draws on this reference, which contains fascinating empirical findings on the economics of politics – particularly with respect to transport and occupational licensing.
32. Ibid., p. 12.
33. Ibid., p. 12.
34. Ibid., p. 11.
35. Ibid., p. 17.
36. Stigler (1971 (b)).
37. Ibid., p. 265.
38. Smith (1976), p. 540.
39. Hayek (1973), p. 12.
40. Ibid., p. 273.
41. Smith (1976), pp. 471–2, emphasis added.
42. Posner (1979). In the United States this takes eight years on average.
43. Rousseau (1968), p. 84.
44. Smith (1976), p. 637.
45. Stigler (1971(b)), p. 273.
46. Stigler recognizes this. Ibid., p. 273, n. 8.
47. Cobban (1965), p. 140.
48. Behrens (1967), p. 26.
49. Smith (1976), pp. 526–7. In fact, price fixing itself could sometimes *generate* a famine.
50. Behrens (1963), p. 460.
51. Turgot (1913), 5: 172.
52. Behrens (1963), p. 462.
53. Ibid.
54. Buchanan (1975), p. 85.
55. Cannan (1896), p. 69, emphasis added.
56. Behrens (1963), p. 465.

57. Ibid., p. 474.
58. Cobban (1965), p. 109.
59. Stigler (1971(a)), p. 18.

9. Rent Seeking and *The Wealth of Nations*

No other writer in the history of economic thought has placed greater emphasis than Smith on the need to promote free market competition and to eradicate all forms of monopolies. In contrast, by the early 1960s the problem of monopolies appeared to have been substantially relegated because new measures of their associated welfare costs conducted at that time appeared distinctly unimpressive. Such findings may well have prompted some observers to ask whether the greatest classical attack on monopolies that appeared with the publication of *The Wealth of Nations* was not, after all, worth the effort. The aim of this chapter is to examine this question by way of a comparative study of classical and neoclassical approaches to the monopoly issue, together with considerable reference to the new public choice doctrine of 'rent-seeking'.

One must acknowledge in advance that many of the 18th-century types of monopolies that occupied Smith, monopolies such as the great overseas trading companies, have long since disappeared. It will be argued, nevertheless, that there is much of the modern public choice approach in Smith's vigorous attack on the more familiar statutory monopolies such as the regulated and licensed industries, as well as on the several continuing forms of foreign trade protection.

The first part of the chapter reviews the modern neoclassical analysis of welfare losses from monopolies in general. An examination of the classical analysis of domestic monopolies will then follow. The third part will analyse the classical economic indictment of the East India Company monopoly, and part 4 will focus upon some hidden costs of monopoly that were recognized by Adam Smith but have since tended to be overlooked. The chapter will conclude by arguing that the modern neoclassical approach is too confined, is too 'institutionally sterile', and ignores important elements in Smith's classical critique.

Figure 9.1   The welfare cost of monopoly

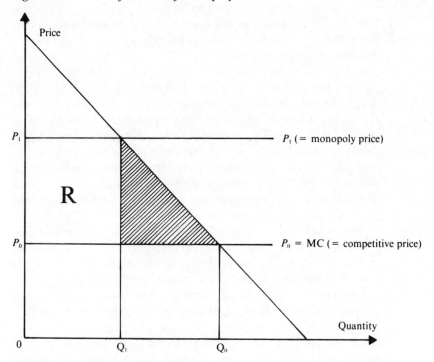

Neoclassical Analysis of Losses

The modern neoclassical method for measuring the welfare losses from monopoly was introduced in 1959 by A.D. Harberger[1] and has since been developed further by others.[2] It can be illustrated here with the most familiar and simple diagram.[3] In Figure 9.1, P_0 represents the competitive price of a commodity. If there are no monopolies the quantity Q_0 will be purchased. The price P_1 is the monopoly price and it will prevail if the monopolist can prevent $Q_1 - Q_0$ from being marketed. Harberger's argument is that such an increase in price involves mainly a transfer from some members of the community to others. It is true that the buyers lose consumers' surplus equal to the triangle *plus* rectangle R. But the rectangle is not *destroyed* income but redistributed income, the recipients being the owners of the monopoly. Thus the only welfare loss from misallocation, is the shaded triangle, described hereafter as Harberger costs.

Modern quantitative studies of the welfare costs of monopolies and tariffs concentrate on simple computations of the value of this triangle. The original numerical estimates of the costs were undramatic and *at first sight* appeared to take the wind out of the sails of the classical attack on monopolies.

It was in his response to Harberger's reasoning that Gordon Tullock, the cofounder of the new discipline of public choice, introduced the concept of rent seeking.[4] Tullock contended that the Harberger (triangle) measure of the social costs of monopoly is biased downwards. This is mainly because resources are wasted in the competitive bidding for the monopoly 'prize' measured by rectangle R. Not only are resources invested in lobbying for the monopoly power (which is usually government bestowed, as for instance with a license or a franchise), but opponents spend money trying politically to prevent the success of the protectionists. 'These expenditures, which may simply offset each other to some extent, are purely wasteful from the standpoint of society as a whole; they are spent not in increasing wealth, but in an attempt to transfer or resist transfer of wealth.'[5] Subsequently, Posner (1975) and others argued indeed that if competition for the monopoly rents is perfect, all of the expected rents from regulation will be converted to welfare losses.[6] Strong criticism of this 'exact rent dissipation' model is now being offered, however. According to Tullock's later analysis the resources devoted to rent seeking can in some circumstances be less than, and in others greater than, the initial rents erected by government policy.[7] Rent-seeking costs will be denoted hereafter as 'Tullock costs'.

Harberger (1959) estimated that the deadweight welfare loss (represented in the shaded triangle in Figure 9.1) from monopoly in the manufacturing sector was equal to 0.1 per cent of GNP at most. Adding the Tullock costs, the subsequent empirical analysis of Posner (1975) suggested it was nearer to 0.6 per cent.[8] More important, Posner argued that monopoly pricing would be more successful in industries where regulatory agencies limited entry and price competition and did not therefore face the problem of having to face charges of collusion under the anti-trust legislation. His estimates of the social costs of monopoly in regulated industries was around 1.7 per cent of GNP. Arguing that government control and licences in underdeveloped countries give rise to considerable rents that are largely absorbed by resources devoted to competitive rent *seeking* activities, Ann Krueger[9] reported in 1974 that in India such rents amounted to 7.3 per cent of national income and in Turkey 15 per cent.

Wenders (1987) argues that there is no re..son why purchasers of products cannot take the offensive by lobbying to obtain monopolies on the buying side (monopsonies). He concludes that, in general, the entire gains from trade in any market, as depicted by the triangle between the demand and supply curves up to their point of intersection, is vulnerable to various kinds of rent seeking, rent defending and political extortion.

Rent Seeking in the 18th Century

Monopoly profits (rectangle R in Figure 9.1) are subject to offsetting by rent-seeking costs only if free entry is allowed into the process of bidding for the politically bestowed rents. The form of bidding, meanwhile, can range from overt auction prices to covert bribes and black markets.[10] In Adam Smith's time covert (or overt) bidding for the monopoly 'prizes' was often out of the question. Certain crafts, for example, often aided by the law, were able to exclude large numbers from many occupations because of membership requirements relating to kinship or geographical origins. The monopoly rents from these occupations, therefore, were not open to political competition. The famous Statute of Apprentices (1563) for instance, was packed with such 'kinship regulations'.

The feasibility of competition for rents of the *illegal* kind, such as bribery, smuggling, and black markets, depends on the severity of the laws against them. In so far as the enforcers' resources are merely substituted for those of potential rent seekers there will be no social savings. The modern literature on the economics of punishment, however, suggests that enforcers' costs can be kept very low by combining severe monetary fines and other punishments with modest resources devoted to apprehending offenders.[11] Such means dramatically increase the expected penalties of rent seeking and therefore reduce the amount of resources it is profitable to invest in the socially wasteful activity.

Smith reminds us in *The Wealth of Nations* that several extant Elizabethan laws for the support of monopolies had been written 'in blood', for the penalties included mutilation and death.[12] In France, the smuggling of salt and tobacco annually sent several hundred people to the galleys, 'besides a very considerable number whom it sends to the gibbet'.[13] In these times, clearly many monopolies bestowed real benefits to their owners that were not eaten up by competitive rent-seeking activities. The practice of granting such monopolies therefore resulted in unambiguous redistribution of income; but the injustice of this alone was a primary social cost in Smith's view, and partly in the sense that it could eventually incite rebellion.

> To hurt in any degree the interest of any one order of citizens, for no other purpose but to promote that of some other, is evidently contrary to that justice and equality of treatment which the sovereign owes to all the different orders of his subjects.[14]

Despite the severity of the laws against illegal rent seeking, opportunities for legal rent seeking were being increasingly recognized and exploited in the late 18th century. Smith, however, detected variations in propensities to seek rents across different groups. The highest propensity occurred among merchants and manufacturers. Smith enters into this subject at the beginning of *The Wealth of Nations*. Thus in the conclusion to Book I he observes:

> To widen the market and to narrow the competition, is always the interest of the dealers. To widen the market may frequently be agreeable enough to the interest of the public; but to narrow the competition must always be against it, and can serve only to enable the dealers, by raising their profits above what they naturally would be, to levy, for their own benefit, an absurd tax upon the rest of their fellow-citizens. The proposal of any new law or regulation of commerce which comes from this order, ought always to be listened to with great precaution, and ought never to be adopted till after having been long and carefully examined, not only with the most scrupulous, but with the most suspicious attention. It comes from an order of men, whose interest is never exactly the same with that of the public, who have generally an interest to deceive and even to oppress the public, and who accordingly have, upon many occasions, both deceived and oppressed it.[15]

This passage clearly recognizes the potential of special interest legislation to restrict entry into a given activity or in Smith's words, 'to narrow the competition'. In terms of Figure 9.1 this implies a restriction of supply from Q_0 and towards Q_1. But the phenomenon was more than a *potential* occurrence. To Smith there was an embarrassing amount of evidence of it in the real world. What is more, he was aware of the extent to which the activity of rent seeking involved a social waste of resources. He observed, for example, that some trades would use resources to *petition* to obtain monopolies that were to the disadvantage of others. And the trade that won the monopoly 'prize' did so usually because its costs of political organization were relatively lower than that of other, more dispersed, trades.

> Country gentlemen and farmers, dispersed in different parts of the country, cannot so easily combine as merchants and manufacturers, who being collected into towns, and accustomed to that exclusive corporation spirit which prevails in them, naturally endeavour to obtain against all their countrymen, the same exclusive privilege which they generally possess against the inhabitants of their respective towns. They accordingly seem to have been the original inventors of those restraints upon the importation of foreign goods, which secure to them the monopoly of the home market.[16]

Because of this assymetry also 'the law gave a monopoly to our boot-makers and shoe-makers, not only against our graziers, but against our tanners'.[17]

There is implicit recognition too, in Smith, of Tullock's observation that the 'excess' costs of monopoly also take the form of defensive lobbying by its potential *victims* who are opposed to existing monopolies or petitions to form new ones. Tanners, for instance, who were less dispersed than graziers, began to retaliate politically and were eventually successful.

> By subsequent statutes, our tanners have got themselves exempted from this monopoly, upon paying a small tax of only one shilling on the hundred weight of tanned leather ... Our graziers still continue subject to the old monopoly.[18]

With respect to the theoretical possibility mentioned by Wenders (above) of purchasers of products taking the offensive and lobbying to obtain monopsony power, Smith reports one conspicuous example. The woollen manufacturers had successfully lobbied parliament to legislate very severe restrictions against the export of wool. The ostensible reason was based on the mercantilist argument that universally recognized fine cloth could be made with the use of English wool only. If, therefore, the export of it could be totally prevented, England could monopolize to herself almost the whole woollen trade of the world. Even if the advocates of this reasoning were correct in their assumption that English wool was the best (which Smith denied), the benefits of the export restriction would accrue not to all citizens in England, but to the wool manufacturers exclusively; for the consequence of the export restrictions was a lower (quasi-monopsonistic) price of wool to the manufacturer buyers.

> Our woollen manufacturers have been more successful than any other class of workmen, in persuading the legislature that the prosperity of the nation depended upon the success and extension of their particular business. They have not only obtained a monopoly against the consumers by an absolute prohibition of importing woollen cloths from any foreign country; but they have likewise obtained another monopoly against the sheep farmers and growers of wool, by a similar prohibition of the exportation of live sheep and wool ... The effect of these regulations has been to depress the price of English wool, not only below what it would naturally be in the present times, but very much below what it actually was in the time of Edward III ... To depress the price of this commodity below what may be called its natural and proper price, was the avowed purpose of those regulations; and there seems no doubt of their having produced the effect that was expected of them.[19]

Smith's argument about the unsophisticated disposition and relatively weak political position of the farmers and 'country gentlemen' is not entirely convincing. He maintained that, country gentlemen were incapable of that 'application of mind' that was necessary to understand the true long-term consequences of any public regulation. This failure was based on the sociological argument that the fact of living off the land and enjoying revenue that 'costs them neither labour or care' made them 'indolent' and easy going.[20] In addition, Smith argued, as we have seen, that the country gentlemen's political influence was relatively weak because they were 'dispersed'.

All these Smithian assumptions are contradicted by Smith's admission concerning the origin of the famous corn laws of 1688.

> In 1688 was granted the parliamentary bounty upon the export of corn ... But the government of King William was not then fully settled. *It was in no condition to refuse anything to the country gentlemen*, from whom it was at that very time soliciting the first establishment of the annual land-tax.[21]

Smith points out that in those days the country gentlemen 'composed a still greater proportion of the legislature than they do at present'.[22]

But though the country gentlemen were successful with the corn bounty legislation, Smith stuck to his argument that they were not shrewd enough to calculate its long-term consequences. As is well known, much to the dismay of Ricardo he maintained that in so far as the legislation succeeded in its purpose of raising the price of corn, this would cause a general inflation. This was so because the price of corn 'by regulating the money price of labour, and of everything that is the produce either of land or labour, must necessarily either rise or fall in proportion to this money price of corn'.[23] The country gentlemen would thus receive higher money income only while their real income would not improve.

Even if we accept the terms of Smith's argument it would be difficult to understand why it took so long for the country gentlemen to realize the mistake in their calculation. The corn laws, after all, had been in operation for 88 years when Smith was writing. Smith himself, however, leaves us with another possible rent-seeking reason for the longevity of the corn legislation. He intimates that a new interest group subsequently appeared and one to whom the benefits from the legislation were unambiguously real.

> There is, perhaps, but one set of men in the whole commonwealth to whom the bounty either was or could be essentially serviceable. These were the corn merchants, the exporters and importers of corn. In years of plenty the bounty necessarily occasioned a greater exportation than would otherwise have taken place; and by hindering the plenty of one year from relieving the scarcity of another, it occasioned in years of scarcity a greater importation than would otherwise have been necessary. It increased the business of the corn merchant; and in years of scarcity, it not only enabled him to import a greater quantity, but to sell it for a better price, and consequently with a greater profit than he could otherwise have made, if the plenty of one year had not been more or less hindered from relieving the scarcity of another.[24]

This passage contains yet another refutable hypothesis and the invitation appears open to future researchers in the history of economic thought to test systematically the proposition that the corn dealers were the decisive lobbyists who secured the continuation and strengthening of the corn laws after 1688. Smith himself goes a little way in this direction with a sentence that follows the previous quotation: 'It is in this set of men [the corn merchants], accordingly, that I have observed the greatest zeal for the continuance or renewal of the bounty.'

One problem with Smith's prediction remains, however. If there were increased rewards for corn merchants they would have caused new entry sufficient to bring the returns back to normal levels. There would be no long-run gains in other words. In contrast, if land is scarce the increased demand for it caused by the corn laws would enhance the net worth of the country gentlemen. On this reasoning it is the latter who would appear to have the strongest rent-seeking motivations.

Rent Seeking and the East India Company

Smith reserved his most severe attack upon rent seeking for the case of the East India Company as restructured after 1757. Following the victory of Clive at Plassey (in Bengal) the company was rewarded with considerable political power. After 1765, for instance, it was given the right to collect taxes over large parts of Bengal and parts of West India. The servants of the company proceeded to enjoy unprecedented opportunities for personal enrichment: 'Those appointed as company tax collectors made fortunes, primarily through the sale of exemptions'.[25]

Smith strongly objected to the diversion from commercial trade to outright extortion. 'He objected to the deflection of the company activities from productive trade to unproductive wealth transfer, from profit seeking to rent seeking.'[26] Normally a company would dismiss employees who were transferring their efforts from their normally contracted duties to corrupt political activities. Astonishing as it may seem, however, the employees in this case became so rich as to be able to purchase enough shareholding votes in the company's general court as to guarantee their appointments.

> Frequently a man of great, sometimes even a man of small fortune, is willing to purchase a thousand pounds share in India stock, merely for the influence which he expects to acquire by a vote in the court of proprietors. It gives him a share, though not in the plunder, yet in the appointment of the plunderers of India; the court of directors, though they make that appointment, being necessarily more or less under influence of the proprietors, who not only elect those directors, but sometimes over-rule the appointments of their servants in India. Provided he can enjoy this influence for a few years, and thereby provide

for a certain number of his friends, he frequently cares little about the dividend; or even about the value of the stock upon which his vote is founded.[27]

It seems clear, therefore, that the votes of shareholders began to enjoy a buyer's market from the increased demand coming from rent-seeking appointees. Meanwhile, by the 1760s the annual income coming to the company from tax revenues had reached about three times the average annual income from trade. The market for tax exemptions sold by individual servants of the company had correspondingly become vigorous and substantial. In the words of Anderson and Tollison 'the company had begun to behave like a legitimatized criminal organization running a gigantic extortion racket'.[28] But this situation is difficult to place in the context of the modern analysis of rent seeking that focuses on Figure 9.1. The demand curve in that diagram assumes a settled constitution with stable expectations stemming from legally-respected property rights and a rule of law. The East India Company situation, in contrast, involved considerable political and legal uncertainty. For the remainder of the 18th century the company had continual struggles with the English government in its endeavour to maintain its territorial rights in India. And eventually in 1834, the company's property was vested in the Crown.

Part of the catastrophic consequences of the East India Company situation stemmed from the unchecked propensity of its servants to spread the disease of monopoly in the foreign countries where their offices were located. Monopolies arose from the discretionary granting of licences, a practice which judging from the work of Krueger (1974) has continued in India down to modern times. This further spread of monopoly reduced demand in the dominated country and restricted world trade correspondingly. The monopoly checked particularly the growth of those commodities which, in a free trade, would be exported to Europe.

> That of the servants tends to stunt the natural growth of every part of the produce in which they choose to deal, of what is destined for home (Indian) consumption, as well as of what is destined for exportation; and consequently to degrade the cultivation of the whole country, and to reduce the number of its inhabitants.[29]

The interest of the trading company, Smith argued, like the interest of any sovereign, is the same with that of the country that is ruled.

This means that the objective should be to open the most extensive market so as to maximize annual produce. In this way, not only will the people prosper, but also the company rulers whose income flows partly from (increasing) land rents, and partly from supplying an expanding market for the British exports of the company. Simple commands from Europe prohibiting the servants from indulging in local trading monopolies were apt to backfire. For the costs of the monopoly were then compounded because new resources were invested in political subterfuge to re-establish the servants' control of inland trade in some underground form.

> They will employ the whole authority of government, and pervert the administration of justice, in order to harass and ruin those who interfere with them in any branch of commerce which, by means of agents, either concealed, or at least not publicly avowed, they may choose to carry on.[30]

Smith believed this situation would incur more welfare loss than would a candid official acknowledgement of the property right of the servants to monopolize trades in their area.[31] But the loss to the present capital value would be enormous nevertheless. This value was based on a probable stream of income in the future. The servants, in contrast, were concerned mainly with their own (shorter) lifetime incomes. Smith could not conceal his contempt for this whole incentive structure.

> It is a very singular government in which every member of the administration wishes to get out of the country, and consequently to have done with the government, as soon as he can, and to whose interests, the day after he has left it and carried his whole fortune with him, it is perfectly indifferent though the whole country was swallowed up by an earthquake.[32]

Unchecked bureaucracies that were thus allowed to spawn their own private monopolies to gouge country after country would obviously 'beggar one's neighbours' more viciously than a simple mercantilist policy that concentrated exclusively upon domestic tariffs and bounties. For the citizens of all countries, the initially positive sum game of trade was in serious danger of turning into negative sum; the spreading disease of monopoly could be a terminal one; and this aspect, to reiterate, can *not* be captured in the geometry of Figure 9.1.

The main argument behind the modern triangular measure of

welfare loss, the argument of a misallocation of resources, was certainly implicit in Smith's analysis of the entire domestic and foreign mercantilist system of monopolies. Smith's term for misallocation was 'derangement', and the derangement was the most striking in the trade with the Indies and America.

> All the different regulations of the mercantile system, necessarily derange more or less this natural and most advantageous distribution of stock [that a system of liberty would produce]. But those which concern the trade to America and the East Indies derange it perhaps more than any other; because the trade to those two great continents absorbs a greater quantity of stock than any two other branches of trade.[33]

But 'derangement' involved more than Harberger costs as will be demonstrated next.

The Hidden Costs

The 20th-century Marxist/Leninist picture of mature capitalist countries being pushed by inevitable economic forces into the role of monopolistic and imperialistic exploiters of their newly-acquired empires, does not quite square with Smith's assessment of events. To him the colonies were an unambiguous liability.

> Under the present system of management, therefore, Great Britain derives nothing but loss from the dominion which she assumes over her colonies.[34]

The 'derangement' of trade had imposed more than the sum of the Harberger and Tullock costs that are indicated in Figure 9.1. First, it had increased the risks of an artifically-concentrated trade, and of a potentially 'disordered' body politic.

> Her commerce in, instead of running in a great number of small channels, has been taught to run principally in one great channel. But the whole system of our industry and commerce has thereby been rendered less secure; the whole state of her body politic less healthful, than it otherwise would have been.[35]

The next concealed cost stemmed from the manufacturing and export constraints imposed on Britain's colonies. Because of the exclusive trading requirements of the navigation acts, the so-called 'enumerated commodities' produced in the colonies could be sent to no other country but England. Other countries were then forced to purchase them from England. Smith argued that the prices of some colonial commodities would be lower in the absence of these restrictions, when a much more extensive market would be available.[36]

The last and most substantial concealed costs of rent-seeking that Smith identified, costs that also cannot be represented in Figure 9.1, arose from certain additional expenses associated with the resultant colonial monopoly system. These consisted of the costs of policing and defending the trade routes and maintaining order in the colonies, all of which fell on the British taxpayer.

> Whatever expense Great Britain has hitherto laid out in maintaining this (colonial) dependency, has really been laid out in order to support this monopoly.[37]

In the late 1760s the ordinary peace establishment of the colonies involved the finance by the British of 20 regiments of foot, artillery, stores, and a large naval force to keep down the smuggling vessels of foreign nations. But more striking still was the expense of colonial wars. The Seven Years War Smith described as 'altogether a colony quarrel' the cost of which should be stated to the account of the colonials. The Spanish War, which began in 1739, was another 'colony quarrel' and the expense of which was in reality, 'a bounty which had been given to support a monopoly'.

The Navigation Act of 1660 was a piece of legislation induced by shopkeepers who had also influenced the setting up of a great empire for the sole purpose of raising up a nation of customers for themselves.

> For the sake of that little enhancement of price which this monopoly right might afford our producers, the home-consumers have been burdened with the whole expense of maintaining and defending that empire.[38]

It is interesting that when Smith begins to make *his* empirical calculations of the 'welfare costs of monopoly' he begins, not with the quantification of some rough equivalent of the triangle and rectangle shown in Figure 9.1, but with these 'externality' costs that are outside the range of such geometry. For the purpose of the same 'little enhancement of price', and for this purpose only, in the last two wars, more than two hundred millions have been spent and a new debt of more than a hundred and seventy millions has been contracted over and above all that had been expended for the same purpose in former wars. The interest of this debt alone is not only greater than the whole extraordinary profit, which, it ever could be pretended, was made by the monopoly of the colony trade, but than the whole value of that trade, or than the whole value of the goods, which at an average have been annually exported to the Colonies.[39]

Smith assessed the cost of the Seven Years War at 90 million pounds – an average of about 13 million pounds per year. Since in those times at least one out of two years was typically spent at war, the cost of hostilities alone came to an average of about 6–7 million pounds annually. The national income in 1760 may be estimated to have been about 130 million pounds.[40] This *partial* measure of the cost of monopoly would already come therefore to around 5 per cent of national income. To obtain estimates of the *total* Smithian costs of monopoly we must first add the average peace time costs of maintaining the 20 regiments of foot, the navy and other military supplies; second, the Smithian cost of greater risks from concentrated trade; third, the decreased health of the body politic; fourth, the 'disorderly conduct' of the servants of the trading companies; and *only* fifth the measures associated with the triangle and rectangle of Figure 9.1. The latter included the costs of home monopolies and regulations – especially labour regulations and the laws protecting some domestic industries against others. The costs of policing and undertaking smuggling into Britain should also be included. Smuggling was a vigorous rent-seeking activity. Smith complained that the administrative costs of collection amounted in some cases to over 30 per cent of the net revenue received by the government. Moreover:

the perquisites of customs house officers are everywhere much greater than their salaries; at some ports more than double or triple those salaries.[41]

Finally, in so far as we treat America before 1776 as part of a composite country that included Britain, the welfare costs of monopoly included the substantial resources that the colonials, as the chief victims of protectionism, invested in their efforts to sabotage or oppose it in peace time, and to finance hostilities in their eventual War of Independence.

The Modern Relevance of Smith

Smith undoubtedly employed the word 'monopoly' in a much wider sense than the modern neoclassical. Harberger confined his welfare triangle analysis to conventional monopolies (single sellers) in manufacturing. Smith focused at least as much on the tariff. While this has been described as 'the mother of the trust', it does not *necessarily* lead to single-seller organization in the home country. Smith was quite different from modern practice too, in his description of land as a monopoly. The fact is that he seemed to equate all restrictions on supply as monopoly. Indeed, in *The Wealth of Nations* the entire subject of misallocation appears to be treated as a monopoly problem.

Such broad usage of the term monopoly will not be admired by neoclassicists. They will complain that there is no gain in understanding or persuasion. And they will demand that the champions of Adam Smith make a case for calling all economic 'sin' monopoly. But what of Smith in his treatment of those monopolies that neoclassicals would accept in their own narrower definition? Their analysis is static while Smith's extends also to the dynamic. He was interested in the process of general, as well as of partial, equilibration. And his general equilibration included, as arguments, political, legal and constitutional factors. Smith was as much interested in the act of *monopolizing* as in monopoly. And he was impressed by the fact that in the process of monopolizing (even in the sense of the strict, neoclassical monopoly) the law and the constitution itself were dependent variables.

It should be remembered, moreoover, that modern neoclassicals do apply the welfare triangle measure of welfare loss to the tariff – even if they do not equate it with monopoly. The measure has also been used to estimate welfare losses from government regulations on domestic industries and utilities (as in Posner's work). From Smith's grand perspective this measure would still fall short, and for reasons previously expressed.

On the basis of this review one may reasonably speculate that Adam Smith's wide list of costs of monopoly, as he defined it, came to at least 10 per cent of the gross national income in his day. This figure is, of course, well above that of Posner's modern estimate for America, and even above Ann Krueger's recent calculation for India. In so far as the welfare burdens of tariffs are the most severe of all restrictions, countries like Britain, whose overseas trade has traditionally accounted for a large fraction of national economic activity, can be expected to have higher costs of protectionism than countries like America. This is true today as well as in the 18th century.

Yet while historical circumstances no doubt contribute some explanation why monopoly was the central focus in the first comprehensive masterpiece in economics, it must be emphasized that Smith's insights still point to important deficiencies in *modern* discussion of the costs of monopoly. The current neoclassical analysis of the 'deadweight triangle' is conducted in an institutional vacuum; individuals pursue their self-interest within given rules that are costlessly imposed. Smith's much broader analysis reminds us that people will use resources to profit themselves by actions outside the rules or directed to changing the rules. Tullock's contribution certainly goes some way in correcting the modern findings. But a study of Adam Smith takes us further. The 'rules' of the competitive game are a delicate but crucial part of the whole economic fabric. Progressive onslaughts of rent-seeking activity that result in more monopolization may ultimately injure the very foundation of the economic constitution. This constitution, which is a system of collective protection of private property rights, is strictly a public good. Monopolizers are in effect free-riders upon it and a multiplication of them will quickly destroy such 'public capital'.[42]

In the real world, the rot could be progressive. In Tullock's words:

> As a successful theft will stimulate other thieves to greater industry and require greater investment in protective measures, so each successful establishment of a monopoly or creation of a tariff will stimulate greater diversion of resources to attempts to organize further transfers of income.[43]

In Smith's words:

> This (the manufacturer's) monopoly has so much increased the number of some particular tribes of them, that, like an overgrown standing army, they have become formidable to the government, and upon many occasions intimidate the legislature.
> ... Every such (monopoly) regulation introduces some degree of real disorder into the constitution of the State, which it will be difficult afterwards to cure without occasioning another disorder.[44]

The fact that it is more difficult to place a precise estimate on such costs of what Smith called declines in 'the health of the body politic', is no reason to ignore them. Also it is necessary, at least openly, to consider the question how much the whole apparatus of customs and excise is directed to the purposes of monopoly or restrictions that favour special interests and indeed how much of the modern defence budget, including that part devoted to protecting international oil supplies, is allocated to this function.

Finally, those who see some 'justice' in a given distribution of property rights should presumably treat as a special cost (as Adam Smith did) any arbitrary interference with it that monopolies (including labour monopolies) incur. This is not simply a psychic cost of pain from arbitrary redistribution, but cost in the sense of the threatened losses to all participants in the social system when that system itself is placed in jeopardy by the ultimate retaliation of victims of monopoly. This will occur when their relative income position in anarchy, or near anarchy, begins to look preferable. In anarchy all statutory monopolies can be expected to collapse, and the benefits from this to the exploited might outweigh the costs peculiar to anarchy itself. This is not to suggest that Western democracies have reached this stage yet; but other countries seem much nearer.

It has been argued that the essence of monopoly to Smith was the ability to exclude. But he also wanted a legal framework that respected property, and property also means the ability to exclude. Property, however, also means the exclusion of predators, whereas monopoly means the exclusion of competitors. Competition *required* property; for this was the basic 'prize' or incentive in the positive sum game that would, for *all* players, improve on the Hobbesian jungle. The danger was that while an initial social contract might set up property rights with the 'proper' kind of exclusion, in some later period, rent-seeking interest groups might effectively rewrite property rights in their own favour and so progressively pervert the constitution.

Smith was under no illusion that one could write the 'perfect constitution'; and it would be a mistake to interpret his measures of monopoly costs in terms of the comparison between the performances of a 'monopoly constitution' and a 'perfect' (monopoly free) constitution. In a sense, the modern 'welfare triangle' approach flirts with this 'nirvana fallacy', because the initial position, P_0 in Figure 9.1, is one of the neoclassical 'perfect competition', a state of the world which is not strictly to be found in Smith. And in this sense, from Smith's standpoint, the modern triangle approach overestimates the welfare loss from monopoly. Yet this approach, to repeat, is a static one, and Smith's major concerns were the 'dynamic' costs of a constitution that was set on a collision course. English monopolies to him, whether manufacturing or labour monopolies, foretold a virulent disease, and one of which the simple geometry of Figure 9.1 offers no signal.

Notes

1. Harberger (1959).
2. Schwartzman (1960), p. 68; Kamerschen (1966); Worcester (1973), pp. 853–70; Bergson (1973), pp. 853–70; Carson (1975) pp. 1008–14.
3. For an exposition using indifference curves see Bergson, op. cit.
4. Tullock (1967), pp. 224–32, although Krueger (1974) was first to coin the title 'rent seeking'.
5. Ibid., p. 228.
6. Posner (1975), pp. 807–27.
7. Tullock (1980).
8. If mining is added to manufacturing. Posner, op. cit., 819, fn. 16.
9. Krueger (1974), pp. 291–303; Kamerschen (1966) developed further Harberger's analysis and obtained a significantly higher welfare loss – 6 per cent of national income. Some of his assumptions, however, such as that advertising is a 100 per cent monopoly element, are debatable.
10. The social costs of bribing stem from the real resources that are drawn into the activity, say, of becoming an official who allocates import licences and who is in a position to receive the bribes. (Krueger 1974, pp. 292–3.)
11. Becker (1968), pp. 168–217.
12. Smith (1976), p. 648.
13. Ibid., p. 903.
14. Ibid., p. 654.
15. Ibid., p. 267.
16. Ibid., p. 462.
17. Ibid., pp. 654–5. Smith also described the manufacturer's as using 'extortion' to obtain concessions from government. If he meant this literally then losses would occur if resources were needed for threats.
18. Ibid., p. 653.
19. Ibid., p. 647, pp. 651–2.
20. Ibid., p. 265.
21. Ibid., p. 215, emphasis added.
22. Ibid., p. 215.
23. Ibid., p. 510.
24. Ibid., pp. 514–15.
25. Anderson and Tollison (1982), p. 1251.
26. Ibid.
27. Smith (1976), p. 752.
28. Anderson and Tollison (1982), p. 1253.
29. Smith (1976), p. 639.

30. Ibid.
31. 'If they are suffered to act as they could wish, they will establish this monopoly openly and directly ... and this perhaps is the best and least oppressive way of establishing it.' Smith (1976), p. 639.
32. Smith (1976), p. 640.
33. Ibid., p. 630.
34. Ibid., p. 616.
35. Ibid., p. 604.
36. Ibid., p. 595.
37. Ibid., p. 615.
38. Ibid., p. 661.
39. Ibid.
40. Mitchell (1962) estimates the British gross national income to have been 232 million pounds in 1801 and 48 million in 1688. Our approximation of 130 million pounds in 1760 is based on reasonable adjustments for population and economic growth between those periods.
41. Smith (1976), p. 896.
42. Buchanan (1975).
43. Tullock (1967), p. 231.
44. Smith (1976), p. 471.

10. Adam Smith's Hypotheses on Religion: Some New Empirical Tests

As mentioned in Chapter 8, David Hume maintained that self-interest is a sufficient basis for the emergence of justice and the embodiment of it in a constitution. Justice emerges after a learning process following which each individual finds himself respecting other people's property provided this respect is reciprocated.

> And even every individual person must find himself a gainer, on balancing the accounts; since, without justice society must immediately dissolve, and everyone must fall into that savage and solitary condition, which is infinitely worse than the worse situation that can possibly be supposed in society.[1]

The implication of Hume's argument is that, by trial and error, man drifts into an ultimate acceptance of the rule of law. Translated into terms of modern game theory we start with a prisoner's dilemma game in which each separate 'player' has an incentive to adopt a non-cooperative strategy. His reasoning is that he will gain if the other player(s) adopt a cooperative strategy by helping, for instance, to pay for some public good, such as a road; for then our player will benefit (from the public good) at no expense to himself. On the alternative assumption, that the other player(s) will also be non-cooperative, it still pays our individual to remain non-cooperative otherwise he will lose by having to devote *his* resources to an expensive public good to which others are not contributing. Because this game is symmetric, every individual, taken separately, reasons similarly. And since the dominant strategy for the individuals is non-cooperation, the social outcome is also one of non-cooperation (or anarchy).

Hume's eventual trial and error solution can then be envisaged in terms of a 'supergame' of prisoner's dilemma situations repeated over and over by the same original players.[2] One outcome that can now emerge is for each participant to play the cooperative strategy so long as the other player(s) does, and then to *punish* the other player(s) for refusing to do so by playing the non-cooperative strategy. This can occur through a series of plays after which the originally non-cooperative players behave cooperatively. Such a solution can occur, even in the absence of direct communication between the players.

The likelihood of the cooperative strategy being adopted universally, however, is greater the smaller the number of players; for then it is easier to learn each other's behaviour and to predict their responses to supergames. With large numbers it is not so easy to detect non-cooperative individuals and to single them out for punishment. In this case, the threat of punishment *of the kind described* becomes more remote and less potentially effective. What is needed then is a more 'exogeneous' type of punishment or threat of punishment. Adam Smith recognized this need; David Hume was more hesitant.

Religion and Self-monitoring

Smith, in fact, saw a role for religion in adopting the required exogeneous punishment function. Indeed the most striking contrast between the two writers is that Smith (as we shall see in detail) strongly preferred a large number of competing sects to one established religion, whereas Hume viewed a multiplicity of sects as socially destabilizing, and favoured an established church for reasons that will subsequently be clarified.

Smith believed that providence had implanted a moral sense in individuals and this was an element quite independent of the notion of utility. In other words, as Levy points out, to Smith the social approval of justice pre-dated the recognition of the utility of justice, and 'our hatred of injustice is something which manifests itself in forms which do not seem to relate to utility'.[3] It is through a slow inductive process that men eventually come to acknowledge a general rule that justice *ought* to be done. Indeed this acknowledgement becomes deeply engrained.

There is scarce any man, however, who by discipline, education, and example, may not be so impressed with a regard to general rules, as to act upon almost every occasion with tolerable decency, and through the whole of his life avoid any considerable degree of blame. *Without this sacred regard to general rules, there is no man whose conduct can be much depended on.*[4]

The last sentence in this quotation suggests that Smith would have had very little faith in the ability of supergames to avoid prisoner's dilemma situations. His inductive process leading to the rules of law and morality implies that the ultimate firm acceptance of them leads to self-monitoring by individuals; and this avoids the enormous cost of external monitoring. It is especially in the early stages of society that religion generates the necessary respect for the rules. Such respect, moreover, comes well before man's full 'scientific' understanding of their usefulness.

Gods were universally represented and believed to be the rewarders of humanity and mercy, and the avengers of perfidy and injustice. And thus religion, even in its rudest form, gave a sanction to the rules of morality, long before the age of artificial reasoning and philosophy. That the terrors of religion should thus enforce the natural sense of duty, was of too much importance to the happiness of mankind, for nature to leave it dependent upon the slowness and uncertainty of philosophical researches.[5]

As is consistent with this reasoning, the word 'duty' plays an increasing role in Smith's scheme of social evolution. But the inculcation of duty takes place through religious instruction. It is thus straightforward to piece together another testable theory in Smith's work. In so far as religion is conducive to social stability and the rule of law, it must also encourage economic prosperity. This follows because, to Smith, the same stability and respect for the law is a necessary condition for liberty,[6] and this, in turn, leads to the efficient operation of decentralized markets. The testable hypothesis then is that the greater the presence of religion the greater is the level of success in the economic sphere.

The Glahe and Vorhies Test

Once again it is unreasonable to have expected from Smith an elaborate formal testing of his hypothesis because systematic data in his time was unavailable. By the late 20th century, however, such data has been collected and was recently used in research by economists Glahe and Vorhies.[7] Their main source of information on religious affiliations by nation was the 1986 *Britannica Book of the Year*. For the purposes of their paper the data was organized into the following groupings: Jewish/ Christian, Muslim, Hindu/Buddhist, Tribal, and Atheist/Non-Religious. Their investigation used as variables both the proportion of believers and the predominant religion in a nation. Their measure of the quantity and quality of economic development was a weighted average of per capita income, life expectancy, adult literacy, and infant survival. The number of countries they examined was 150.

Among the findings of Glahe and Vorhies was a particularly strong empirical relationship between Judaeo-Christianity and economic development. The authors conjectured that an important explanation was the encouragement that Judaeo-Christianity gives to private ownership of capital. In general, the authors drew upon some of their previous work which, like that of Scully (1988), found a positive and significant relationship between liberty and economic development. Their next task was to search for a relationship between religion and liberty. Judaeo-Christianity again received a high score. The remaining nations exhibited no significant meaningful relationship between political liberty and development.

In one sense, however, these findings appear to be reasonably consistent with Smith's 'predictions'. His necessary conditions for best performance in terms of the growth of the wealth of nations, after all, included not only legal and political stability, which was fostered by the presence of religion, but the existence also of 'natural liberty'.

In another sense, the findings of Glahe and Vorhies are not pertinent to a *general* proposition that, because religion universally fulfills the need of an exogenous threat of punishment, it promotes stability and economic growth. It is true that their results suggest that non-religious countries are not very successful economically. It is also true, nevertheless, that their evidence shows that some religious countries also have low scores. The evidence, in other words, is consistent with the proposition that *selected* types of religions or religious organizations are conducive to economic prosperity. But this calls for specific explanations as to which religious structures have the requisite qualifications. As we shall see, Smith, indeed, was himself anxious to rule out *some* systems of religion since he saw them as having a negative influence on growth and stability.

Smith was concerned that religion can sometimes become corrupt, in which case it leads to what he called a 'very gross perversion of our natural sentiments'. In *The Wealth of Nations* he argues that the greatest danger of such corruption occurs within government-established religions. The argument is set in the context of a long examination of Hume's conclusion that non-established religions result in civil unrest. Smith rejected Hume's reasoning 'because it ... confused religion *per se* with religion that has access to state power'.[8]

Religion as an Individual Investment

Before examining this important issue further, however, it will be helpful to make one or two observations on what Smith identified as the economic incentives inducing individuals to join religious denominations. As a preliminary, it is necessary to refer to Smith's treatment of the economic value of an individual's personal reputation. As Anderson has shown, Smith has, in effect, a human capital theory of reputation.[9] One context where this is revealed is that of medicine.[10] When asked whether he thought there should be restrictions placed on the sale of medical degrees in some Scottish universities, Smith answered in the negative because he maintained that the demand for physician's services was a function of their professional reputations. Generally, the higher one's reputation the higher the fee one's clients are willing to pay and therefore the higher one's income.

Reputations in medicine, of course, depend upon an efficient flow of information to clients concerning each physician's successes and failures. Smith believed the barriers were few.

> That Doctors are sometimes fools as well as other people, is not in the present times, one of those profound secrets which is known only to the learned.[11]

On the subject of education, meanwhile Smith argued similarly that the payment of student fees to teachers 'must always depend more or less upon their industry and reputation'.[12]

Smith recognized, however, that the flow of information about a potential employee's reputation was an inverse function of the size of the population in which he dwelt. Thus a man 'of low condition' who lived in a village could generate information about himself with little difficulty since his actions were easily observed by his neighbours. 'In this situation, and in this situation only, he may have what is called a character to lose.'[13] When the same 'low condition' individual migrates to a large town, however, it is easy for him to get lost in the much larger society so that general information about his morals and reputation approaches zero. The result is that '... as soon as he comes into a great city, he is sunk in obscurity and darkness'.[14] If he is a man of moral virtue he now requires some kind of institution that can signal or vouchsafe this fact. Accordingly, it is by joining one of the small religious sects (which Smith treats in effect as clubs) that he finds his search successful.

> He, from that moment acquires a degree of consideration which he never had before. All his brother sectaries are, for the credit of the sect, interested to observe his conduct, and if he gives occasion to any scandal, if he deviates very much from those austere morals which they almost always require of one another, to punish him by what is always a very severe punishment, even where no civil effects attend it, expulsion or excommunication from the sect.[15]

As Anderson concludes, by joining such a club, an individual with little wealth and no established reputation and references, was able to signal information to potential employers, lenders and service providers that he or she represents a relatively low risk in terms of potential transactions.

> Hence, the overt participation by individuals in religious sects that apply strict rules of conduct for their members is represented as a rational investment ... By providing valuable, reliable information concerning the level of risk attached to dealings with particular individuals, religious sects both benefit their members in a tangible way and also improve the efficiency of the allocation of human resources.[16]

Smith's Critique of Established Religions

Having established the private economic motives for religious membership we now return to the issue whether religion had unintended wider or social effects. To Smith the most important of these was that of enforcing the natural sense of duty so that legal stability, and hence economic prosperity, ensued. It has been shown that the evidence of Glahe and Vorhies (1989) suggests that the presence of religion may be a necessary condition for successful economic development. At the same time they find that the relationship works with some types of religion only. And it is in this context that it is interesting to note that Adam Smith discriminated carefully among religions before granting his approval.

Smith reserved his strongest criticisms for religions that were established by the State. He insisted that *these* were the ones that encouraged intolerance and religious fanaticism, and not, as Hume believed, the numerous small sects that natural liberty brought forth. To Smith, free entry into the religion 'market' and the absence of substantial subsidies would provide a socially useful check on religious arrogance. Teachers who depended for their living upon the fees of their pupils were likely to be zealous and industrious. In contrast, those teachers who enjoyed payment from some other fund – such as a tithe, a land tax, an established salary, or a stipend – were more prone to 'giving themselves up to indolence'. Established church systems resulted in this very outcome. They gave their teachers financial support independent of their 'customers'; as a result, they subsequently became lazy and inefficient. This weakness led them to be complacent even in defending their own doctrines against the attacks of new religions and new teachers whose income *was* dependent upon their immediate customers – their 'common people' listeners.

> In this respect the teachers of new religons always had a considerable advantage in attacking those ancient and established systems of which the clergy, reposing themselves upon their benefices, had neglected to keep up the fervour of faith and devotion in the great body of people; and having given themselves up to indolence, were become altogether incapable of making any vigorous exertion in defence even of their own establishment.[17]

It may be asked whether, after all, the problem of monopoly religion would thus ultimately solve itself. Unfortunately, Adam Smith argued, this was not so. The gradual encroachment of new religions subsequently forced the established one into vicious over-reaction. The established clergy would eventually call upon the civil magistrate to persecute, destroy, or drive out their new adversaries.

It was thus that the Roman Catholic clergy called upon the civil magistrate to persecute the protestants; and the Church of England, to persecute the dissenters; and that in general every religious sect, when it has once enjoyed for a century or two the security of a legal establishment, has found itself incapable of making any vigorous defence against any new sect which chose to attack its doctrine or discipline.[18]

Times of violent religious controversy were often times of equally violent political faction. Rent seeking abounded, each political party allying itself with someone or other of the contending religious sects. The sect that supported the winning political party would then want some share in the spoils of office. 'Their first demand was generally, that he [the civil magistrate] should silence and subdue all their adversaries; and their second, that he should bestow an independent provision on themselves. As they had generally contributed a good deal of the victory, it seemed not unreasonable that they should have some share in the spoil.'[19] If politics had never called in the aid of religion, and never adopted the tenets of one sect more than those of another, Smith insisted, it would probably have dealt equally and impartially with all the different sects. Every person would have been able to choose his/her own priest and religion as he/she thought proper. But then comes a further shrewd and characteristic Smithian prediction.

There would in this case, no doubt, have been a great multitude of religious sects. Almost every different congregation might probably have made a little sect by itself or have entertained some peculiar tenets of its own. Each teacher would no doubt have felt himself under the necessity of making the utmost exertion, and of using every art both to preserve and to increase the number of his disciples. But as every other teacher would have felt himself the same necessity, the success of no one teacher, or sect of teachers, could have been very great. The interested and active zeal of religious teachers can be dangerous and troublesome only where there is, either but one sect tolerated in the society, or where the whole of a large society is divided into two or three great sects; the teachers of each acting by concert under a regular discipline and subordination. But that zeal must be altogether innocent where the society is divided into two or three hundred, or perhaps into as many thousand small sects, of which no one could be considerable enough to disturb the public tranquility. The teachers of each sect, seeing themselves surrounded on all sides with more adversaries than friends, would be obliged to learn that candor and moderation which is so seldom to be found among the teachers of those great sects, whose tenets, being supported by the civil magistrate, are held in veneration by almost all the inhabitants of extensive kingdoms and empires, and who therefore see nothing round them but followers, disciples, and humble admirers.[20]

If the plan had been adopted of no ecclesiastical government, a plan put forward by the Independents in England toward the end of the English Civil War, it would, argued Smith, have produced 'the most philosophical good temper and moderation with regard to every sort of religious principle'. Smith's hypothesis, of course, needed all the contemporary evidence he could muster. Accordingly, he quoted the case of Pennsylvania where the predicted happy result had occurred because 'the law in reality favours no one sect more than another'. And relative tranquility prevailed even though the Quakers happened to be in the majority.

Provided, then, that the sects were sufficiently numerous, excessive zeal could not lead to much harm. On the contrary, there could be several good consequences. Smith believed that membership of little religious sects, especially in the towns, was conducive to successful civilization: 'In little religious sects, accordingly, the morals of common people have been almost remarkably regular and orderly: *generally much more so than in the established church*'.[21]

From the quotations and observations presented so far, Laurence Iannaccone has concluded:

> Smith's analysis lays the foundation for an economic theory of religion, a theory in which self-interest motivates clergy just as it does secular producers; market forces constrain churches just as they do secular firms; and the benefits of competition, the burdens of monopoly, and the hazards of government regulation are as real as in any other sector of the economy.[22]

The Iannaccone Test

Iannaccone focuses on the fact that Smith's reasoning amounts to a genuine testable hypothesis and he proceeds with a 20th-century test of it. His investigation is based on data from multi-nation surveys conducted between 1968 and 1976. He confined his analysis, however, to 18 Western, developed nations because comparable data were available for only a few less developed or non-Western nations.

To measure the degree of monopoly in religion, Iannaccone employed an index (Herfindahl) of religious concentration for each nation:

$H_j \equiv \sum_i S^2_{ij}$

where i, the index of summation, runs over all denominations in country j, and S_{ij} is the market share of denomination i in country j. The symbol H equals the probability that two people with religious affiliation, selected at random, share the same denomination. Thus, the higher the coefficient the greater the degree of religious monopoly. Iannaccone discovered enormous differences across otherwise similar nations. The concentration ratio for the Catholic countries Italy, Portugal and Spain is 0.98 or more. Similarly, Norway, with its established Lutheran Church, has a ratio of 0.95. In contrast, are countries with completely open religious competition among which the US is the most extreme with its concentration ratio as low as 0.12.

Measures of religious belief and behaviour employed by Innaccone included the per cent of the population attending church each week, the per cent claiming belief in God and the per cent claiming their religious beliefs are 'very important' to them. All three variables were obtained from Gallup surveys.

Iannaccone's regression analysis produced the striking result that the expected church attendance rate among Protestants declines from around 40 per cent in a freely-competitive market to 2 per cent in a country monopolized by a single Protestant denomination. His Figure 1, reproduced as Figure 10.1 here, plots each nation's attendance rates against the Protestant contribution to total market concentration. It shows that the inverse relationship between concentration and attendance applies to the entire sample. Iannaccone's additional regression results show that it is not just church attendance but also private piety (defined as declared belief in God and the perceived importance of religion) that declines as religious monopoly increases.

The evidence reported, however, suggests that there is no significant effect of monopoly on religiosity in the case of Catholicism. Catholics attend church, for instance, at roughly the same rate independently of the proportion it is of the national religious market. Adam Smith appears to have recognized this strength of Catholicism in his own time. But it was not incompatible with his economic reasoning because, in effect, he maintained that Catholics in the 18th century managed their monopoly better than other religions. Catholic leaders were apparently well aware of Smith's point that the zeal of teachers was in direct proportion to the degree

Figure 10.1   Attendance vs. concentration

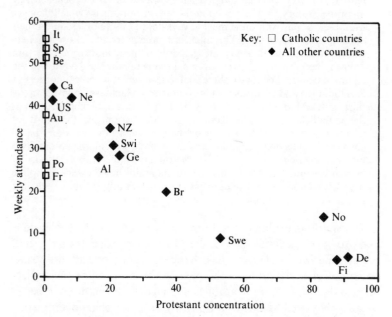

Notes: Al = Australia, Au = Austria, Be = Belgium, Br = Britain, Ca = Canada, De = Denmark, Fi = Finland, Fr = France, Ge = West Germany, It = Italy, Ne = Netherlands, NZ = New Zealand, No = Norway, Po = Portugal, Sp = Spain, Swe = Sweden, Swi = Switzerland, US = United States.

of their dependence on the fees of their pupils, whereas teachers who depended for their incomes on some other fund, such as a tithe or an established salary were likely to be much less diligent. Knowing this, Smith argued, the Catholic church rationally attempted to harness the motive of self-interest among its 'inferior' clergy. His argument appears in one of the most fascinating, but neglected, passages in *The Wealth of Nations*:

> In the church of Rome, the industry and zeal of the inferior clergy is kept more alive by the powerful motive of self-interest, than perhaps in any established protestant church. The parochial clergy derive, many of them, a very considerable part of their subsistence from the voluntary oblations of the people; a source of revenue which confession gives them many opportunities of improving. The mendicant orders derive their

whole subsistence from such oblations. It is with them, as with the hussars and light infantry of some armies; no plunder, no pay. The parochial clergy are like those teachers whose reward depends partly upon their salary, and partly upon the fees or honoraries which they get from their pupils, and these must always depend more or less upon their industry and reputation. The medicant orders are like those teachers whose subsistence depends altogether on their industry. They are obliged, therefore, to use every art which can animate the devotion of the common people. The establishment of the two great mendicant orders of St. Dominick and St. Francis, it is observed by Machiavel, revived, in the thirteenth and fourteenth centuries, the languishing faith and devotion of the catholick church. In Roman Catholick countries the spirit of devotion is supported altogether by the monks and by the poorer parochial clergy. The great dignitaries of the church, with all the accomplishments of gentlemen and men of the world, and sometimes with those of men of learning, are careful enough to maintain the necessary discipline over their inferiors, but seldom give themselves any trouble about the instruction of the people.[23]

The Smithian explanation of the relative success of Catholicism is likely to have much less force in the 20th century when the pattern of use of donations (oblations) has changed. Iannaccone admits he has no *empirical* explanation to the phenomenon but offers the conjecture that 20th-century Catholics manage their monopoly better because they are less easily co-opted by their national governments.

> The Catholic Churches of Spain, Austria, or even Italy, can never be as much a part of the state as the Lutheran Churches of Sweden, Norway or Finland. In these latter countries, the national churches are effectively branches of the government, financed by the state, run by civil servants, and hence plagued by the same inefficiencies as other state monopolies. The ties between Catholic Church and the state are by comparison never as close, its status never as secure, and hence its employees never as poorly motivated.[24]

This conjecture is quite consistent with Smith's main argument that the *State* monopoly religions tended to lose touch with 'the great body of the people'.

Clearly, if Catholicism, unaided by the state, is unable to use the force of law to restrict newcomers, then the religion market is continuously contestable. The ever-present possibility of free entry of competing religions must act as an ongoing and effective incentive to keeping up the fervour of faith among all 'ranks' in society. And, arguably, this proposition is just as true today as it was in Smith's time.

US Supreme Court Decisions in a Smithian Perspective

Smith's authority has recently been invoked in connection with US Supreme Court decisions on religion. Since Smith inferred that the more religious sects there were, and hence the smaller each one was on average, the more effective would religion be in regulating behaviour, one implication is that legal regulations that have the effect of multiplying rather than concentrating religious organization may improve the moral tone of society. Richard Posner argues accordingly that the US Supreme Court's aggressive secularist stance must, on Smith's reasoning, have done just this.[25] Judicial decisions, for instance, that forbid prayer in schools spark demands for private religious schooling of all kinds. More to the point, the court's morality decisions help those churches whose relationship with the government is competitive rather than complementary.

> Churches closely identified with the political 'establishment' (used in its nonreligious sense), such as the mainline Protestant churches, have trouble distancing themselves from the public schools and other government institutions with which they have for so long been entwined. When those schools and institutions turn secular, as they have in recent decades – in part under judicial prodding – the position of the mainline churches is eroded. Since the non-mainline denominations tend also to attract the more intense believers, the effect of the morality decisions on competition with the religious sector seems clear and is consistent with the growth of these denominations in recent years.[26]

Conclusion: Hume vs. Smith

To end this chapter on an issue in the history of economic thought we return to David Hume's expressed support for an established religion. Contrary to first impressions, his position is not inconsistent with Smith's argument that competition in religion is as effective as competition elsewhere. Hume favoured an established church for the very reason that, being a non-competitive system that placed clergymen on government payrolls, like other civil servants, they would lose their zeal and religion would become devitalized and therefore innocuous. Hume, after all, was hostile to religions of all kinds; Smith was not. But Hume's proposition that competing religions are a destabilizing influence and therefore at odds with the harmony and prosperity of nations, appears to be refuted by the new empirical tests described in this chapter. Pending further research, therefore, we must tentatively conclude that it is Smith's hypothesis, not Hume's, that so far survives the new evidence.

Notes

1. Hume (1888), p. 497.
2. Ordeshook (1986), Chapter 10.
3. Levy (1978), p. 672.
4. Smith (1969), Part III, Chapter 3, emphasis added.
5. Ibid.
6. Smith (1976), p. 722.
7. Glahe and Vorhies (1989).
8. Levy (1978), p. 673.
9. Anderson (1988), p. 1070.
10. See the letter from Smith to William Cullen in 1774 reproduced and analysed in West (1976), pp. 188–92.
11. Ibid, p. 189.
12. Smith (1976), p. 798.
13. Ibid. p. 795.
14. Ibid.
15. Ibid.
16. Anderson (1988), p. 1072.
17. Smith (1976), pp. 788–9. The economics of monopolized religious organization in Smith is expounded in West (1976c).
18. Ibid. p. 789.
19. Smith (1976), p. 792.
20. Ibid, pp. 792–3.
21. Smith (1976), p. 796.
22. Iannaccone (1987), p. 2.
23. Smith (1976), pp. 789–90.
24. Iannaccone (1987), p. 8.
25. Posner (1987).
26. Posner (1989), p. 58.

11. *Laissez-Faire* Revisited

This final chapter attempts to chart the career of public policy that, in popular language, has come to be known as '*laissez-faire*'. The treatment here requires considerable reference to 20th-century literature in the history of thought as well as to substantial direct comparisons between Smith and his immediate classical economist successors. In keeping with the overall theme of our book, however, the discussion is conducted wherever possible in the light of current economic analysis.

Several modern analysts are pointing to technical weaknesses in the invisible hand reasoning that were not suspected in the 18th and 19th centuries. It is now argued for example that, if the invisible hand is to work perfectly, there must be sufficient opportunities for intertemporal and contingent intertemporal trade. If contingent markets are *not* complete (and this seems descriptive of reality), markets will be associated with much more uncertainty than otherwise. Other scholars have replied that the modern rational expectations hypothesis might take care of the problem in the sense that, as Hahn expresses it, each individual 'somehow has learned how the invisible hand would have performed if it had been given [complete] markets in which to perform'.[1] But many others are questioning the real world plausibility of such a process.

Before examining other sophisticated modern attacks on the invisible hand it will be helpful to review the verdicts of modern historians of thought on the reasons for some conspicuous classical departures from *laissez-faire* as the classical economists understood the term.

The Viner Tradition in the History of Thought

The picture of the English classical economists as die-hard defenders of pure *laissez-faire* is now typically dismissed by historians of economic thought as a popular caricature. Quoting evidence especially from the second generation of classical writers, and particularly from the works of Jeremy Bentham, James Mill, John Stuart Mill, and Nassau Senior, several scholars emphasize that there has been a common confusion between their writings and those of the Manchester School plus the early 19th-century Anti-Corn Law League.

One recent illustration of this argument is provided in D.P. O'Brien's interesting work *The Classical Economists* (1978). But the tradition is an old one and it goes back at least to an influential article written in the 1940s by Jacob Viner.[2] Viner emphasized that John Stuart Mill, Torrens, Cairnes, Jevons, Sidgwick, Marshall and Edeworth had all to deny repeatedly and forcefully that the Cobdenites had any authority to invoke the 'Laws of Political Economy' to stop government intervention in the aid of the poor. And, according to O'Brien, an accurate reading of the classical economists reveals an entirely pragmatic attitude towards legislation. The criterion for intervention was simply that of 'general expediency', to use J.S. Mill's words.

The writer who comes closest to having given classical economics the reputations of pure *laissez-faire* advocacy was, of course, Adam Smith. O'Brien's emphasizes, however, that we must remember that *The Wealth of Nations* was primarily a vigorous critique of mercantilism which Smith saw as the regulation of economic activity by the State in the interests of the merchant classes:

> and it is the classical economists' attacks upon mercantilism which have helped to create the impression of their being totally opposed to state activity, which they were not. What they were mainly criticising was the use of government power in the interests of a small minority to create for themselves privileged conditions.[3]

Nevertheless, one difficulty with the argument that the classical economists' attitude to intervention was 'pragmatic', or based on 'expediency' is that the same could be argued for the system of 'mercantilism'. This being so, the territory between the mercantilists and the classical economists begins to narrow and one starts to wonder what was the nature of the classical economic revolution after all. Certainly the 'expediency' of mercantilist policies was based on an argument that emphasized the benefits to nation states rather than to the majority of working people within them. The 'expediency' of the 19th-century classical economist, in contrast, was such as to include, if not give priority to, the interests of the poor. It is true, also, that the classicals condemned policy proposals that were likely to create monopolies or trade restrictions. Yet, according to the O'Brien/Viner thesis, the pragmatism of the classical economists' proposals for legislation included a disposition to create something of their own regulatory state. Regulated industries, however, can ultimately reproduce the effects of monopoly and/or involve a whole 'standing army' of administrators and inspectors. It was this kind of world, surely, that Smith set out to attack. For in his philosophy there was a presumption in favour of *minimum* government.

Smith's invention of the 'invisible hand', after all, was offered to supersede the mercantilist notion that governments needed to act in every corner of the economy in order to achieve growing wealth and welfare. He argued that a decentralized price system would take care of those objectives, but with much greater efficiency, and much less corruption. Certainly there would not be perfection; but the economy would be far less imperfect than if controlled by 'pragmatic' government regulation.

Adam Smith and *Laissez-Faire*

In reply to those who describe Smith as the doyen of the 'free market school', several scholars offer the reminder of Viner's essay: 'Adam Smith and *Laissez-Faire*', published in 1928. As explained in Chapter 7, Viner referred to Smith's exceptions to spontaneous harmony in a list of recommended public projects to be found in *The Wealth of Nations* that included education, the post office, the public mints, roads, and canals. He concluded: 'The modern advocate of laissez-faire who objects to *government participation in business* on the ground that it is an encroachment upon the field reserved by nature for private enterprise cannot find support for this argument in *The Wealth of Nations*'.[4] Similar arguments have been put forward by Robbins (1952) and Crouch (1967).

As also explained in Chapter 7, however, Viner and others seem to have overlooked that the thrust of most of Smith's prescription for new public works, was the extension of private provision by way of public companies enjoying new privileges of joint stock and limited liability. It should be noted that there is no problem with Smith proposing the functions of government that include defence and security. It is readily acknowledged that his system of markets depended upon a suitable legal framework that is appropriately policed, so that such policing and such vision of law is not inconsistent with *laissez-faire*, but underpins it. The debate concerns the extent to which Smith went beyond the provision of these central and indispensible 'public goods'.

The crucial issue is the legitimacy of 'government participation in business' to use the words (in our italics) in the above quotation from Viner. The fact is that most of Smith's discussion of the need for 'public works', upon which Viner focuses, results in proposals to extend by legal means the sphere of *private* activity. This is a different thing altogether from government *participation in business*. Of the 'public works' that 'facilitated the commerce' of any country, Smith gave the examples of bridges, navigable canals, harbours and marine insurance. The sequence of his argument leads to a discussion of the need for (private) *joint-stock* enterprise so as to allow 'extra large' canal companies, and so on. If intervention by the sovereign was required, it was in terms of adjusting the legal framework and sets of property rights so that new larger-scale markets were possible.

Smith's reasoning about the 'third duty of the sovereign' (to promote public works) was couched in terms of extending the privilege of joint-stock organization in order to allow large amounts of capital to be accumulated and employed within one firm in cases where it was deemed necessary. In this way the 'public work' of banking, Smith argued, required a special form of contract because large banks, especially those expected to support public credit and to lend to governments, required a greater capital than could easily be collected into any 'private co-partnery'. Similarly, canals and water supplies were argued to qualify for joint-stock status and again on the grounds of the large capital requirement. There was also need for accumulating capital in the fire and marine insurance business and this too was not practical without the privilege of the joint-stock institution. It is true that in the case of roads, Smith came down in favour of public trustees, but as explained in Chapter 7, his argument here is somewhat obscure. On the whole, however, Smith's reasoning is strongly against government *participation in business* as distinct from government granting legal privileges that allow private business to work more effectively.

Classical Economists as Reformers

In his book *The Economist in Parliament* (1980), Frank W. Fetter surveys the influence of economists in Parliament in the classical period from 1780. The individuals studied include Ricardo, J. S. Mill, Torrens, Fawcett, Horner, Lauderdale, Scrope, Thompson and Thornton. Also examined is an assembly of others to whom the title 'economist' is rather generous. This list comprises Brougham, Cobden, Goschen, Hume, Huskisson, Overstone and Horton. The voting record of these writers is examined on a large number of contemporary issues including the Corn Laws, the Navigation Acts, the Combination Acts, the Factory Acts, the Usury Laws, Education, the Poor Laws and the regulation of railways and banks. Fetter concludes that most of the parliamentary economists up to 1850 were strongly anti-establishment reformers. And in Parliament it was the authority of Adam Smith, not Ricardo, that was most often appealed to.

But it is a mistake to conclude that because Adam Smith and his immediate followers were reformers they were all of a politically progressive disposition. As James Buchanan has observed, it is one thing to undertake politically-orchestrated attempts to 'do something' by making changes through *ordinary politics* and quite another to be a reformer in the sense of urging changes in the basic rules of ordinary politics (i.e., the constitutional rules).[5] The emphasis in this chapter (as also in Chapter 8) is upon classifying Adam Smith and his followers as reformers in the second (constitutional sense) primarily, while arguing that the philosophic radicals of the 19th century, especially those associated with John Stuart Mill, were increasingly disposed to be reformers in the first sense, that is in 'doing something' by way of urging legislation on day-to-day affairs within the existing rules of the constitution.

The key personages in the changeover from the Smithian type of classical economy to that of John Stuart Mill, were his father James Mill and Jeremy Bentham. The case of Bentham is somewhat complex. In many ways he and his disciples engineered reforms of the basic constitution, and so there were strong Smithian leanings in this respect. Indeed, Bentham could be said to have been more influential than Smith in leading to profound reforms of the legal framework. These included fundamental law reform in various branches; reform in colonial governments; legalization of trade unions; free speech and free press; a civil service appointed and promoted on merit; general registration of titles to property; and reform of local government. Indeed in one instance, the case of usury laws, Bentham not only corrected Smith in terms of the internal economic logic of *The Wealth of Nations*, but was actually influential in the repeal of the legislation.

The parliamentary economists surveyed by Fetter, moreover, were also, on the whole, reformers of the basic rules of society. The following issues, upon which they pronounced, could certainly be classified as 'constitutional' in Buchanan's sense: the relation between Church and State, civil rights and religious disabilities, the abolition of the slave trade, the criminal law, the problems of Ireland, the Corn Laws, the Combination Acts, the Factory Acts, the Navigation Acts and issues of taxation.

But with Bentham came another strand of thought, and one that was quite unSmithian. This was the Benthamite science of ethics, an ethics that should be followed by moral leaders and could not be accepted by the ordinary man. In Bentham's word, this science could appeal 'only to lofty minds with whom the public welfare has become a passion'.[6] Although Bentham presented three grounds for a general rule against government activity: 1 Individuals know their own interests better than government can; 2 They are more skillful in the pursuit of their own interests than government; 3 Intervention means coercion and therefore 'pain' and is therefore an evil; nevertheless he argued that 'indiscriminate generalizations' were an error. Indeed he presented an elaborate taxonomy of cases where the government should not ('non-agenda'), and those under which it should ('agenda') intervene. He approved, for instance, of government aid in the construction of canals, railways, public hospitals and workhouses. He also advocated public health activities on a large scale.

It was the view of Elie Halevy that Bentham's work contains a central contradiction because it relies upon government to create an *artificial* harmony of individual and public interest and this conflicts with the spontaneous harmony of interests implied by his *laissez-faire* conclusions.[7] Viner, however, argued strongly against Halevy's opinion. It was unfounded, he insisted, mainly because there was no trace in Bentham's writings of a doctrine of natural harmony.[8] And this was understandable, according to Viner, because the idea of the continuous intervention of a beneficent Author of Nature would have been in basic conflict with Bentham's juristic theories and cosmological outlook.

One implication of this verdict, however, is that Bentham did not fully appreciate the basic Smithian insight which was that of the invisible hand in the *metaphorical* sense and not in the sense of supra-natural or divine intervention. The concept was an attempt to explain, in positive terms, a system of decentralized decision-making linked together by the constant 'feedback' of market prices. The mechanism, moreover, was seen by Smith, not primarily as a means of achieving a static 'optimum' distribution of resources, but rather as a dynamic means of widening markets, developing the division of labour, and promoting growth. The spontaneous linking of free men throughout the world via decentralized market processes and prices, created results that individuals as such could never fully comprehend. If Bentham and his followers did *not* fully grasp the extent of this insight, then the argument that there was a serious division between the classical economists seems well founded.

Robbins's response to Halevy's criticism was that in fact there is no dualism in the work of the classical economists; that is there is no distinction between legal regulation and the workings of the market. Robbins emphasized that a necessary condition for the Smithian market system to work was a legal framework that guaranteed respect for contracts and property.[9] This condition certainly describes Adam Smith's position. We return to the question, however, whether many of the second generation of economists did not go further than making proposals that concern the constitutional legal fabric which sets the basic rules for the economic game, a game whose outcome has to be determined by the participants. It is strongly arguable, as we shall see, that Bentham, or at least his ardent followers, wanted to go further and influence not only the characters of the players, but also the end results of the game.

At the same time it is possible to argue that Bentham recognized circumstances where the invisible hand fails for technical reasons. But, today, evidence of such failure is not a sufficient argument for government intervention since economists also recognize failures in politics. It is necessary, in other words, also to identify and to compare circumstances of *government* failure.

It is interesting that towards the end of his trenchant technical criticism of the invisible hand as a philosophy for today, Hahn concedes that his verdict does not warrant the conclusion 'that there is some social device which will perform more satisfactorily or that we should cut off the hand altogether'.[10] He admits that it remains to be demonstrated 'that "Government failure" is less damaging than market failure'. Consequently, while there may be a prima facie ground for intervention when the invisible hand 'trembles', and no such ground when it does not, 'there is some arguing and thinking to be done before a case for intervention has been clinched'.[11] But since Hahn fails to follow up with the 'arguing and thinking' that he deems so necessary, he is left in an agnostic position. And because, moreover, Adam Smith at least made the attempt, the *scope* of his overall reasoning was at least more comprehensive than is that of today's typical economic technician.

Compared with Smith, Bentham was somewhat naïve in his faith in real world democratic government to act as a superior corrective instrument. Buchanan argues, indeed, that the relative neglect of the discipline of 'public choice' in the UK is partly traceable to a Benthamite utilitarianism 'which provided idealized objectives for governmental policy to the neglect of institutional structure'.[12] The British, Buchanan continues, 'held on longer than most people to the romantic notion that government seeks only to do good in some hazily defined Benthamite sense, and, furthermore, to the hypothesis that government could, in fact, accomplish most of what it set out to do'.[13]

There can be no doubt that the growing pressure and popular support for democracy in the 19th century coloured the extent to which political economists viewed state intervention. As new population cohorts were granted the franchise, so came the political temptation to use policies for special interest groups. For this reason continued insistence upon the old minimal government prescription of Adam Smith became less popular with policy makers and political entrepreneurs.

James Mill's Theory of Public Choice

Curiously enough, it was Bentham's associate James Mill who *began* (albeit crudely) to develop an economic theory of public choice in the modern manner of viewing 'political markets' in parallel to conventional markets. Mill's contribution appeared in the 'Essay on Government' first published in 1820 in the *Encyclopaedia Britannica*, and, as Ernest Barker has said, it was 'the classic statement of the political theory of the Benthamites'. It will be helpful to examine closely this early study of 'the economics of politics that failed' because it provides an important explanation of subsequent departures from *laissez-faire*.

Mill proceeded to deduce a theory of government from the nature of man, and that nature, he argued, was self-interest. Because of this characteristic, members of aristocracies and monarchies would use political power at a cost to other men in society. Mill concluded that 'the community itself must check those individuals, else they will follow their interest and produce bad government'.[14] The great difficulty, he acknowledged, consisted in finding the means of constituting a checking body, the power of which would not be turned against the community for whose protection it was created. The question was, therefore, how the interests of the representatives were to be identified with those of the community.

Mill wanted to extend the franchise to below the middle classes but was willing to confine it to males over forty. 'The great principle of security here is that men of forty have a deep interest in the welfare of the younger men ... the great majority of old men have sons, whose interests they regard as an essential part of their own.'[15] Similarly, Mill was content to let the interests of women be cared for by the male votes. The most important check that he claimed to have invented was that of reduced duration of government, that is frequent elections. The reason was: 'The smaller the period of time during which any man retains his capacity of representative, as compared with the time in which he is simply a member of the community, the more difficult it will be to compensate the sacrifice of the interests of the longer period by the profits of misgovernment during the shorter'.[16]

At the end of his essay, Mill attempted to assuage those who feared that the extension of the franchise would result in excessive and coercive redistribution from the rich to the poor. He argued that the people would act, after all, according to the directions of the middle class, members of whom they had always resorted to for advice.

In his famous rebuttal of Mill's essay, T.B. Macaulay, writing in the March 1829 issue of the *Edinburgh Review*, ridiculed it primarily for its reliance on the a priori method. In particular, he attacked mercilessly Mill's assumption that legislators regularly and predictably pursue their selfish interests. In terms of the modern economic debate on methodology Macaulay's critique concentrated therefore on 'the realism of assumptions'. One well-known modern reply to this, of course, is that the only relevant test of the *validity* of hypothesis is not the realism of assumptions but the comparison of its predictions with the evidence. It must be acknowledged, however, that this Friedman-type methodology itself is not without its own problems.[17]

Friedman would have demanded from James Mill sustained and systematic empirical data to see if it refuted his hypothesis. Macaulay himself insisted on only one half of the Friedman requirement, that is he called for the evidence alone, without any reference to a model or hypothesis (which was in any case dismissed as a priori reasoning). The result was a call for crude inductionism. In Macaulay's words: 'The very circumstances which he [Mill] mentions, irresistably prove that the a priori method is altogether unfit for investigations of this kind, and that *the only way to arrive at the truth is by induction*'.[18] James Mill certainly presented only the slightest anecdotal material as evidence. But Macaulay himself failed to deliver facts that were systematically arranged with reference to an hypothesis. Interestingly, Adam Smith, who also surveyed the various political organizations in search of the most effective, supported his theories with an ordered series of rich references to historical sources, although, as Blaug observes, Smith's methodology was more often that of verifiability than falsifiability.[19]

Ironically, 20th-century empirical research by the modern school of 'public choice' is now supplying a constant stream of work that supports one part of James Mill's thesis.[20] This developing analysis and evidence is consistent with Mill's assumption that individual participants in the political process *are* motivated primarily by their self-interest, the assumption that was most attacked by Macaulay.

But Mill had an additional 'countervailing power' theory. Government, he argued, would be efficient and protective of the public interest so long as members of the middle and lower classes were truly represented. His argument was that if the governing class was a minority, there would be rich spoils to be divided among a small number. If the governing body comprised the majority representatives, the spoils per member of the majority would be less and even these 'benefits of misrule' may be counterbalanced by the benefits of good government to all classes, including the minority.

Unlike Smith, Mill seems to have overlooked that élites can still emerge in the form of 'majorities within majorities'. As well, the modern 'economics of democracy' argues that the benefits of political activity are concentrated among supply interest groups whereas the costs (e.g., of taxes to provide subsidies to such groups) are diffused over a wide number of voters whose incentive to resist is thereby quite low.[21] This Smithian perspective incidentally is pertinent to the economist Wittman's conclusion (1989) that democracy produces efficient results even when it is concerned mainly with transfers to special interests. Wittman seems to have ignored the fact that since these interests are given the right to determine the disposition of wealth created by others, property rights are correspondingly attenuated. Smith's efficiency-generating invisible hand via market exchange, however, depends crucially upon property rights that are well-defined and unattenuated.

To Adam Smith, as we have seen, the use of simple majority voting was more conducive to monopoly than to anything else; it was in fact one of the keys to statutory protectionism. To him the vote was a property right that could violate other more legitimate property rights. The evidence for this view is Smith's reference to statutory regulations that enabled members of the same trade to tax themselves to provide sickness and welfare funds. By giving them a common interest to manage, Smith observed, the regulation 'renders such assemblies necessary'. After that, a simple majority vote is given statutory respect and this, in turn, is followed by a severe setback to the Smithian system since 'the majority of a corporation can enact a by-law with proper penalties, which will limit the competition more effectually and more durably than any voluntary combination whatever.'[22] Another Smithian example of perverse results from majority voting is to be found in the Glasgow Lectures.[23]

The failure to recognize what Smith had grasped so clearly, and the subsequent influence of James Mill's 'romantic' model of democracy, was probably responsible for much of the impatience with predominant reliance on the free market by later economists. For it encouraged the simple belief that *laissez-faire* was only to be resorted to when politics was inefficient, i.e., when Mill's democratic machinery was absent. Meanwhile, the actual constitutional reform via an extended franchise in the direction of Mill's model, as happened in 1832, probably did much to add momentum to the wave of optimistic confidence in politics, at least among the philosophic radicals.

Writers in the Smithian Camp

Despite the fact that Malthus and Ricardo made significant modifications to Smith's theoretical system, the bias of both writers remained strongly in the *laissez-faire* tradition. Questioning the ability of the free market system to maintain aggregate employment (Say's Law), Malthus certainly conceded a larger role for government in *this* respect. Nevertheless, the conclusions from his theory of population were explicitly *laissez-faire*. He argued, for instance, for the termination of parish relief for anyone born after a certain date to be specified by Parliament. And his views on population resulted in much pressure, a pressure that culminated in the Poor Law Reform Bill of 1834. We shall see, however, that this Bill did not incorporate Malthus's desire for a gradual termination of relief, only a reorganizing of its administration along Benthamite lines.

With respect to Ricardo, Ellen Paul believes that despite his substantial theoretical disagreements with Smith's economic principles, 'he did not draw conclusions from these changes which would enhance the role of government in the economy'.[24] Ricardo's pure theory of rent and its suggestion of antagonistic class interests, and ultimately a stationary state with landlords enjoying the highest relative incomes, did not lead Ricardo to demand more government intervention. Ricardo's strongest agitation was directed at the repeal of the Corn Laws with the aim of establishing free trade. It was ultimately the later Fabian socialists and the followers of Henry George who drew the conclusions from Ricardo's rent doctrine that land should be nationalized and that the payment of rent should be made to the government.

Despite Ricardo's warning of an eventual stationary state, Hollander (1979) has emphasized that the practical Ricardo was, in fact, more of an optimist. He argued that in the progress of society there were two opposite causes operating on the value of corn. The first was the increase of population which ultimately raised costs. The second stemmed from what Ricardo called 'improvements in agriculture, or the discovery of new and abundant foreign markets, which always tend to lower the value. Sometimes one predominates, sometimes the other, and the value of corn rises and falls accordingly.'[25] In this respect, Ricardo is nearer to the optimism of Adam Smith, for whom the stationary state was a far distant problem. In Smith's reasoning, also, technological improvements were endogenous to his system. They automatically accompanied capital accumulation and the growing divisions of labour that featured the developing market system. In Smith too there is a key assumption concerning population: population increases with a lag as the quantity of capital increases and thus in such a dynamic economy the pressure on wages is always upwards and the Malthusian spectre is absent. But the accumulation of capital and the growing divisions of labour that would keep the wolf at bay, depended on non-interference, or minimal government.

Ricardo is often accused of having been overly preoccupied with maximum output. Yet Hollander insists that, as with Adam Smith, distribution was of the very first importance. Both writers were interested in high and rising per capita income. Working-class living standards were specified in the statement of end. But again the primary instrument that both relied upon was, as Hollander observes, that of the market. Ricardo, in other words, shared Smith's belief that rising working-class standards would best result from a competitive process working within an appropriate institutional and legal framework.

In Parliament, Ricardo emphasized Smith's dictum that 'consumption is the sole and purpose of all production' and he also agreed with Smith that any reform to remove traditional protection should be introduced gradually. On the subject of the security of property, Hollander has demonstrated too that it is difficult to exaggerate the Smith-like emphasis in Ricardo's work. Also stressed is the fact that Ricardo received with scepticism many of the arguments pressed on him by the Benthamites who believed that society could be better directed by utilitarian 'scientific legislators'. And Ricardo, like Malthus, wanted the ultimate *abolition* of the Poor Law rather than its better administration. The latter was desired by the utilitarians and under the leadership of Chadwick it found expression in the New Poor Law of 1834.

As a final candidate for membership of the Smithian camp, J.R. McCulloch has strong qualifications. McCulloch opposed the new Poor Law but argued for a continuation of the old Poor Law with some modifications. He was, however, strongly opposed to the philosophic radicals and showed general affinity with Adam Smith even though he allowed for a somewhat larger role for the state. He was opposed to public works in the sense of government *production* of services (which was generally not Smith's sense of public works). 'The State would not find profitable investment opportunities which private industry had not.'[26]

The Revolutionaries: Nassau Senior and John Stuart Mill

With the passage of the Reform Act of 1832, and the ascendency of the Whig Party, there was an increasing temptation for politicians to pass legislation supportive of the new special interest groups. It was in such an environment that the classical writers Nassau Senior and John Stuart Mill became sensitive to the attacks on the validity of Smithian economics. Ellen Paul argues, 'they themselves were instrumental in re-evaluation and ultimately banishing the previous connection between political economy and the system of laissez-faire. Thus the received doctrine suffered considerable assault both from its avowed enemies and its putative supporters.'[27]

Marion Bowley also maintains that the attitude of Senior and J.S. Mill marked an important breach with the preceding generation:

> It is one thing to maintain, as a principle, that the duty of Government is to keep out except in special cases, however literally that phrase is interpreted. It is quite another to assert the right, duty and possibility of intervention for the common good, and that the only limit to the duty of Government is its power, without any first principal limiting that power. This is what Senior and effectually J.S. Mill were asserting in 1847.[28]

According to his book *An Outline of the Political Economy*, published in 1836, Senior argued that economics should consist solely of the positive analysis of wealth and should be silent on normative matters. Thus the economist must never offer his opinion on the effect of the economy on happiness, morals, or income distribution. Be this as it may, it is ironic that, subsequently, Senior himself has been remembered less for his contribution to economic theory (which were several) than for his efforts on the boards of various government commissions starting with the Poor Law Enquiry Commission of 1832. It was Senior who (with the help of Chadwick) was the architect of the Bill that reformed the Poor Law in 1834. The other commissions for which he is most remembered are the Royal Commission on the Distress of the Hand-Loom Weavers of 1841, and the Royal Commission on Popular Education in 1858 (The Newcastle Commission). In the contributions that Senior made to these bodies, he seems not to have been restricted by his recommendations of the astringently 'pure' duty of the political economist as laid down in his *Outline*.

Paul has argued, nevertheless, that Senior 'deployed principles drawn from the science of political economy to lend authority to his arguments in this field of art, an art whose existence he had denied in his treatise'.[29] And according to Marion Bowley, Senior apparently found it just as impossible as other economists to refrain from giving advice, 'but he had never explained the status of such advice, whether it had all the weight of economics behind it or not'.[30]

When professor of economics at Oxford in 1847, Senior wrote down some revealing personal thoughts on the relation of economic analysis to policy. In the first of three lectures on the subject he asserted that the business of government extends beyond the provision of protection and the punishment of internal or external violence or fraud:

> The only rational foundation of government, the only foundation of a right to govern and of a corollative duty to obey, is expediency – the general benefit of the community. It is the duty of a government to do whatever is conducive to the welfare of the governed. The only limit to this duty is its power.[31]

In Bowley's opinion this quotation implied that the sacred and respected rule of non-interference was thrown overboard as a principle. The departure from Smith could not have been more clear.

In the remaining two lectures, under the headings 'The Power of Government to Decrease the Desirability of Wealth' and 'The Power of Government to Mitigate the Hardships of Poverty', Senior elaborated further. Under the first he produced the usual classical exposition of the police functions of government, the preservation of freedoms, and Adam Smith's canons of taxation. This discussion was at the level of the design of constitutions, a level that Chapter 8 argued was the primary dimension in Smith's work. It was the lecture under his second heading, however, that Senior broke new ground by outlining several novel measures of social reform. On the subject of 'bad housing' he provided particularly striking evidence of the new mood.

> No one denies the right in the state to interfere to prevent a man from injuring others. It exercises this right when it forbids him to build a row of undrained cottages. But the right of the state to interfere to prevent a man from injuring himself supposes that the legislator knows better how to manage the affairs of an individual than the man himself does. In the present case this supposition is true.[32]

The new attitude, it seems, was one that encouraged a romantic view of government wherein it was believed that it could abolish scarcity simply by legal fiat. As Bowley observes, the supreme difficulty of providing for the rehousing of the inhabitants at rents they could afford was still unsolved, 'and to a large extent is unsolved to the present day.[33] (One is reminded of several disastrous 20th-century attempts in the US to undertake 'urban renewal'.) Senior himself was fond of emphasizing that it was remarkable that the difficulty of scarce resources is one which legislators often refuse to take into account. This concession, however, suggests another problem with Senior's logic. For if it is admitted that the difficulty of government provision lies in the scarcity of income (resources), it cannot be unambiguously demonstrated that the inhabitors of houses are 'ignorant'. There is, in other words, an identification problem. We cannot really deduce that people are ignorant until their poverty has been removed and choice of action becomes possible for them. The disposition of Adam Smith was to concentrate first on removing poverty. And this would best be done by increasing the wealth of the nation via the invisible hand principle.

But perhaps the most important contrast in the economics of Senior and Smith lies in the difference in empirical emphasis. As we have seen, Smith's approach was overwhelmingly inductive and indeed can be seen sometimes in the light of the 20th-century practice of offering hypotheses that are formally refutable by evidence. According to Anderson and Tollison he even employed evidence available in his own time to test his own hypotheses concerning joint-stock enterprises (see Chapter 5). In contrast, although Senior sat on several official commissions he did not seem to be able to marshall the abundant evidence gathered with the same effectiveness. Indeed he often seemed unimpressed with the idea of gathering data relevant to his economic arguments. The most striking example is his own failure to collect evidence on his firm prediction, as expressed in a letter to Lord Ashley, that 'a Ten Hour Bill would be utterly ruinous'. Senior lived for 17 years after the passage of the act yet failed to undertake an examination of its actual effects.

Despite J.S. Mill's reaction against Benthamism, especially after the attack upon it by Macaulay, he ultimately endeavoured to rebuild the central core of utilitarianism in a way that made it less rigid and more human or aesthetic in its appeal. Bentham's pleasure-pain motivation of individuals had been too narrow, Mill argued, because it had precluded the ability of men to pursue spiritual perfection and to be guided by the ideal of excellence. But Mill's vision of a world in which individuals were more prompted by human fellow-feeling and benevolence than by narrower self-interest caused him to entertain the idea of men living in a social state in which collective interest would predominate. The main requirement was education. And here, once more, as with Senior, we enter the new world of paternalism. Both Mill and Senior, it seems, required the participants of their social economy to receive prior 'conditioning' before ultimate freedom could be allowed. And they believed that the machinery of a state education system offered the most promising avenue.

It may be objected that this is not such a break from Adam Smith because in *The Wealth of Nations* there is also a programme for state education. As pointed out in Chapter 7, however, while Smith's verdict on education is certainly given as an illustration of another potential case for 'public institutions or works' there is ultimately no recommendation of free schooling. Like canals and water supplies, educational institutions could finance themselves from their own revenue. After acknowledging the public benefits of education, Smith proceeded to argue indeed that their existence was not always a reason for government finance. His reticence to recommend subsidies was based on his belief that they were typically non-productive, if not counter-productive.

Although expenditure on institutions for education and religious instruction was no doubt beneficial to the whole society, Smith concluded, and while it may be defrayed by the general contribution of the whole society, it 'might perhaps with *equal propriety, and even with some advantage, be defrayed altogether* by those who receive the immediate benefit of such education and instruction, or by the *voluntary contribution* of those who think they have occasion for either the one or the other'.[34]

More important in the present context, Smith upheld the principle of free choice in education. He disliked both state training of teachers and a system of pedagogic licensure operated by a self-governing teaching profession. People were to be left free to choose since 'they will soon find better teachers for themselves than any whom the state could provide for them'.[35]

The Whig victory of 1832 brought in a period of legislative enthusiasm inspired especially by the utilitarians. J.A. Roebuck introduced an education bill in 1833 that was to start the first of the annual grants to education that have remained to this day. Roebuck's arguments, and also the later utterances of Edwin Chadwick concerning the educational opportunities and responsibilities facing the new Poor Law Commissioners, drew the special praise of J.S. Mill. While the vast legislative reform machinery of the Benthamites was explicitly heralded as promotion of the cause of individual freedom, they intuitively recognized that education was a political prize of the first order.

It was from the experience of the 'scientific administration' of the Poor Law establishments after the Poor Law Reform Act of 1834 that Chadwick, as Secretary to the Poor Law Commission, announced the practical success of Benthamite pedagogic principles. At last the utilitarians had the chance of controlling individuals from birth so as to provide the correct environment that would lead to happiness. During this experimental period, Chadwick was in constant communication with Senior and J.S. Mill, both of whom were duly impressed and gave him much encouragement.

Also appointed to the Poor Law Commission (as an assistant commissioner) was James Kay (later Kay-Shuttleworth). Kay was introduced by Senior to Chadwick and the Mills with whom there was much subsequent intellectual discourse. Chadwick delegated Kay to produce reports on the training of pauper children and these, with Chadwick's clear approval, were published by the government in 1841. Kay's enthusiasm and success with the educational work of the Commission caused him to be appointed the first secretary of the committee of the Privy Council on education in 1839. Kay's committee, in effect the first ministry of education, purchased increasing influence over independent schools by offering subsidies in return for school inspection and regulation. But Kay's greatest ambition was to establish a system of teacher training by the state, an ambition that was eventually realized. Kay obviously differed strongly from Smith's view that people 'will soon find better teachers for themselves, than any whom the state could provide for them'.

As a member of the Royal Commission on Popular Education which reported in 1861, Senior gave Chadwick the task of supplying him with certain evidence. On the basis of such information, much of which seemed anecdotal, he severely opposed the proposal of a fellow commissioner that education was a matter that should be left in the hands of the parents. Experience with other activities showed that they could not be trusted:

> For fifty years they have been managing their own trade unions. There is not one that is not based on folly, tyranny and injustice which would disgrace the rudest savages. They sacrifice their wives', their childrens' and their own health and strength to the lowest sensuality. The higher the wages the worse seems, in general, to be the condition of the families.[36]

Senior's own Commission, however, produced more systematic data. It reported that there were about two and a half million attending school in 1858 and that nearly all children were having some schooling. The figures showed that the growth of voluntary schooling (i.e., schools run by private enterprise and also by churches) over the previous 30 years had been remarkable. Furthermore, the figures easily matched those of European countries where, unlike England and Wales, compulsory state education prevailed.

In the face of this evidence, Senior directed his criticism against the quality rather than the quantity of education. And in this he seems to have been strongly influenced by James Kay-Shuttleworth. His criticism of free parental choice was based on his complaint that 'too many people' were choosing non-inspected schools, the standards of which, according to his advisors, were very inferior. Parents could not be trusted to select the best kind of schools, that is, schools of Benthamite design or preference. Even though the fees were subsidized by the State, too many parents, according to Senior, thought that these schools were vulgar 'or their boy had been punished there, or he is required to be clean, or to be regular, or the private school is half a street nearer, or is kept by a friend, or by someone who will submit his teaching to their dictation'.[37]

Mill versus Smith on Education

In his *Principles of Political Economy* John Stuart Mill confronted the question whether the buyer is always qualified to judge of the commodity and concluded that: 'If not, the presumption in favour of the competition of the market does not apply to this case'.[38] Medicine was an obvious example of this sort of market failure. Even if the patient could be relied upon to purchase some minimum amount at his own expense, and from his own free will, this would not necessarily imply that the patient would select the right medicine without assistance. Similarly with education: 'The uncultivated cannot be competent judges of cultivation'.[39]

It is interesting that, in contrast, Adam Smith had maintained that people were not such children in the choice of their doctors, as the would-be paternalists (usually the less patronized doctors) were fond of believing. 'That doctors are sometimes fools as well as other people, is not, in the present time, one of those profound secrets which is known only to the learned.'[40]

Adam Smith obviously had a far different understanding of institutional realities. Whereas the utilitarians believed that government educational enterprises could do things more efficiently than the market, it was Adam Smith's view that:

> Those parts of education, it is to be observed, for the teaching of which there are no public institutions, are generally the best taught ... the three most essential parts of literary education, to read, write and account, it still continues to be more common to acquire in private than in public schools; and it very seldom happens that anybody fails of acquiring them to the degree in which it is necessary to acquire them.[41]

It should be mentioned, however, that by 'public institutions' Adam Smith meant generally those establishments that received subsidies so that their employees were not fully dependent on their incomes from their customers. Such establishments included the endowed private schools, that is schools receiving private subsidies from bequests. There is no reason to believe, however, that Smith would have different views about institutions receiving subsidies from government.

Mill's opinion was in striking contrast:

> Now any well-intentioned and tolerably civilized government may think, without presumption, that it does or ought to possess a degree of cultiva-

tion above the average of the community which it rules, and that it
should therefore be capable of offering better education and better
instruction to the people, than the great number of them would spontaneously demand. Education, therefore, is one of those things which it is
admissable in principle that a government should provide for the people.[42]

It should be noticed that the words 'well-intentioned and tolerably
civilized' to describe government is illustrative of the increasing faith
in the reformed democracy that Mill hoped was arriving by the mid-
19th century.

In the report on the hand-loom weavers in 1841, which was largely
written by Nassau Senior, it was observed that 'if the State be bound
to require the parent to educate his child it is bound to see that he
has the means to do so'. In his *Principles* published seven years later,
John Stuart Mill similarly argued:

> It is therefore an allowable exercise of the powers of government to
> impose on parents the legal obligation of giving elementary instruction
> to children. This, however, cannot fairly be done, without taking mea-
> sures to insure that such instruction shall always be accessible to them
> either gratuitously or at a trifling expense.[43]

Despite the evidence, Mill believed that 'the end not being desired,
the means will not be provided at all'; that is he seems to have
believed that the majority of people were not already educating their
children at schools. But apart from the fact that he was factually
wrong in this supposition,[44] there remains the same error of reasoning that occurs in Senior's argument. It is unsatisfactory to contend
that parents are somehow irresponsible because the evidence shows
them to be underpurchasing education and, at the same time, to
argue they cannot afford it anyway.

Laissez-Faire and the Distribution of Income

Perhaps the most significant innovation in political economy that
appeared in Mill's *Principles* was his separation of production from
distribution (Part I of his book is devoted to Production and Part II
to Distribution). According to Ellen Paul this was a complete change
from the perspective of Adam Smith to whom all production had as
its purpose the satisfaction of human needs: consumption was the

sole end of production. 'By treating production as a primary, almost a given, Mill was able later in his discussion of distribution to treat the products of industrial society as almost pre-existing entities, there to be distributed by those in authority.'[45] The result of this was to 'sever the connection between the laws of economics and the political prescriptions associated with the laissez-faire doctrine'.[46]

Mill tells us in his *Autobiography* that he believed that the production distribution distinction was the original element in his *Principles*. The laws of production, he argued therein, have the properties of natural laws and the laws of distribution are subject to human invention and institutions. And if the laws of distribution are man-made then existing property relations can be interfered with on the principle of equity. It was in this way that Mill introduced the search for practical means of redistribution as a crucial part of the political economist's task. Another justification, in Mill's view, for departing from *laissez-faire* was thus introduced. The practical problem, in his words, was to determine which 'institutions of property would be established by an unprejudiced legislature, absolutely impartial between the possessors of property and the nonpossessors'.[47] Our discussion of public choice (Chapter 8) and rent seeking (Chapter 9), in contrast, throws serious doubt on Mill's confidence in finding a legislature that is 'unprejudiced' and 'absolutely impartial' concerning the distribution of property.

Closely connected with issues of redistribution were Mill's arguments on trade unions. He conceded that union activity would in all probability produce a fall of wages or loss of employment to non-unionized labourers.

> For ... there is no keeping up wages without limiting the numbers of competitors for employment. And all such limitations inflict distinct evil upon those whom it excludes – upon that great mass of labouring population which is outside the Unions; an evil not trifling, for if the system were rigorously enforced it would prevent unskilled labourers or their children from ever rising to the condition of the skilled.[48]

But despite this 'evil' Mill championed the unions because he believed they represented the more responsible sections of the population, sections of individuals who were more foresighted and less likely to have large families. Whether this kind of redistribution is acceptable on any principle of equity is surely doubtful. But the fact that Mill was reconciled to imposing a serious institutional restriction on many members of the poorer classes, a restriction imposed by unions on their ability to sell their labour, is again in striking contrast to Adam Smith who denounced such a barrier as 'a plain violation of the most sacred property'.[49]

The Grounds and Limits of *Laissez-faire* in 1848

In the final book of the *Principles*, first published in 1848, Mill argued the inadequacy of the *laissez-faire* school which limited the province of government to the protection of person and property against force and fraud. It is difficult to know, however, which member or members of the 'school' he had in mind. We have argued above that Smith was engaged in the search for the 'rules of the game' that would be most conducive to an increase in wealth of the nation to the benefit of all ranks of society. This fairly wide political scope that Smith gave himself, nevertheless, had little room for government itself *participating in business*.

Mill broke away from this tradition. First he distinguished undesirable or *authoritative* interference which referred to intervention that controlled the free agency of individuals. The other kind of intervention he described as *non-authoritative*. An example of it would be intervention that, while leaving individuals free to use their own means of pursuing any object of general interest, 'the government, not meddling with them, but not trusting the object solely to their care, establishes, side by side with their arrangement, an agency of its own for a like purpose'.[50] Under this rubric Mill argued the legitimacy of government participating in their business *as a general principle*, but in a way that he believed avoided any degree of 'meddling'. He offered the following illustrations: 'There might be a national bank, or a government manufactory, without any monopoly against private banks and manufactories. There might be a post-office, without penalties against the conveyance of letters by other means ... There may be public hospitals, without any restriction upon private medical or surgical practice'.[51] With respect to education Mill argued: 'Though a government, therefore, may, and in many cases ought to, establish schools and colleges, it must neither compel nor bribe any person to come to them'.[52]

He advocated that a public (government) school should exist: 'as one among many competing experiments, carried on for the purpose of example and stimulus, to keep the others up to a certain standard of excellence'.[53] What is interesting here is Mill's a priori confidence that the government schools would always be the superior pace-makers.

With benefit of hindsight, such propositions today, seem naïve. Experience has shown that when a government enters a particular profession or industry there are automatic and apparently unavoidable restrictions placed on the private competitors. For one thing the public enterprise has the extra advantage of having the reliance on government tax revenue and access to loans that rest on the public credit. The individuals connected with the public supply, moreover, often become a political constituency in their own right and are able to press successfully for further degrees of protection. A post office that exists 'without penalties against the conveyance of letters by other means' does not conform to reality. The penalties are both economic, for the reasons of special financial advantage just mentioned, and political, since usually post offices have also secured *legal* sanctions against mail delivery by third parties.

Adam Smith's vision was of quite a different nature to Mill's in these respects. Smith argued, for instance, that unsubsidized private schools were in an unfortunate minority because the salaries of the public school teachers:

> put the private teachers who would pretend to come into competition with them, in the same state with the merchant, who attempts to trade without a bounty in competition with those who trade with a considerable one.[54]

Smith, it seems, had grasped the phenomenon of what modern economic literature calls the 'crowding out' of the private by the public institutions and was anxious to avoid its dangers at all costs.

The above interpretation of J.S. Mill may appear somewhat severe to some readers. This is probably because he always gives the impression of making a careful examination of two sides of any question. For those who do not follow him carefully and thoroughly to the end of his argument there is some difficulty in seeing the side of it on which he comes down. His Chapter XI 'Of the grounds and limits of the laissez-faire or non-interference principal' is a case in question. He sets out the pros and cons in a way that will appeal to most reasonable men. For the 19th-century 'orthodox economist', for instance, Mill was very reassuring when he readily acknowledged that the non-interference principal, that is, *laissez-faire*, should be the general principle, departures from which must be justified by the claim of overriding expediency.

The 'orthodox economist' might well have been tempted to put down the book with satisfaction at this point. This is the more so because Mill, himself, goes through a process of recognizing many of the disadvantages of public participation in industry. Every increase in the government's functions, he argues, necessarily increases its power, and that trend is to be guarded against with every vigilance. Again he concedes that things tend to be done worse by government than by private agencies. And he returns to the conclusion that: 'Laissez-faire, in short, should be the general practice: every departure from it, *unless required by some great good*, is a certain evil'.[55]

One can sympathize, however, with writers such as Ellen Paul who regards the words in italics in the previous quotation as the operative ones. For here was the *implicit* advocacy of the utilitarian standard. Paul concludes that:

> In the final analysis, Mill really has one standard, expediency, not two as would appear from the way in which his argument unfolded. By the end of his argument, the expediency standard reigned supreme, and the laissez-faire principle is almost completely discarded. Mill declared, finally, that the government can do anything important to the general interest.[56]

According to John Gray (1979) the recent revisionist wave of Mill scholarship has shown him to be 'far more complex and subtle, far more acutely aware of obvious counter-arguments, than exponents of the traditional view habitually allow'.[57] This conclusion can be granted here without detriment to our present opinion that, on the subject of *laissez-faire* Mill did make a strong final judgement. The fact is that ultimately he was strongly distrustful of Smith's invisible hand. Each individual by pursuing his own interest would *not necessarily* be led by the invisible hand to take the course that would be most beneficial to society. For Mill questioned, time and again, whether the individual could be the best judge of his own interests, especially if he belonged to the poorer classes.

Our main account is almost at an end. It could be continued by examining Mill's disciples, J.E. Cairnes and Henry Sidgwick, but space does not permit a full treatment. Suffice it to say that in Cairnes the misunderstanding of Smith's invisible hand seems to be complete. Cairnes interpreted the principle to mean that people not only follow their own interest but that interest is coincident with that of other people, an assumption that he vigorously denied. Yet it was no part of the concept of Smith's invisible hand that men necessarily pursue mutually similar interests. Men can have different interests and yet mutually beneficient results will occur. Adam Smith's clearest expression of this view is to be found in Part II, Section II, of *The Moral Sentiments*:

> Society may subsist among *different* men as among different merchants, from a sense of its utility, without any mutual love or affection; and though no man in it should owe any obligation, or be bound in gratitude to any other, it may still be upheld by a mercenary exchange of good offices according to agreed evaluation.[58]

By the time we get to Sidgwick we have the Millian views expressed more openly as utilitarian. Each government intervention was to be judged on the utility standard and according to whether it furthered or obstructed general happiness or 'social utility'. And Sidgwick took J.S. Mill's approach towards small-scale government participation such a step further that we appear to be on the threshold of Fabian socialism. (Although, as Gray observes, there was quite a distinction between Mill's position and that of the Fabians.)[59] Sidgwick believed in a gradual expansion of the government's role in the economy and the nationalization of industries in which competition had become markedly imperfect. Mill's argument that protection can, in some cases, benefit the protecting nation was also pushed further in that it was argued to be of potential benefit also to the whole world. At this point, of course, we have come a complete circle away from the system of Smithian free trade and back once more towards a kind of mercantilism, neo-mercantilism in fact.

Laissez-faire and Natural Law

It will be helpful now to examine another dimension of the debate, the argument that the erosion of natural law was the central explanation of the decline of *laissez-faire*. In attempting to answer the question why 19th-century orthodox political economists greatly relaxed the limitations on government that their founder, Adam Smith, had laid down, Ellen Paul (1979) emphasizes the revolution in moral principles. Smith's moral outlook, she argues, was based on a natural law philosophy and his suspicion of government was 'natural rights inspired'. Utilitarianism, which succeeded him, shared *initially* (under Bentham) his presumption that the individual is the best judge of his own interests. Yet it was grounded on the very different moral principle of pleasure maximization.

It was only a matter of time before the utility principle undercut the general rule of non-interference. The eventual desire of the utilitarians was to instruct the legislature in any demonstrated instance where the greatest happiness was not being furthered by individualistic means. But all this was a change in morals and political philosophy. When intervention was eventually justified (under J.S. Mill) on the utilitarian principle of 'expediency', all vestiges of a philosophy of natural rights were removed.

But this conclusion that it was a sequential shift from natural rights to utilitarianism that explains the reaction action against *laissez-faire*, is open to some debate. It is interesting especially to compare Hayek's views in his essay 'Individualism: True and False' (1948) with those of Paul. Consider, for instance, her contrast of Bentham's utilitarian position, comprising its potential for intervention, with the writings of both Smith *and* the physiocrats. The latter pair are grouped together by Paul on the ground that both had natural law underpinning their doctrines. Hayek, in contrast, stresses that the physiocrats espoused an individualism that is based on Cartesian rationalism with its emphasis on human design (planning). Smithian individualism is different in that man is only partly guided by reason and in any case an individual's reasoning frequently is limited and imperfect. Instead of Paul's *sequence* from Smith to utilitarianism, the conflict of two different philosophies, one favouring social planning and the other opposing it, was there right from the 18th century.[60]

J.S. Mill, Senior, Cairnes, Jevons, Sidgwick and Wicksteed and company may therefore, on Hayek's reasoning, trace some ancestry to the French thinkers. A partial explanation for their departure from Smith's individualism may be that their understanding of it was too superficial. In addition, they may well have allowed themselves to be influenced by the growing 19th-century popular caricature of *laissez-faire* that sketched it as a world of egotistical and isolated money-making individuals, a description to which Marx was especially prone. Yet Smith's individualism, Hayek insists, was primarily intended as a *theory of society*, a theory that tries to understand the forces that shape the social life of man. The spontaneous collaboration of free men creates things that are greater than their individual minds can ever fully comprehend. It was in this way that Smith's invisible hand mechanism had deeper scope and intentions.

The more we read Paul's book the more we realize a striking failure of the later 19th-century economists to have understood or matched the comprehensiveness with which Smith developed his theory of interaction of individuals. For he pursued the theme to the innermost portals of governments. Governments, like markets, were collections of self-interested men.[61] How naïve, in contrast, do we find such authors as J.S. Mill and Jevons who look to the legislator who is prompted purely by the public interest. And how unsatisfactory seems Wicksteed's criticism of Smith's system for its neglect of distribution and justice. The redistribution through government that Smith reported to be taking place in his time was, in his view, usually to the detriment of the poor. And today he would be impressed that the largest part of redistribution that takes place through government auspices (after much wasteful political 'rent seeking') is a redistribution from and to the middle class or to those subgroups within it who are most organized politically.[62] In addition, the author of *The Wealth of Nations* detected a considerable redistribution from the ruled to the rulers. The important point is that Smith, unlike his successors, had a rudimentary understanding of political as well as conventional markets and one that was much more penetrating and consistent than that, for instance, of James Mill.

Ellen Paul's book might well have developed these points had she not restricted herself so tightly to the British writers. Many continental scholars at the turn of the 19th century were returning to the non-romantic notions of government. The Swedish economist Knut Wicksell's warning in 1896 that economic policy is made by self-interested politicians who are participating in a legislative process might especially have reminded some of them of Smith's counsel.[63] So while the change among British economists might be partially accounted for by a change in moral perspective, there is much also to be said for the view that the main explanation was a growing asymmetry in the application of the analytical tools of economics.

Conclusion: The Two Invisible Hands

The concept of '*laissez-faire*' has never been very precise, and controversy over the interpretation of different classical economists in terms of it can quickly become frustrating if not semantic. Nevertheless, it is surely the case that some kind of revolution in thinking occurred in 1776 with the publication of *The Wealth of Nations*. And it is reasonable to argue that the same revolution was effected by the supersession of mercantilist reasoning by the paradigm of the invisible hand. Smith argued that the decentralized price system was more efficient at increasing the wealth of nations than were the legions of government regulations that featured the mercantilist state.

Yet, 20th-century literature on the history of thought is divided. On the one hand, scholars such as Viner, O'Brien and Robbins place all the economists from Smith to J.S. Mill into one common group wherein differences occur only in a small degree. On the other hand, writers such as Bowley, Hayek, Hollander, West and Paul, detect a fundamental schism between the Smithian 'camp' (which included Malthus, Ricardo, and McCulloch) and the Senior/Mill group (with followers that included especially Cairnes and Sidgwick). As we have seen, one suggested reason for the schism is the 19th-century change in ethics, notably the replacement of natural law with the principle of utility. A second reason that we have offered, is that there developed a special belief in democracy (of the James Mill variety) and a new confidence in the ability to find dispassionate and ultra-intelligent legislators.

O'Brien (1978) argues that the vigour with which mercantilism was attacked produced the mistaken impression that the classical economists were totally opposed to state activity. What they *were* opposed to mainly 'was the use of government power in the interests of a small minority to create for themselves privileged conditions'. But, in fact, the modern economics of democracy (Downs, 1957) shows that simple majority voting systems that James Mill prescribed, result *predictably* in a series of small minorities (special interest groups) creating for themselves 'privileged conditions'.

Adam Smith's invisible hand appears to have been increasingly misunderstood as the 19th century progressed. Most important of all, Senior, James and John Stuart Mill, and their followers never seemed to realize that Adam Smith had in effect recognized *two* invisible hands. In the first an individual *in the conventional market*, who 'intends only his own gain', is led by an invisible hand to promote an end that was no part of his intention. 'Nor is it always the worse for society that it was no part of it. By pursuing his own interest he frequently promotes that of the society more effectually than when he really intends to promote it.'

To understand the second invisible hand, consider again the example of the woollen manufacturers discussed in Chapter 8. Their propaganda about the benefits to England from prohibiting wool exports convinced well-meaning statesmen to undertake the restrictive legislation. The consequence was a benefit to the private interest of the manufacturers but an injury to all consumers as well as to wool suppliers. Incentives to produce the propaganda were embedded in the political process. The benefits to the lobbyists were concentrated among them since they obtained their livelihood from the economic activity that stood to gain. The costs of lobbying, meanwhile, were relatively low because the manufacturers were clustered in towns while the raw wool suppliers were dispersed. Smith's second invisible hand therefore operated in the opposite direction from his first. It can be summarized in parallel terms: an individual who intends only to serve the public interest by fostering government intervention is led by an invisible hand to promote private interests which was no part of his intention.[64]

A commonly alleged technical defect in the applicability of the first kind of invisible hand theorem today (see Hahn, 1982), is that it is at risk the moment monopoly power appears. Smith seems to have believed that all the serious forms of monopoly depended for their survival on legislation by the very government that critics of '*laissez-faire*' usually rely upon to correct things. But these monopolies were the result of organized 'rent seeking', a phenomenon that would increase progressively via the second 'invisible hand'.

As has been argued in Chapters 8 and 9, Smith foreshadowed much of the new brand of economics called public choice in recognizing that the political organization of any given industry results in concentrated and differentiated legislative benefits. The costs of political organization, however, vary according to the accidents of geography and other circumstances. Country gentlemen and farmers dispersed in different parts of the country, 'cannot so easily combine as merchants and manufacturers ... They accordingly seem to have been the original inventors of those restraints upon the importation of foreign goods, which secure to them the monopoly of the home market.'[65]

Nowhere in James Mill's essay on government is there any such degree of political perspicacity. Similarly, recognition of the 'rent-seeking' phenomenon in politics is absent from the writings of J.S. Mill and Senior. The case for constitutionally protected *laissez-faire*, it seems, is much more cogent when the *two* invisible hands are recognized. And it was the decline of the recognition of the second (rent-seeking) invisible hand that surely accounted, more than anything else, for the increasing 19th-century classical departures from Smith's prescription of minimal government.

Notes

1. Hahn (1982).
2. Viner (1949), see also Coats (1971), p. 144.
3. O'Brien (1978), pp. 273–4.
4. Viner (1928).
5. Buchanan (1982).
6. Quoted in Viner (1949).
7. Halevy (1928).
8. Viner (1949), p. 369.
9. Robbins (1952), pp. 190–2.
10. Hahn (1982), p. 9.
11. Ibid., p. 9.
12. Buchanan (1978), p. 3.
13. Ibid., p. 4.
14. Mill (1955), p. 67.
15. Ibid., p. 75.
16. Ibid., p. 70.
17. See Milton Friedman (1953), 'Essay on the Methodology of Positive Economics', and Mark Blaug (1980), p. 104.
18. Macaulay (1829), p. 101, emphasis added.
19. Blaug (1980), p. 13.
20. See, for example, McCormick and Tollison (1980), Stigler (1971) and Mueller (1989).
21. Downs (1957). Mill failed to consider another safeguard to democracy, the one that was to be developed later in the century by Wicksell, namely the requirement of voting rules that demand more than a 50 per cent majority, and indeed in some cases even approach 100 per cent (unanimity). It is for all these reasons that it is probably fair to describe Mill's attempt as 'the economics of politics that failed'. And it failed not for the reasons Macaulay presented.
22. Smith (1976), p. 145.
23. Hutchison (1966), p. 7.
24. Paul (1979), p. 103.
25. Quoted in Hollander (1979), p. 628.

26. O'Brien (1970), p. 290.
27. Paul (1979), p. 121.
28. Bowley (1949), p. 276.
29. Paul (1979), p. 139.
30. Bowley (1949), p. 276.
31. Quoted in Bowley (1949), p. 265.
32. Ibid., p. 267.
33. Ibid.
34. Smith (1976), p. 301, emphasis added.
35. Ibid., p. 281.
36. Senior (1861), p. 258.
37. Ibid., p. 39.
38. Mill (1848), p. 953.
39. Ibid.
40. Quoted in West (1976), p. 189.
41. Smith (1976), p. 254.
42. Mill (1848), p. 953.
43. Op. cit., p. 954.
44. West (1975).
45. Paul (1979), p. 160.
46. Ibid.
47. Ibid., p. 174.
48. Mill, *Essays* (1967), Vol. 5, p. 663.
49. Smith (1976), p. 23.
50. Mill (1848), p. 942.
51. Ibid.
52. Op. cit., p. 956.
53. Mill, *On Liberty*, p. 240.
54. Smith (1976), p. 265.
55. Mill, (1848), p. 950, emphasis added.
56. Paul (1979), p. 194.
57. Gray (1979), p. 34.
58. Smith (1969), p. 166, emphasis added.
59. See Gray (1979), p. 22.
60. Hayek (1948), pp. 9–11.
61. Stigler (1971) thinks Smith did not recognize this point thoroughly or consistently enough; but see West (1976).
62. Buchanan, Tollison and Tullock (1980).
63. Wicksell, 'A New Principal of Just Taxation' reproduced in Musgrave and Peacock (1958).
64. Friedman (1980), pp. 5–6.
65. Smith (1976), p. 42.

References

Alchian, A. and Harold Demsetz (1972), 'Production, information costs, and economic organization', *American Economic Review*, Vol. 62.

Alchian, A. (1976), 'On Corporations: A Visit with Smith', Foundation for Research in Economics and Education, Los Angeles, Cal.

Anderson, A. (1964), *Historical and Chronological Deduction of the Origin of Commerce*, Kelly, New York.

Anderson, Gary M. and Robert D. Tollison (1982), 'Adam Smith's analysis of joint-stock companies, *Journal of Political Economy*, 90, No. 6.

Anderson, Gary M. (1988), 'Mr. Smith and the Preachers: The Economics of Religion in *The Wealth of Nations*', *Journal of Political Economy*, Vol. 96, No. 5, October.

Arrow, Kenneth (1951), *Social Choice and Individual Values*, John Wiley, New York.

Barro, Robert J. and David Gordon (1983), 'Rules, Discretion and Reputation in a Model of Monetary Policy', *Journal of Monetary Economics*, Vol. 12, pp. 101–21.

Barzel, Yoram and Ben T. Yu (1984), 'The Effect of the Utilization Rate on the Division of Labor', *Economic Inquiry*, Vol. XXII, No. 1.

Baumgardner, James R. (1988), 'Physicians' Services and the Division of Labor across Local Markets', *Journal of Political Economy*, Vol. 96, No. 5.

Becker, Gary (1968), 'Crime and Punishment: An Economic Approach', *Journal of Political Economy*, 76, No. 2, April.

Behrens, Betty (1963), 'Nobles, Privileges and Taxes in France at the end of the Ancient Regime', *Economic History Review*, 2d, ser. 15.

Behrens, Betty (1967), *The Ancient Regime*, Thames Publishers, London.

Bergson, A. (1973), 'On Monopoly Welfare Losses', *American Economic Review*, December, Vol. 63.

Berle, Adolph, A. and Gardiner C. Means (1932), *The Modern Corporation and Private Property*, Macmillan, New York.

Black, Collison, R. D. (1975), 'Review of Robert Eagly's *The Structure of Classical Economic Theory*', in *History of Economic Thought*, Newsletter, Autumn.

Black, Collison, R. D. (1976), 'Smith's Contribution in Historical Perspective', in *The Market and the State Essays in Honour of Adam Smith*, T. Wilson and J. A. Skinner (eds.), Oxford.

Black, Duncan (1958), *Theory of Committees and Elections*, Cambridge, Mass.

Blaug, Mark (1975), 'Kuhn versus Lakatos, or Paradigms versus Research Programmes in the History of Economics', *History of Political Economy*, Vol. 7, No. 4.

Blaug, Mark (1980), *The methodology of economics*, Cambridge University Press.

Blaug, Mark (1985), *Economic Theory in Retrospect*, Richard Irwin Inc., Homewood.

Bloomfield, A. I. (1975), 'Adam Smith and the Theory of International Trade', in *Essays on Adam Smith*, A. Skinner and T. Wilson (eds.), Oxford.

Bowley, Marion (1949), *Nassau Senior and Classical Economists*, Augustin Kelly, New York.

Bowley, Marion (1971), Discussion on Samuel Hollander's "Adam Smith and the Industrial Revolution"', in *History of Economic Thought Newsletter*, Autumn.

Bowley, Marion (1975), 'Some Aspects of the Treatment of Capital in *The Wealth of Nations*', in A. Skinner and T. Wilson, *Essays on Adam Smith*, Clarendon Press, Oxford.

Buchanan, James, M. (1972), 'Review of Rawls' *Theory of Justice*' in *Public Choice*, 13: 123.

Buchanan, James, M. (1975), *The Limits of Liberty: Between Anarchy and Leviathan*, The University of Chicago, Chicago.

Buchanan, James M. (1976), 'Public Goods and National Liberty', in *The Market and the State: Essays in Honour of Adam Smith*, T. Wilson and A. Skinner, (eds.), Oxford.

Buchanan, James M. (1978), 'History of Neglect "Public Choice" in U.K.' in *The Economics of Politics*, London Institute of Economic Affairs Readings, 18.

Buchanan, James M., Robert D. Tollison and Gordon Tullock

(1980), *Toward a Theory of the Rent-Seeking Society*, Texas, A&M, College Station.

Buchanan, James (1982), Foreword to *Tomorrow, Capitalism*, by Henri Lepage, Open Court Publishing Co., London.

Buchanan, James M. and Robert D. Tollison, eds. (1984), *The Theory of Public Choice II*, The University of Michigan Press, Ann Arbor.

Bush, Winston C. (1972), 'Individual Welfare in Anarchy', in *Explorations in the Theory of Anarchy*, G. Tullock (ed.), Center for the Study of Public Choice.

Cannan, Edwin (ed.) (1896), *Lectures on Policy, Justice, Revenue and Arms by Adam Smith*, Oxford University Press.

Carson, Richard (1975), 'On Monopoly Welfare Losses: Comment', *American Economic Review*, December, 65.

Clifford, F. (1885) *A History of Private Bill Legislation*, Butterworth, London.

Coase, R. H. (1974) 'The Lighthouse in Economics', *Journal of Law and Economics*, 17, 357–76.

Coats, A. W. (1969), 'Is There a "Structure of Revolutions" in Economic Thought?' *Kyklos*, Vol. 22.

Coats, A. W. (1971), *The Classical Economists and Public Policy*, Methuen, London.

Cobban, Alfred (1965), *History of Modern France*, Braziller, New York.

Corry, Bernard (1971), 'Discussion on Samuel Hollander's "Adam Smith and the Industrial Revolution' in *History of Economic Thought Newsletter*, Autumn.

Cropsey, Joseph (1957), *Polity and Economy*, The Hague, Martinus Nijhoff.

Cropsey, Joseph (1975), 'Adam Smith and Political Philosophy', in A. Skinner and T. Wilson, op. cit.

Crouch, R. L. (1967), 'Laissez Faire in 19th Century Britain: Myth or Reality?' *Manchester School*, 35, pp. 119–215.

Demsetz, Harold (1983), 'The Structure of Ownership and the Theory of the Firm', *The Journal of Law and Economics*, Vol. XXVI(2), June.

Demsetz, Harold and Kenneth Lehn (1985), 'The Structure of Corporate Ownership: Causes and Consequences', *Journal of Political Economy*, Vol. 93, No. 6, December.

Dixit, A. K. and V. Norman (1980), *Theory of International Trade*, Nisbet, Cambridge.

Dow, Sheila C. (1987), 'The Scottish Political Economy Tradition', *Scottish Journal of Political Economy*, Vol. 34, No. 4, November.

Dowd, Kevin (1985), 'Adam Smith and the 'Real Bills' Doctrine', Ontario Economic Council, Toronto, March.

Dowd, Kevin (1988), *Private Money: The Path to Monetary Stability*, IEA, *Hobart Paper* 112.

Downs, Anthony (1957), *An Economic Theory of Democracy*, Harper and Row, New York.

Eagly, Robert V. (1974), *The Structure of Classical Economic Theory*, Oxford University Press.

Edwards, Brian K. and Ross M. Starr (1987), 'A Note on Indivisibility, Specialization, and Economies of Scale', *American Economic Review*, Vol. 77, No. 1, March.

Ekelund, R. E. (jr) and R. T. Hebert (1990) *A History of Economic Theory and Method*, McGraw-Hill, New York.

Elliot, John E. (1975), 'Professor Robert's Marx; On Alienation and Economic Systems', *Journal of Economic Issues*, Vol. IX, No. 3, September.

Eswaran, Mukesh and Ashok Kotwal (1989), 'Why are Capitalists the Bosses?' *Economic Journal*, 99, March.

Fama, Eugene F. and Michael Jensen (1983), 'Separation of Ownership and Control', *The Journal of Law and Economics*, XXVI(2), June.

Friedman, Milton (1953), *Essays in Positive Economics*, University of Chicago.

Friedman, Milton (1976), 'Adam Smith's Relevance for 1976', International Institution for Economic Research Original Paper, Los Angeles.

Friedman, Milton and Rose (1980), *Free to Choose*, Harcourt Brace Johanovich, New York.

Garrison, Roger (1985), 'West's "Cantillon and Adam Smith": A Comment', *The Journal of Libertarian Studies*, Vol. VIII, No. 2, Fall.

Gastil, Raymond D. (1982), *Freedom in the World*, Greenwood, Westport, CT.

Glahe, Fred and Frank Vorhies (1989), 'Religion, liberty and economic development: An empirical investigation, *Public Choice*, 62, No. 3, September.

Goldberg, V. P. (1976) 'Regulation and Administered Contracts', *Bell Journal of Economics*, 7, pp. 426–48.

Gordon, D. F. (1965), 'The Role of the History of Economic Thought in the Understanding of Modern Economic Theory', *American Economic Review*, Vol. 55, May.

Gray, John (1979), 'John Stuart Mill: Traditional and Revisionist Interpretations', *Literature on Liberty*, Vol. 11, No. 2, April-June.

Haberler, G. (1959), *International Trade and Economic Development*, National Bank of Egypt, Cairo.

Hahn, Frank (1982), 'Reflections on the Invisible Hand', *Lloyds Bank Review*, London, No. 144, April.

Halevy, E. (1928), *The Growth of Philosophic Radicalism*, London, Faber, English translation by M. Morris.

Harberger, A. D. (1959), 'Using the Resources at Hand More Effectively', *American Economic Review*, Vol. 49.

Hayek, Friedrich A. (1948), *Individualism and Economic Order*, University of Chicago.

Hayek, Friedrich A. (1973), *Economic Freedom and Representative Government*, IEA Occasional Paper 39, London.

Herber, B. P. (1971) *Modern Public Finance: The Study of Public Sector Economics*, Richard D. Irwin, Homewood.

Hicks, J. R. (1965), *Capital and Growth*, Oxford.

Hollander, Samuel (1973), *The Economics of Adam Smith*, University of Toronto Press, Toronto.

Hollander, Samuel (1977), 'Adam Smith and the Self-Interest Axiom', *Journal of Law and Economics*, XX(1), April.

Hollander, Samuel (1979), *The Economics of David Ricardo*, University of Toronto Press, Toronto.

Hume, David (Oxford 1888), *Treatise of Human Nature*.

Humphrey, Thomas M. (1983), *Essays on Inflation*, 4th ed, Federal Reserve Bank of Richmond, Richmond, VA.

Hunt, B. C. (1968), *The Development of the Business Corporation in England 1800–1867*, Russell and Russell, New York.

Hutchison, Terence (1966), *Markets and the Franchise*, London I.E.A., Occasional Paper 10.

Hutchison, Terence (1988), *Before Adam Smith: The Emergence of Political Economy 1662–1776*, Basil Blackwell, London.

Iannaccone, Laurence (1987), 'Testing Smith's Theory of Religious Markets', Santa Clara University, Department of Economics, November.

Ippolito, Richard A. (1977), 'The Division of Labor in the Firm', *Economic Inquiry*, Vol. XV, No. 4, October.

Jadlow, Joseph M. (1977), 'Adam Smith on Usury Laws', *The Journal of Finance*, Vol. XXXII, No. 4, September.

Jones, Frank J. (1975), 'The Division of Labour is Limited by the Extent of Alienation', *The American Economist*, Fall.

Kamerschen, David R. (1966), 'An Estimation of the "Welfare Losses" from Monopoly in the American Economy', *Western Economic Journal*, No. 4, June.

Kim, Sunwoong (1989), 'Labor Specialization and the Extent of the Market', *Journal of Political Economy*, Vol. 97, No. 3, June.

Krueger. Anne (1974), 'The Political Economy of the Rent Seeking Society', *American Economic Review*, 64, June.

Krugman, Paul R. (1987), 'Is Free Trade Passé?' *Economic Perspectives*, Vol. 1, No. 2, Fall, pp. 131–144.

Kuhn, T. S. (1970), *The Structure of Scientific Revolutions*, 2nd ed, Chicago University Press, Chicago.

Lachman, Ludwig M. (1977), Review of 'Method and Appraisal in Economics', by J. Spiro Latsis, *Journal of Economic Literature*, XV, 3, p. 934, September.

Laidler, David (1981), 'Adam Smith as a Monetary Economist', *Canadian Journal of Economics*, 14, May.

Lancaster, Kelvin (1980), 'Intra-industry Trade Under Perfect Monopolistic Competition', *Journal of International Economics*, 10, pp. 151–175.

Lepage, Henri (1982), *Tomorrow Capitalism*, Open Court Publishing Co., London.

Levy, David (1978), 'Adam Smith's "Natural Law" and Contractual Society', *Journal of the History of Ideas*, September.

Macaulay, T. B. (1829), 'Mill's Essay on Government: Utilitarian Logic and Politics', *Edinburgh Review*, No. xcvii, Article vii.

Mansfield, Edwin (1976), *Microeconomics – Theory and Application*, (shorter 2nd ed.), W. W. Norton, New York.

Marglin, S. A. (1974), 'The Origins and Functions of Hierarchy in Capitalist Production', *Review of Radical Political Economics*, No. 6.

McCormick, Robert E. and Robert Tollison (1980), 'Wealth Transfers in a Representative Democracy' in James M. Buchanan et al. *Toward a Theory of the Rent-Seeking Society*, Texas A&M, College Station.

McMulty, Paul J. (1967), 'A Note on the History of Perfect Competition', *Journal of Political Economy*, pp. 395–399.

McNulty, Paul J. (1984), 'On the Nature and Theory of Economic Organization: The Role of the Firm Reconsidered', *History of Political Economy*, 16 (2).

Meek, R. L. (1954), 'Adam Smith and the Classical Concept of Profit', *Scottish Journal of Political Economy*, Vol. 1.

Mill, James (1955), *An Essay on Government*, Bobbs-Merrill Company Inc., New York.

Mill, John Stuart (1848), *Principles of Political Economy*, Augustin Kelley reprint, New York 1969.

Mill, John Stuart (1967), *Essays on Economics and Society*, in J. M. Robson (ed.), Collected Works, Vols. 4 and 5, University of Toronto Press, Toronto.

Mints, L. W. (1945), *A History of Banking Theory in Great Britain and the United States*, University of Chicago Press, Chicago.

Mitchell, B. R. (1962), *Abstract of British Historical Statistics*, Cambridge.

Mueller, Dennis C. (1989), *Public Choice II*, Cambridge University Press, Cambridge.

Musgrave, R. A. and A. T. Peacock (1958), *Classics in the Theory of Public Finance*, Macmillan, London.

Musgrave, R. A. (1976), 'Adam Smith on Public Finance and Distribution' in *The Market and the State: Essays in Honour of Adam Smith*, T. Wilson and A. Skinner (eds.).

Myint, H. (1948), *Theories of Welfare Economics*, Longmans, London.

Myint, H. (1977), 'Adam Smith's Theory of International Trade in the Perspective of Economic Development', *Economica*, Vol. 44, September.

Niskanen, William A. (1971), *Bureaucracy and Representative Government*, Chicago.

O'Brien, D. P. (1970), *J. R. McCulloch: A Study in Classical Economics*, George Allen and Unwin, London.

O'Brien, D. P. (1976), 'The Longevity of Adam Smith's Vision: Paradigms, Research Programmes and Falsifiability in the History of Economic Thought', *Scottish Journal of Political Economy*, Vol. XXIII, No. 2, June.

O'Brien, D. P. (1978), *The Classical Economists*, Clarendon Press, Oxford.

Ordeshook, Peter (1986), *Game Theory and Political Theory: An Introduction*, Cambridge University Press, Cambridge.

Paul, Ellen Frankel (1979), *Moral Revolution and Economic Science: The Demise of Laissez-Faire in Nineteenth-Century British Political Economy*, Greenwood Press, Westport, Conn. and London.

Peacock, A. T. (1975), 'The Treatment of the Principles of Public Finance in *The Wealth of Nations*' in *Essays on Adam Smith*, A. Skinner and T. Wilson, (eds.), Oxford.

Perlman, Morris (1989), 'Adam Smith and the Paternity of the Real Bills Doctrine', *History of Political Economy*, 21:1, Spring.

Petrella, Frank (1968), 'Adam Smith's Rejection of Hume's Price-Specie-Flow Mechanism: A Minor Mystery Resolved', *Southern Economic Journal*, January.

Posner, Richard A. (1975), 'The Social Costs of Monopoly and Regulation', *Journal of Political Economy*, No. 83, August.

Posner, Richard A. (1979), 'A Statistical Study of Antitrust Enforcement', *Journal of Law and Economics*, No. 87, October.

Posner, Richard A. (1987), 'The Law and Economics Movement', *American Economic Review*, Papers and Proceedings, Vol. 77, No. 2, May.

Posner, Richard A. (1989), 'An Economic Approach to Issues of Religious Freedom', *The University of Chicago Law Review*, Vol. 56, No. 1, Winter.

Rashid, Salim (1986), 'Adam Smith and the Division of Labour', *Scottish Journal of Political Economy*, Vol. 33, No. 3. August.

Rashid, Salim (1989), 'Does a Famous Economist Deserve Special Standards? A Critical Note on Adam Smith's Scholarship', *History of Economics Society Bulletin*, Vol. 11, No. 2, Fall.

Rawls, John (1971), *A Theory of Justice*, Harvard University Press.

Rees, A. (1975), 'Compensating Wage Differentials', in *Essays on Adam Smith*, Andrew Skinner and Thomas Wilson (eds.), Clarendon Press, Oxford.

Richardson, G. B. (1975), 'Adam Smith on Competition and Increasing Returns' in *Essays on Adam Smith*, A. Skinner and T. Wilson (eds.), Oxford.

Robbins, Lionel (1952), *The Theory of Economic Policy in English Classical Economy*, Macmillan, London.

Rosen, Sherwin (1983), 'Specialization and Human Capital', *Journal of Labour Economics*, Vol. 1, No. 1.

Rosenberg, N. (1960), 'Some Institutional Aspects of *The Wealth of Nations*', *Journal of Political Economy*, December.

Rosenberg, N. (1965), 'Adam Smith and the Division of Labour: Two Views or One?', *Economica*, February.

Rosenberg, N. (1976), 'Another Advantage of the Division of Labour', *Journal of Political Economy*, Vol. 84, August.

Ross, Stephen A. (1972), 'The Economic Theory of Agency: The Principal's Problem', *American Economic Review*, 67 (1).

Roumasset, James A. (1974), 'Institutions, Social Contracts and Second Best Pareto Optimality', Paper presented at the Public Choice Society Meetings, 21 March.

Rousseau, J. J. (1968), *The Social Contract*, Cranston (ed.), Penguin Books.

Runciman, W. G., and A. K. Sen (1965), 'Games, Justice and the General Will', *Mind*, Vol. No. 22, April.

Samuels, Warren L. (1966), *The Classical Theory of Economic Policy*, Ohio, Cleveland.

Samuels, Warren L. (1973), 'Adam Smith and the Economy as a System of Power', *Review of Social Economy*, Vol. 21, October.

Samuelson, Paul (1977), 'A Modern Theorist's Vindication of Adam Smith', *American Economic Review*, Vol. 67, No. 1, February.

Schumpeter, J. (1955), *History of Economic Analysis*, Oxford University Press, New York, p. 472.

Schwartzman, D. (1960) 'The Burden of Monopoly', *Journal of Political Economy*, December.

Scott, W. R. (1912), *The Constitution and Finance of English, Scottish and Irish Joint-Stock Companies to 1720*, Cambridge University Press, Cambridge.

Scully, Gerald W. (1988), 'The Institutional Framework and Economic Development', *Journal of Political Economy*, Vol. 96, No. 3, June.

Senior, N. (1861), *Suggestions on Popular Education*, London.

Shughart, William F. and Robert D. Tollison (1983), 'Preliminary Evidence of the Use of Inputs by the Federal Reserve System', *American Economic Review*, Vol. 73, No. 3, June.

Skinner, Andrew (1974), *Adam Smith and the Role of the State*, Glasgow University Press, Glasgow.

Skinner, Andrew and T. Wilson (1975), *Essays on Adam Smith*, Clarendon, Oxford.

Smith, Adam (1896), *Lectures on Policy, Justice, Revenue and Arms*, Edwin Cannan (ed.), Clarendon Press, Oxford.

Smith, Adam (1950), *The Wealth of Nations*, Vols. I and II, Edwin Cannan (ed.), Methuen, London.

Smith, Adam (1969), *The Theory of Moral Sentiments*, Bohn (ed.), (1853); reprinted, Liberty Fund, Indianapolis.

Smith, Adam (1976), *An Inquiry into the Nature and Causes of the Wealth of Nations*, reprinted in two volumes, R. H. Campbell, A. S. Skinner and W. B. Todd (eds.), Clarendon Press, Oxford.

Spengler, Joseph (1977), 'Adam Smith on Human Capital', *American Economic Review*, Vol. 67, No. 1, February.

Stigler, George (1951), 'The Division of Labor is Limited by the Extent of the Market', *Journal of Political Economy*, LIX, June.

Stigler, George (1957), 'Perfect Competition, Historically Contemplated', *Journal of Political Economy*, LXV, February.

Stigler, George (1969), 'Directors' Law', *Journal of Law and Economics*, Vol. 12.

Stigler, George (1971a), 'The Theory of Economic Regulation', *Bell Journal of Economics and Management Science*, 2, No. 1.

Stigler, George (1971b), 'Smith's Travels on the Ship of State', *History of Political Economy*, 3.

Stigler, George (1976), 'The Successes and Failures of Professor Smith', *Journal of Political Economy*, 84, No. 6, December, p. 1208.

Stiglitz, J. E. (1974), 'The Demand for Education in Public and Private School Systems', *Journal of Public Economics*, 3, pp. 349–85.

Stiglitz, Joseph E. and Andrew Weiss (1981), 'Credit Rationing in Markets with Imperfect Information', *The American Economic Review*, Vol. 71, No. 3, June.

Stiglitz, Joseph E. (1987), 'The Causes and Consequences of the Dependence of Quality on Price', *Journal of Economic Literature*, Vol. XXV, March.

Summers, Robert and Alan Heston (1984), 'Improved International Comparisons of Real Product and Its Composition: 1950–1980', *Review of Income and Wealth* 30, June, pp. 207–62.

Thweatt, William O. (1988), *Classical Political Economy: A Survey of Recent Literature*, Kluwer, Boston.

Tucker, Rev. Josiah (1756), *Elements of Commerce*, as reproduced in

Josiah Tucker: A Selection of his Economic and Political Writings, Columbia University Press, New York, 1931.

Tullock, Gordon (1967), 'The Welfare Costs of Tariffs, Monopolies and Theft', *Western Economic Journal*, No. 5, June.

Tullock, Gordon (ed.) (1972), *Explorations in the Theory of Anarchy*, Center for the Study of Public Choice, Blacksburg.

Tullock, Gordon (1980), 'Efficient Rent Seeking' in *Toward a Theory of the Rent Seeking Society*, J. Buchanan, R. Tollison and G. Tullock (eds.).

Turgot, A. R. J. (1913), *Oeuvres*, Schelle (ed.), Paris.

Vickers, D. (1975), 'Adam Smith and the Status of the Theory of Money' in *Essays on Adam Smith*, A. Skinner and T. Wilson (eds.), Oxford.

Viner, J. (1928), 'Adam Smith and Laissez Faire', in *Adam Smith 1776–1926*, University of Chicago, Chicago.

Viner, Jacob (1949), 'Bentham and J. S. Mill: The Utilitarian Background', *American Economic Review*, Vol 39 (3), June.

Viner, Jacob (1965), *Guide to John Rae's Life of Adam Smith*, reprinted, New York.

Walker, Kenneth (1946), 'The Psychological Assumptions of Economics', *The Economic Record*, XII, June.

Watkins, Frederick (1951), *Hume: Theory of Politics*, Nelson, London.

Wenders, John (1987), 'On Perfect Rent Dissipation', *American Economic Review*, Vol. 77 (3), June.

West, E. G. (1964), 'Adam Smith's Two Views on the Division of Labour', *Economica*, February.

West, E. G. (1969), 'The Political Economy of Alienation: Karl Marx and Adam Smith', *Oxford Economic Papers*, Vol. 21, March.

West, E. G. (1969), *Adam Smith*, Arlington Press, New York.

West, E. G. (1975), 'Adam Smith and Alienation: A Rejoinder', *Oxford Economic Papers*, Vol. 27, July.

West, E. G. (1976a), 'Adam Smith's Economics of Politics', *History of Political Economy*, Vol. 8, No. 4, November.

West, Edwin G. (1976b), *Adam Smith: The Man and His Works*, Liberty Press, Indianapolis.

West, Edwin G. (1976c), *Nonpublic School Aid: The Law, Economics and Politics of American Education*, D. C. Heath, Lexington, Mass.

West, E. G. (1977), 'Adam Smith's Public Economics', *Canadian Journal of Economics*, Vol. X, No. 1, February.

West, E. G. (1978), 'The Burdens of Monopoly: Classical versus Neoclassical', *Southern Economic Journal*, Vol. 34, No. 2, April.

West, Edwin G. and R. Hafer (1979), 'Alienation and the Production Fucntion', *The American Economist*, Vol. 25.

West, Edwin G. (1985), 'Richard Cantillon and Adam Smith: A Reappraisal', *Research in the History of Economic Thought and Methodology*, Vol. 3, Lansing, Michigan.

White, L. H. (1984), *Free Banking in Britain: Theory Experience and Debate, 1800–1845*, Cambridge University Press, Cambridge.

Williamson, Oliver E. (1980), 'The Organization of Work: A Comparative Institutional Assessment', *Journal of Economic Behaviour and Organization*, Vol. 1, No. 1.

Wittman, Donald (1989), 'Why Democracies Produce Efficient Results', *Journal of Political Economy*, 97, December.

Worcester, D. A. (Jr.) (1973), 'New Estimates of the Welfare Loss to Monopoly; U.S. 1956–60', *Southern Economic Journal*, 40, October.

Young, A. A. (1928), 'Increasing Returns and Economic Progress' *Economic Journal*, 38, No. 6, December.

Zashin, Elliot M. (1974), 'The Logic of Collective Action: Rousseau's *Social Contract* Revisited', Paper presented at the Public Choice Society Meetings, 21 March.

Zeisel, Joseph S. (1958), 'The Workweek in American Industry 1850–1956', *Monthly Labor Review*, 81, January.

Index